THE APOLOGY RITUAL

Christopher Bennett presents a theory of punishment grounded in the practice of apology, and in particular in reactions such as feeling sorry and making amends. He argues that offenders have a 'right to be punished' – that it is part of taking an offender seriously as a member of a normatively demanding relationship (such as friendship or collegiality or citizenship) that she is subject to retributive attitudes when she violates the demands of that relationship. However, while he claims that punishment and the retributive attitudes are the necessary expression of moral condemnation, Bennett's account of these reactions has more in common with restorative justice than traditional retributivism. He argues that the most appropriate way to react to crime is to require the offender to make proportionate amends. His book is a rich and original contribution to the debate over punishment and restorative justice.

CHRISTOPHER BENNETT is a Lecturer in the Department of Philosophy, University of Sheffield.

THE APOLOGY RITUAL

A Philosophical Theory of Punishment

CHRISTOPHER BENNETT

CAMBRIDGE UNIVERSITY PRESS
Cambridge, New York, Melbourne, Madrid, Cape Town, Singapore, São Paulo, Delhi

Cambridge University Press
The Edinburgh Building, Cambridge CB2 8RU, UK

Published in the United States of America by Cambridge University Press, New York

www.cambridge.org
Information on this title: www.cambridge.org/9780521880725

First published 2008

Printed in the United Kingdom at the University Press, Cambridge

A catalogue record for this publication is available from the British Library

Library of Congress Cataloging in Publication data
Bennett, Christopher, 1972–
The apology ritual: a philosophical theory of punishment/Christopher Bennett.
p.   cm.
Includes bibliographical references and index.
ISBN 978-0-521-88072-5 (hardback)
1. Restorative justice.   2. Punishment–Philosophy.   I. Title.
HV8688.B46   2008
364.601–dc22
2008015648

ISBN 978-0-521-88072-5 hardback

For Sue

Contents

Acknowledgements

The first draft of the present manuscript was completed with the help of an AHRB Research Leave Scheme grant during 2005–6. But the ideas expressed here are ones that I have been working on for what now seems like rather a long time. Because it has taken so long to write I am afraid I cannot hope to acknowledge or thank everyone who has helped me in some way to develop the ideas presented here. This does not mean that I am not grateful to those who have taken the time to ask difficult or encouraging questions, or with whom I have had enlightening discussions. But there are some people I would like to mark out for thanks, starting with Tom Pink, Bob Stern, Leif Wenar and David Owens, who provided immeasurable help in the early stages of this project. I would also like to give particular thanks to Antony Duff for his generous support, advice and encouragement over the years.

I would also like to thank those who volunteered to look at drafts of the book, either as a whole or as sets of chapters: Linda Radzik, Leo Zaibert, Kimberley Brownlee, and John Tasioulas. I am also grateful to Richard Holton, John Skorupski, Gerry Johnstone, Matt Matravers, Andrew Schaap, Suzanne Uniacke, Rowan Cruft, Jim Dignan, Mick Cavadino, Julie Brownlie, Simon Anderson, Thom Brooks, Daniel Van Ness, Gwen Robinson, Joanna Shapland, Pedro Tabensky and Richard Dagger, audiences at Durham and Glasgow Philosophy Departments and Birkbeck College Law Department. Thanks also to an anonymous referee for Cambridge University Press who provided helpful and incisive comments. I am also grateful to my colleagues in Sheffield, who have continued to provide a supportive and stimulating research environment, as well as an object lesson in philosophical argument.

In addition I would like to record a special debt of gratitude to Sandra Marshall, with whom I had many formative philosophical discussions: I hope she recognises her influence in these pages.

Closer to home I would like to thank my parents and my brothers for support, encouragement and stimulation of many kinds. And finally of course the biggest 'thank you' goes to Sue, Sarah and Lois for putting up with having a philosopher in the house.

Introduction

After a hard day at the office Bryson gives in to the cajoling of a couple of his colleagues and decides to join them for a drink. Stretching out his legs in the pub he savours the atmosphere, the chat and the sheer leisure of having nothing to do until the next morning, while the alcohol courses into his blood and makes the world appear that little bit rosier. The only problem is, he drives to work, and will need to drive home again. This fact hovers constantly more or less into focus in his mind, and he makes it clear to his mates that he will not be staying with them for long. Nevertheless, as he is about to get up to leave, having had as much to drink as he ought to in the situation, they persuade him to stay for one more. It is not that Bryson is naturally reckless or that he does not care about the danger he might be to others when he is under the influence: this fact has been more or less present to his mind all along. It is just that, after he has had a couple of drinks, this aspect of the situation slips out of his awareness under pressure from his friends. In the delicious relaxation of the moment he assures himself that he is not really going to be a danger to anyone.

Eventually Bryson does get to his car. He is nowhere near legless, but he should not be driving. But at this point he is feeling good and in control of all situations. As he sets off, he puts on the car stereo and winds down the window. Soon he is driving, with care but unjustified confidence, past rows of tenement blocks along the busy and often congested roads that lead out of the city. Having queued for what seems like ages he is suddenly presented with a stretch of relatively open road and he puts his foot down. In his sporty car he is soon up to 40 mph; but this is a 30 mph limit, and other road users are expecting cars to be moving slowly. When the cyclist swings out across the road she assumes that she can complete her manoeuvre before Bryson catches her. But she misses her pedal at the crucial moment and falters, leaving her momentarily stranded in the middle of the road. He is travelling too fast, and her sudden pause catches him unawares. Despite his confidence his reactions do not come quickly enough. Though he brakes and tries to steer away, he cannot help but catch her squarely and knock her from her bike.

Fortunately for Bryson, the cyclist sprawled on the pavement – call her Judith – is very much alive. But she is seriously injured, with broken legs and shattered hips. Judith will probably walk again, but not without difficulty. As a shocked Bryson gets from his car and goes over to his victim, a bystander calls the police and ambulance. Bryson's immediate unthinking reaction is to say sorry, though he is aware that that cannot be enough. He tries – clumsily in his shocked state – to find something that he can do for this woman who has become his victim. A bystander better informed about first aid shoos him away, but he hovers close by, his tense posture expressing his wish that everything could be all right. Soon Bryson's nervous attempts to help Judith are interrupted and he is bundled into a police car, while an ambulance rushes the cyclist to casualty.

DEALING WITH CRIME: TWO SCENARIOS

What should happen to Bryson as a result of what he has (recklessly) done to the cyclist? What happens in our society at the moment is that, with the arrival of the police car, Bryson is taken away from contact with his victim and enters into a system with its own procedures, assumptions and language: in short its own culture or way of doing things. He will meet police officers, prison warders, solicitors, lawyers, probation officers: various agents of the state and others with official status in the system. But the system will shield him from any contact with Judith. He will be charged, tried if need be, and then sentenced. The charge might be the fairly serious one of dangerous driving. The sentence might be custodial or he might get a fine. In some cases he might be sentenced to community service.

But why do we think that this is what should happen to Bryson? When taken away by the police car, Bryson was in the middle of an apology to the victim, an apology that he no doubt sees as quite inadequate to the situation, but which he feels compelled to make nevertheless. He is immediately and strongly concerned for Judith, and it is inarticulately but fundamentally apparent to him that he owes her something of which an apology is only the start. More than anything, his whole impulse at this point is to do something for her. Indeed we can all recognise the appropriateness of this kind of response. It is because Bryson feels compelled to make it that we can regard him as, despite his misdemeanour, a basically decent human being.

Some theorists have criticised our criminal justice system because it severs rather than builds on this disposition in the decent offender.[1] Under our present system, the police bundle Bryson off and from that point on he has little or no chance to have contact with Judith, or to act on his impulse to do something for her. But the system also has features that militate against the victim getting anything from the offender. First of all, we have a range of such severe and disruptive sanctions that they give offenders strong incentive to deny the offence. By doing so it encourages the offender to think self-interestedly rather than morally, and the criminal justice process turns into one of opposing 'sides' attempting to manipulate each other in order to get the result they want, rather than an arena in which all parties attempt to deal together with the aftermath of the offence.[2] The offender is threatened with a sanction that, sorry as he is, will be severe enough and cause sufficient havoc to his life (particularly if it involves a custodial sentence) that he will do what he can to evade the charge. Thus the severity of the sanction may make it less likely that he ever expresses how sorry he is to his victim when they do come face-to-face in court, and provides offenders with a strong incentive to disguise rather than show their remorse. Secondly, the severity of what will be done to Bryson should he be convicted means that we need a high standard of proof before inflicting this sanction. The charge must be proven beyond reasonable doubt before the whole terrible weight of the state apparatus comes down on an offender. Again, this means that it is less likely that the victim will get the satisfaction that comes from a conviction.[3]

On the basis of features such as these, critics claim that the present criminal justice system neglects victims and treats crimes as though they

---

[1] For instance proponents of restorative justice, see e.g. N. Christie, 'Conflicts as Property', *British Journal of Criminology* 17 (1977), pp. 1–15; J. Braithwaite, *Crime, Shame and Reintegration* (Cambridge: Cambridge University Press, 1989); H. Zehr, *Changing Lenses: A New Focus for Crime and Justice* (Scottdale, Pa.: Herald Press, 1990); M. Wright, *Justice for Victims and Offenders: A Restorative Response to Crime*, 2nd edn (Winchester: Waterside Press, 1996); G. Johnstone, *Restorative Justice: Ideas, Values, Debates* (Cullompton: Willan, 2002).

[2] The latter part of this sentence draws on a widely quoted formulation of restorative justice. See T. Marshall, 'Restorative Justice: An Overview', in G. Johnstone (ed.), *A Restorative Justice Reader* (Cullompton: Willan, 2001), pp. 28–46.

[3] Johnstone, *Restorative Justice: Ideas, Values, Debates*, p. 69. Johnstone attributes this point to Martin Wright.

were only the business of the state. Rather than the incident described above fundamentally involving Bryson and Judith, it is rather the state that must take action. And rather than taking action to ameliorate the situation, it narrowly takes action against Bryson. The concern of the state is simply to ascertain whether Bryson has done something for which he can be punished. That – according to the narrative that underpins our criminal justice institutions – is the overriding interest in this situation. The official line is that there is a public interest in dealing with crime that overrides individual interests. And indeed, this is the way the system seems to explain itself. Criminal cases are '*R.* v. *Jones*' rather than '*Smith* v. *Jones*' (even the 'v.' indicates the assumed adversarial rather than collaborative nature of the process). And even if there is a conviction, what Bryson will end up doing is what is described appropriately as 'being detained at Her Majesty's pleasure': he will end up doing something for the crown rather than for Judith. Furthermore, what he will end up doing for the crown will not have much to do with any sense of remorse he may still have. In other words, sitting in a cell or paying a fine to the state will not appear to him a particularly meaningful way of expressing his remorse or making amends. What he wants to do, if he is feeling bad for what he has done, is to do something for the victim. But the criticism is that the punitive system corrupts and stifles that important impulse and leaves the claims of victims unaddressed.

As a result, critics say, the experiences of those like Bryson and Judith in the criminal justice system end up being meaningful only in the most attenuated sense. What happens is that, once what takes place between Bryson and Judith is defined as a crime, the situation is taken out of their hands. Bryson is driven away in the police car, contact between victim and offender is severed, and the bureaucratic machinery of the state lumbers into action. Police and lawyers get involved, with their own languages and procedures, their own institutional perceptions of the parties involved; Bryson and Judith may well feel that they are being carried along by the bureaucracy and its own ends – a tiny part of a huge machine. They become bit players in their own story, rather than at the centre of the narrative. And yet, when Bryson gets out of his car and steps over to Judith to begin a shocked apology, his victim and his response to her *is* the centre of his world: this is all, at that moment, that matters to him.

Imagine, then, an alternative form of justice: one in which the response of offender to victim *is* put at the heart of things. On such a view, let us say, if Bryson pleads guilty when charged, he enters into a process in which he is able to make good on that initial impulse to apologise; he attends a meeting with his victim when he is able to have an exchange with her, and when she can tell him what effect the offence has had on her, and he can make the necessary response. Such a process might be an element of what is called *restorative justice*.[4] The basic idea behind restorative justice is often thought to be the following: it is a process in which the 'stakeholders' to some offence get together and decide what has to be done in its aftermath.[5] In other words, those actually affected by what has been done are able to decide how the action ought to be addressed. Rather than the victim and offender being taken up by a bureaucracy that has its own momentum and its own culture, they are able to keep themselves at the centre of the story. In the language sometimes used by its proponents, in restorative justice they retain *ownership* of the process: it is the direct concern of those who are most affected, not the business of the crown in which they have only a narrowly circumscribed role. They can 'own' the process in a way that the formal procedures of the present system make impossible.[6]

On this restorative alternative, Bryson and Judith should be given a chance to have such a meeting, though proponents of this alternative usually stress that any involvement in this process has to be voluntary. Also involved in – or invited to – this meeting can be other interested parties. For instance, although the obvious and direct victim of the crime is Judith, the character of the offence is such that members of the local community could also count themselves as having a legitimate claim to have been harmed by the offence. For although they were not themselves hit by the car, they (and their children or their elderly relatives) were unjustifiably put at risk by Bryson's recklessness. And because of this they have a legitimate complaint to make of him. And further, the character of their neighbourhood is changed if people drive fast down their main street: crossing such a road becomes an increasingly risky business (particularly if one is in any way vulnerable, such as the young or the elderly or the disabled), and one side of the road thus becomes effectively cut off from the other. The 30 mph limit is in place to protect the residents' legitimate interests in not being put at risk and in not having their

---

[4] My understanding of restorative justice has been greatly furthered by Daniel Van Ness's extraordinary attempt to imagine what a city might look like if it attempted to respond 'as restoratively as possible to all crimes, all victims and all offenders.' See www.rjcity.org.

[5] See e.g. the widely quoted definition in Marshall, 'Restorative Justice: An Overview'.

[6] For an account of the aims and realities of restorative justice, see e.g. J. Shapland *et al.*, 'Situating Restorative Justice in Criminal Justice', *Theoretical Criminology* 11 (2006), pp. 505–32.

neighbourhood cut in two by a fast road. The harm that Bryson does to *these* interests is of a less dramatic character than what he does to the cyclist, but it is an aspect of the crime, and so there are good grounds for allowing representatives of the local community a place at the meeting. As usually conceived, there should also be an official at the meeting who is charged with facilitating the discussion, keeping order, and leading the discussion through its various stages (crudely, perhaps, from recrimination to agreement on reparation).

Imagine then that such a process is really staged. In the meeting, Bryson listens to what the various parties have to say about the impact the offence has had on them (or in the case of the representatives of the local community, the effect of widespread speeding on their community), and gains an insight into his behaviour as seen and felt from the outside. When it is his turn to speak, he is moved by what he has heard, and is able to make it clear to Judith how badly he feels about what he has done to her; and to make it clear to the group that he intends never again to get into a car drunk or to drive recklessly over the limit. His experience, he can tell them, has given him a new insight into the importance of the speed limit: before he had just thought of it as a busybody rule it was fine to ignore. As a group, the meeting can then decide on a course of action whereby Bryson can make reparation to the cyclist and, if this is appropriate, to the local community. Of course, he can never put things back to the way they were or undo the harm caused by his offence. But he can do something that expresses his wish that he could. Thus he might agree, for instance, to pay for some equipment that aids the cyclist's efforts to relearn to walk, or that helps her cope with impaired mobility; and he might agree to give a programme of talks to schoolchildren on the dangers of reckless driving. Thus he expresses his wish that he had never done what he did by doing something that helps his victims, perhaps in ways related to the harm caused by his offence. He is able to make some kind of reparation for what he has done in a way that benefits the victims.

Proponents of restorative justice argue that this sort of procedure, based as it is on the fundamental impulse to apologise and make amends when one has wrongfully caused harm, can be more meaningful to victims, offenders and the local community than the current system of trial and imprisonment.[7] Such theorists often conceive of restorative justice as

---

[7] See Zehr, *Changing Lenses*; H. Strang, 'Justice for Victims of Young Offenders: The Centrality of Emotional Harm and Restoration', in Johnstone, *A Restorative Justice Reader*, pp. 286–93. Not all proponents of something like restorative justice base it in conceptions of apology: see e.g. R. Barnett, 'Restitution: A New Paradigm for Criminal Justice', *Ethics* 87 (1977), pp. 279–301.

an alternative, not just to the trial and imprisonment scenario I described briefly above, but also to retributive justice and to punishment more generally conceived. Retributive punishment, it is said, is backward-looking and concerned with making the offender suffer for what he or she has done; whereas restorative justice would be concerned with making things better for all parties for the future. The restorative justice alternative raises a number of important questions. What, if anything, would be lost if criminal justice became a form of restorative justice, taking the alternative scenario briefly sketched above? Is there a sense in which crimes *are* actions that are a legitimate and necessary concern of the state and hence should not just be regarded as the business of private individuals? And is the ritual of apology really as free from retributive ideas of justice as is sometimes imagined? Is restorative justice necessarily all that different from retributive justice?[8]

RETRIBUTIVE, RESTORATIVE AND CRIMINAL JUSTICE

In this book I am concerned with these questions of the proper role of apology in criminal justice. Like some proponents of restorative justice, I see apology as our fundamental means to 'make things right' in the face of having done wrong. However, unlike many proponents of restorative justice, I believe that the right theory of the importance of apology will lead us to understand properly the importance of *punitive* responses to wrongdoing. On my view, understanding apology will give us an answer to the question of why hard treatment is a necessary part of a response to wrongdoing. Thus I will depart from those who think of restorative justice as being a non-punitive response to crime.

I will also depart from those who think that restorative justice is different from punishment in being an essentially informal response to crime rather than one delivered by the state. I am sympathetic to the idea that criminal justice would do well to harness the power of our informal reactions to wrongdoing, but I see this as being part of a state system of censure of crime rather than a form of community justice.[9] I argue that

---

[8] We address these questions as we go on. But see K. Daly, 'Restorative Justice: The Real Story', *Punishment and Society* 4 (2002), pp. 55–79, for some sceptical issues relating to the claims of restorative justice.

[9] For the idea that the state has a duty to issue authoritative condemnation of crimes, see e.g. J. Feinberg, 'The Expressive Function of Punishment', in his *Doing and Deserving* (London: Princeton University Press, 1970), pp. 95–118; A. von Hirsch, *Censure and Sanctions* (Oxford: Oxford University Press, 1993); R. A. Duff, *Punishment, Communication and Community* (Oxford: Oxford University Press, 2001).

collective censure of wrongdoing is a necessary action of the state; and that we should resist the view on which crime becomes a private 'conflict' between two individuals rather than something that is of appropriate concern to their fellow citizens as a whole. In chapter 6 we will see the problems that arise for the restorative alternative when it has to deal with offenders who – unlike Bryson – do not willingly comply with the restorative process. Any justice system needs to say what it is going to do with such non-compliant offenders. Trying to give a satisfactory answer to this question will lead us to see that there has to be more to justice than the restorative alternative tends to allow.

What this book sets out, therefore, is a retributive theory of punishment, but one that pays attention to the challenge presented by restorative justice. In the end I agree with those who argue that there is a legitimate public interest in censuring crime. However, I argue that in order to do its job such censure has to be *symbolically adequate*. And I argue that the appropriate symbols are to be found in the practice of apology. My account of the punishment and retribution is therefore based in the importance of apology, and for this reason it shares something with restorative justice. But it argues that in the end the imposition of proportionate sanction on offenders is a morally necessary response to those actions that are crimes.

So why, on my account, is hard treatment a necessary part of responding to wrongdoing? My defence of retribution is distinctive because I claim that retributive reactions are necessary to do justice *to the offender*. In part II of this book I offer an interpretation of the Hegelian idea that the wrongdoer has a 'right to be punished'. This is to say that punishment is *owed to* the wrongdoer; in the absence of punishment we would be failing to respect the status of the wrongdoer as a moral agent. The key intuition, on my account, is that sometimes 'making allowances' for a person – not subjecting them to a range of retributive reactions – is incompatible with maintaining a valuable sort of relationship with them. Making allowances – when it is taken too far – can involve a failure to take the person seriously as someone of whom certain behaviour can legitimately be expected. Other things being equal, then, we owe it to wrongdoers to blame them and to expect them to apologise. Expressing the need for apology is the central motivation of punishment, an account of which I give in part III.

In everyday life a meaningful apology has to be one that is made sincerely and of the offender's own free will as an expression of remorse or guilt. But punishment is obviously something the state imposes on offenders regardless of their willingness to accept it as deserved. And one might think that it would be unacceptable to insist on genuine remorse (that is, demonstrably genuine remorse) before we allow that an offender has adequately 'done her time'. Therefore punishment can only ever be *modelled* on the process of apology: there is a limit to the extent to which the state can require offenders actually to apologise. However, this is why I call my account the Apology Ritual. A ritual, in this usage, is an act the form of which expresses the attitude that a participant ought to have in performing it (think of kneeling in order to pray). The idea is that, by requiring offenders to undertake the sort of reparative action that they would be motivated to undertake were they genuinely sorry for what they have done, the state condemns crimes in a way that is symbolically adequate and hence more meaningful than simple imprisonment or fining.

The theory of punishment that we end up with provides a critical perspective both on criminal justice as conventionally understood, and on restorative justice. In order to know *how* justice ought to be carried out, I argue, we need to know *why* it needs to be carried out: this practical question implies a philosophical foundation. However, it is a corollary of this that when we ask the philosophical question about why we punish, our answers will be blinkered if we have a narrow view of what sort of thing we count as punishment – for instance, if we only have in mind imprisonment or fining. Whether punishment is justified depends on what we mean to do to an offender by way of punishing: the why question implies something about the how. Thus I will argue – and attempt to exemplify the claim – that an argument about punishment has to pay attention to the practical question of how punishment is to be carried out, just as claims about our practical arrangements for carrying out criminal justice rest on deeper assumptions about the purpose of the institutions and the nature of the human beings who can be made accountable to such institutions.

PART I

Justifying punishment

CHAPTER I

The problem of punishment and the restorative alternative

TODAY'S CRIMINAL JUSTICE: A LEGITIMATION CRISIS?

Penal justice can be described as a set of institutions in search of a narrative or a 'practice without a policy'.[1] Many writers talk of a crisis in the system. This crisis has a number of aspects – for instance, how to cope with overcrowded prisons; how to cope with perceptions of rising crime that seem to be independent of the evidence; how to sustain liberal and progressive values in the face of an entrenched popular 'law and order' mentality that politicians use for their own advantage – that I will not deal with here. What I want to address might rather be called a crisis of *meaning*.[2] It seems that for many victims and offenders, and often for the officials who run the institutions, it is not clear what the system is actually meant to be doing, what the overall purpose of criminal justice is – or whether the officially given purposes are really compelling ones. In this section I will give an explanation of this state of affairs by looking at some of the persistent problems plaguing the central justifications of penal institutions. I propose that one of the reasons for a loss of faith in the penal system stems from the fact that none of these narratives is able to attract and sustain the overall support of those who are involved in it. This disillusion can be traced to deficiencies, apparent or real, in the narratives themselves.

So what are the main justifications of the penal institutions, and why is it that many think that they are problematic? The debate has often been

---

[1] A. Speller, *Breaking Out* (London: Hodder and Stoughton, 1986), quoted in M. Schluter, 'What Is Relational Justice?' in Johnstone, *A Restorative Justice Reader*, p. 303. See also A. E. Bottoms and R. H. Preston (eds.), *The Coming Penal Crisis* (Edinburgh: Scottish Academic Press, 1980); D. Garland, *Punishment and Modern Society* (Oxford: Clarendon Press, 1990), pp. 3–10; J. Dignan and M. Cavadino, *The Penal System: An Introduction*, 3rd edn (London: Sage, 2002), ch. 1.
[2] Dignan and Cavadino, *The Penal System*, pp. 22–4.

characterised as having two main parties: the retributivist, who takes it that punishment of a person who is responsible for some moral wrong is a good thing in itself; and the instrumentalist,[3] who argues that if punishment is good at all it is only so by virtue of some further happy state of affairs (such as lower crime) that it tends to bring about. Retributivists see punishment as somehow justified in its own right: for instance, as being necessary to vindicate or avenge victims; or to restore justice; or to express the justified outrage of reasonable people. Instrumentalists, on the other hand, see punishment purely as a technique for solving a social problem (or perhaps a range of social problems), such as the impact of the fear and harm caused by crime on general welfare. On the instrumentalist view, then, there is nothing important about punitive institutions in their own right, but a range of broadly punitive institutions such as prisons can be used for purposes that might reduce crime. These purposes might include *deterrence*, individual or general (on the grounds that imprisonment is seriously unpleasant and almost everyone, whatever their other motivations, has a strong motive to avoid it); *incapacitation* (in that one obvious way to reduce the threat posed by dangerous people is to lock them away); and *rehabilitation* (in that having offenders in prisons can make them a captive audience for various sorts of education or resocialisation).

One way to summarise the difference between the retributivist and the instrumentalist is by saying that while the former finds the justification for punishment by looking *back* to the crime committed, the latter looks *forward* to the good that will come from punishment. Another way of putting it is that the retributivist sees punishment as essentially charged with emotion and symbolism, while for the instrumentalist – who perhaps regards the retributive view as rather 'primitive' – it is a technical, administrative question of how to solve the social problem of crime.

It has seemed to many people that ultimately it must be the instrumentalist who has it right. Consider, for instance, how much it costs to run the criminal justice system, and then consider how much we would benefit were that money transferred to other priorities such as health, welfare and education. It is plausible to many that this vast expenditure would be well enough justified if, as the instrumentalist claims, it is necessary in order to protect our welfare and security. But would spending such vast sums of public money really be appropriate

---

[3] As I understand it here, the term 'instrumentalist' can be used interchangeably with 'consequentialist'.

simply in order to ensure that offenders were given their just deserts? The key problem here for the retributivist is to say why it is that the state has an interest in meting out justice that is so strong that it outweighs the benefits that would come from diverting the money to health, welfare or education. This is part of a wider problem, which is for the retributivist to say why it is that giving people their just deserts is important at all. But asking why retribution should be an aim specifically of the state (particularly a liberal state) sharpens the question.

However, if instrumentalists seem to start off at an advantage, there are also problems ahead for them. On their way of thinking, the crucial thing that we want from our penal institutions is that they should neutralise the threat that individuals who are prone to crime pose. One range of problems with this form of justification therefore has to do with the empirical matter of showing that punishment *is* the most efficient means of reducing crime. For although incapacitation is clearly an effective way of preventing crime (at least while criminals are physically locked away) it is not clear that many criminals are sufficiently dangerous to make incapacitation a necessary or cost-effective option; while the evidence on whether deterrence or rehabilitation are effective remains controversial and inconclusive at best.[4]

The other kind of problem stems from the thought that there is something unacceptable about the methods of instrumentalist punishment *in principle*, *regardless* of the results they achieve. For instance, there is the notorious problem that instrumentalists would be willing to assent to the punishment of an innocent person if that were necessary to bring about the best results. Furthermore, the problem here seems to have its roots deep within the forward-looking approach. If the point of punishment is really to promote the social good, then punitive institutions are not essentially different from institutions like the NHS or social security or other welfare agencies. The penal system is to be thought of – and assessed – as a systematic and institutional way of minimising, containing and perhaps ultimately eradicating the problem of crime, that is, a great social ill that, like poverty, sickness and

---

[4] For accounts of the available evidence, see e.g. Braithwaite, *Crime, Shame and Reintegration*; M. Bagaric, *Punishment and Sentencing: A Rational Approach* (London: Cavendish, 2001); D. Nagin, 'Deterrence and Incapacitation', in M. Tonry (ed.), *The Handbook of Crime and Punishment* (New York: Oxford University Press, 1999), pp. 345–68; D. Beyleveld, 'Deterrence Research and Deterrence Policies', in A. von Hirsch and A. Ashworth (eds.), *Principled Sentencing*, 2nd edn (Oxford: Hart, 1998), pp. 66–79.

ignorance, can blight the lives of many. But the analogy between penal and non-penal institutions suggested by the instrumentalist approach makes it seem as though penal interventions, like those in health and education, are or ought to be driven by outcomes, that is, they ought to aim to discover and implement the most efficient way of dealing with the problem. However, this makes it problematic that the penal institution, regulated by the criminal law, appears to be individual- rather than outcome-centred. In other words, the penal institution appears at first sight to be a response to individual *wickedness* or *fault*. I say this because it operates with a fundamental notion of *culpability*. In other words, one has to have responsibly broken a law in order to become punishable. For this reason it might be claimed that there is a basic lack of fit between the instrumentalist's view of the purposes of criminal justice and the form that criminal justice has traditionally taken, hence the worry that the instrumentalist approach makes the culpability requirement dispensable.

Now instrumentalists can find reasons to adopt the culpability requirement. Thus, in response to this kind of problem, some theorists have put forward 'hybrid' strategies, often effectively a kind of rule-consequentialism.[5] They have argued that a system with the culpability requirement has better consequences than that which does not; and that the culpability requirement is needed in order to balance the demands of social stability with those of individual freedom. However, on these accounts it remains only a contingent matter that the general justifying aim of punishment is best realised by punishing all and only the guilty. And hence it may be that, in a particular set of circumstances (and assuming that the knowledge of what had been done would never come out), framing and punishing an innocent person would be easier and have just as good an effect – or an even better one – as trying to track down the guilty party. In that case what would a good and conscientious official within the system do? What, if the instrumentalist account gives the whole story of the morality of punishment, *should* such an official do? She realises, we assume, the importance of the culpability requirement. But she realises also that the general justifying aim of punishment is the reduction of crime; and that in the final analysis it is the general justifying aim that justifies whatever importance the culpability requirement has. Can we not imagine situations in which a good instrumentalist police

---

[5] See e.g. H. L. A. Hart, 'Prolegomenon to the Principles of Punishment', in his *Punishment and Responsibility* (Oxford: Oxford University Press, 1968), pp. 1–27; J. Rawls, 'Two Concepts of Rules', *Philosophical Review* 64 (1955), pp. 3–13; and for a recent defence, M. Clark, 'The Sanctions of the Criminal Law', *Proceedings of the Aristotelian Society* 97 (1997), pp. 25–39.

officer would feel that she had to take it upon herself to bend the rules in order to get the right result?[6]

For these reasons many have thought that these hybrid responses fail to address the deeper problem at the heart of the instrumentalist line of thought. The problem of punishing the innocent, such critics charge, is merely symptomatic of the fact that instrumental approaches justify punishment, not as a response to him or her as an individual, but as something to be imposed on her in order to promote some further overall good.[7] And this means, these critics say, that instrumentalists see it as relatively unproblematic that the innocent person can be sacrificed for the sake of social order; that the offender is treated as a social problem that must be neutralised; and that the body of (presumably innocent) citizens as a whole has the criminal law wielded over it like a big stick, threatening each of us with bad consequences should we step out of line.[8] The reason that the instrumentalist narrative for criminal justice fails to gain widespread support, it might be claimed, is that it sees criminal justice as something like public health, a large matter for social engineering, and does not capture the human significance of crime for individuals.

Let us explore in a bit more depth whether this really is a problem at the heart of instrumentalism. The reason that instrumentalism is said to be essentially vulnerable to the problem of neglecting the individual is that its key principle is that the rightness of actions is to be judged only by their consequences for our fundamental interests.[9] Opponents of instrumentalism charge that some actions – like punishing the innocent – are absolutely wrong and cannot be redeemed by their bringing about good effects. In this way instrumentalism is said to neglect the absolute character of individual moral *status* or *rights*: it involves treating people as mere means to an end. However, in response to such criticisms the instrumentalist is wont to dream up 'catastrophe scenarios' in which we might agree that punishing the innocent is, all things considered, the thing to do in order to prevent some huge amount of suffering. And this,

[6] This is essentially the same problem for rule-consequentialism as is posed (from a utilitarian viewpoint) by J. J. C. Smart in his 'Extreme and Restricted Utilitarianism', *Philosophical Quarterly* 6 (1956), pp. 344–54.

[7] R. A. Duff, *Trials and Punishments* (Cambridge: Cambridge University Press, 1986), ch. 6.

[8] For these criticisms, see e.g. G. W. F. Hegel, *Elements of the Philosophy of Right*, trans. H. B. Nisbet (Cambridge: Cambridge University Press, 1996), §99 Addition; H. Morris, 'Persons and Punishment', *Monist* 52 (1968), pp. 475–501; Duff, *Trials and Punishment*, ch. 6.

[9] These fundamental interests need not be thought of, as in the utilitarian tradition, in terms of happiness. The republican theory put forward by Braithwaite and Pettit takes our fundamental (politically relevant) interest rather to be freedom or 'dominion'. See Braithwaite and Pettit, *Not Just Deserts: A Republican Theory of Criminal Justice* (Oxford: Clarendon Press, 1990).

the instrumentalist argues, shows both that such actions are not absolutely wrong and that what ultimately makes an action morally right or morally required is its consequences.

However, this instrumentalist response ignores the moral depth of such catastrophe scenarios, a depth that one can only appreciate if one recognises that bringing about the best available consequences does not make an action right. Even where punishing the innocent is, all things considered, the thing to do it remains wrong.[10] The instrumentalist claims victory by arguing that in these catastrophe scenarios punishing the innocent is straightforwardly the right action. But in fact the catastrophe case makes it clear why instrumentalism is inadequate: precisely because such an action can never be *straightforwardly* right. To the instrumentalist, punishing the innocent in such a case looks unproblematic as long as it is the necessary means to a necessary end: for instrumentalism that is the only sort of consideration that is morally relevant. Of course, if we can pursue this end without resort to anything quite as damaging as punishing the innocent, then that is what we should do. But the instrumentalist is committed to the view that if some action *is* the most efficient way to bring about the best available result then it is the right action. However, this is to ignore the consideration that makes a case of the necessary punishment of the innocent an agonising one: the fact that in doing so we would be treating someone as he ought never to be treated.

The thing is that we can only see what is really wrong with the way we treat the innocent person in such a case if we see that we have responsibility to treat him with a certain consideration that is not reducible to producing good states of affairs – and is therefore not simply outweighed by the good outcome produced by his being punished. In this situation we are, by hypothesis, producing the best available state of affairs. But we are doing the person involved a serious wrong. This suggests that in order fully to understand the morality of the catastrophe situation we need to recognise that as well as considerations of how efficiently one meets one's ends, morality contains issues of *status* or *respect* or *appropriate treatment*. The reason that the problem of punishing the innocent reveals a deep problem with instrumentalist approaches is that it reveals this neglect of any moral issues that do not reduce to that of producing good states of affairs. And hence the instrumental approach

---

[10] This is one of the main issues in the case of Jim discussed in B. Williams, 'A Critique of Utilitarianism', in J. J. C. Smart and B. Williams, *Utilitarianism: For and Against* (Cambridge: Cambridge University Press, 1973).

can never do justice to the value that individuals ought to have for us, since it is blind to the idea that individuals may have moral status that requires respect. If this is correct, then the least that we can say in favour of the critics of instrumentalism is that any theory of punishment based only on instrumental considerations will always leave out much of what is morally relevant. It will regard some actions as justified when they are not, and it will sometimes fail to pick out the real reason why an action is right or wrong. Of course precisely what one thinks is left out by the purely instrumental approach will depend on what one thinks we owe to individuals by virtue of their moral status. For instance, if there is a duty not to coerce or manipulate, as Kantians claim, a duty that we owe to individuals by virtue of their status as rational agents,[11] and which would constrain the legitimate role of the criminal law,[12] then the instrumental-ist theory will only be able to accommodate it if it can be reduced to something that produces good states of affairs. This is the heart of the criticism that the instrumentalist approach is happy to treat the subjects of criminal law as mere means to an end. We explore these themes in some more detail in chapter 3.

Those who put forward these criticisms of the instrumentalist approach to justifying punishment could be abolitionists: they could believe that there are therefore no good grounds for punishment. But more often, these arguments have come from thinkers who take it that there are indeed grounds for punishing, but that these must be retributive. The thought is that retributive punishment avoids these problems because it is directed towards the individual as a result of a failure for which she is responsible, not for the sake of some result she can be used to promote. Thus retribu-tive punishment shows the offender due respect as a responsible moral agent.[13] But if this makes retributivism appear to have the moral high ground over the consequentialist, there are two major worries for the retributivist as well. One lies in saying exactly why it is that treating someone as a responsible agent requires that some hardship, suffering or deprivation be inflicted on them. For even if the arguments from human dignity do succeed in ruling out consequentialist punishment, it is not clear that they help at all to prove the need for its retributive counterpart.

[11] See e.g. C. Korsgaard, 'The Right to Lie: Kant on Dealing with Evil', in *Creating the Kingdom of Ends* (Cambridge: Cambridge University Press, 1996), pp. 133–58.
[12] Cf. Duff's argument that the criminal law ought not to be understood as offering us 'content-independent' reasons for action in *Punishment, Communication and Community*, pp. 56–9.
[13] This is a theme, for instance, in the early work of Jeffrie Murphy. See e.g. his 'Marxism and Retribution', *Philosophy and Public Affairs* 2 (1973), pp. 217–43.

To press this point, consider that there are various responses to wrongdoing – from ignoring it, to arguing with the wrongdoer, to making some non-retributive symbolic show of disapproval (naming and shaming; waving a red flag) – that all appear, on the face of it, to be compatible with respect for the wrongdoer's identity as a moral agent. Yet, crucially, none of these strategies would involve purposefully harming the wrongdoer's interests or depriving him of his rights. The retributivist therefore has the hard job of explaining why it is more than mere vindictiveness to punish offenders rather than use these seemingly more humane alternatives.

The other worry lies in justifying the claim that offenders are responsible agents, responsible at any rate in a way that would justify retributive punishment. In order to *deserve* hard treatment, we tend to think, offenders have to have brought it upon themselves in some way. But many have doubted whether it can be shown that we have the free will that would make us responsible in this way. After all, human beings are not self-made: they are products of various factors. Although not merely a mechanical response to stimuli, human behaviour is conditioned through and through by influences that were never chosen by the agent herself. Whether through Nature or Nurture our behaviour is not the product of pure free will. So how can it be fair to impose suffering on us when we behave badly? I look at these arguments against retributivism in more detail in the next two chapters.

RESTORATIVE JUSTICE: A PROMISING ALTERNATIVE?

The arguments sketched above give some account of why neither retributive nor instrumentalist approaches have been able to attract and sustain the rational support of those involved in criminal justice. Neither of them, at least on the basis of my sketch, gives a clearly acceptable answer to the question of why we should punish. And without a convincing basic purpose, it will be hard to answer further questions such as: why we should punish in particular ways (the question of sentencing); why individuals should accept that punishment should be left to the state rather than taking it into their own hands; why the interest in punishment outweighs the importance of other goods (such as liberty) that are incompatible with it. However, the theorist who is interested in reforming criminal justice might argue that the criticisms of traditional justifications sketched above give some prima facie support for some criminal justice alternative like restorative justice.

We introduced this alternative briefly in the introduction. Let us say some more about it now. The central ideas of restorative justice might be summarised as follows:[14] (a) criminal justice should be more focused on the needs of victims than it presently is; (b) criminal justice should be more focused than it presently is on the needs of offenders to gain reacceptance or reintegration into the community;[15] (c) offenders have a responsibility to make reparation to victims; and (d) these aims can best be met when matters of justice are left as far as possible for citizens to sort out for themselves.[16] Restorative justice is often carried out by direct or indirect mediation between victim and offender in the presence of a facilitator, sometimes with other 'supporters' of the participants present. The role of these mediation meetings is for the victim and others to testify to how the crime has affected them, to put these points to the offender, to listen to the offender's side of the story and to decide collectively how to address the consequences of the crime. Ideally, perhaps, the process can draw a reparative response (apology, offer of amends, determination to reform) from the offender.[17]

How does my sketch of the pros and cons of retributive and instrumentalist justifications of punishment lend support to this sort of alternative? If successful, the arguments canvassed above cast doubt on the attractiveness of consequentialist punishment – as it violates the dignity of citizens as moral agents and is not clearly necessary to reduce crime – and

---

[14] See e.g. Zehr, *Changing Lenses*; Braithwaite, *Crime, Shame and Reintegration*; Johnstone, *Restorative Justice: Ideas, Values, Debates*; A. E. Bottoms, 'Some Sociological Reflections on Restorative Justice', in A. von Hirsch *et al.* (eds.), *Restorative Justice and Criminal Justice: Competing or Reconcilable Paradigms?* (Oxford: Hart, 2003), pp. 79–114. What follows is really the briefest sketch of these themes and grossly simplifies ideas and debates. My justification, however, is that what I need at this stage in the book is just to give a sketch of this alternative.

[15] See, for instance, the *Declaration of Leuven*: 'Reactions to crime should contribute towards the decrease of . . . harm, threats and challenges [caused by crime]. The purely retributive response to crime not only increases the total amount of suffering in society, but is also insufficient to meet victims' needs, promotes conflict in community and seldom promotes public safety.' In Johnstone, *A Restorative Justice Reader*, p. 478.

[16] On this point the *Declaration of Leuven* claims that the role of public authorities in responding to crime should be limited to 'contributing to the conditions for restorative responses to crimes'; 'safeguarding the correctness of procedures and the respect for individual legal rights'; and 'imposing judicial coercion, in situations where voluntary restorative actions do not succeed and a response to crime is considered to be necessary'; though it does also allow that public authorities can also have a role in 'organising judicial procedures in situations where the crime and the public reactions to it are of such a nature that a purely informal voluntary regulation appears insufficient'. It is this latter point that I will seek to exploit in chapter 6 when we return to look at restorative justice in some more detail.

[17] There are various conceptions of how the restorative process should work. For a survey, see e.g. B. E. Raye and A. W. Roberts, 'Restorative Processes', in G. Johnstone and D. W. Van Ness (eds.), *The Handbook of Restorative Justice* (Cullompton: Willan, 2006), pp. 211–27.

they rule out retributive punishment, as it inflicts hardship for no good reason. But more positively these arguments do suggest the need for a response to crime that will promote social order while respecting citizens as moral agents. One reason for being interested in restorative justice is therefore that it represents an increasingly well-thought-out alternative to traditional forms of criminal justice that can meet some of the major criticisms of traditional justifications of penal intervention. After all, restorative justice is in some way forward-looking, orientated towards meeting the needs of victims of crime and reforming offenders while, it might be argued, not treating the offender as a mere means to an end. It does not relegate the offender to a mere means because of its focus on *moral communication*: the restorative process engages the offender, with his victim and other affected parties, in a dialogue about how to address the crime and the factors that led to the crime. (For this reason restorative justice can be thought of as a form of what Adam Crawford has called 'deliberative justice'.[18]) Thus while restorative justice sees the crime as a problem (for the victim, for the offender and for the community) that has to be solved – and thus potentially shares something with the instrumentalist approach – there are grounds for thinking that it could do so in a way that sees the offender as a morally aware individual who has to be reasoned with rather than simply controlled.

Furthermore we might think that the fact that restorative justice treats offenders as moral beings is something that might actively contribute to its effectiveness in reducing crime. We can illustrate these points by looking at John Braithwaite's theory of 'reintegrative shaming'.[19] Braithwaite thinks that the restorative justice process should aim to induce shame in the offender: this is what happens when the offender takes responsibility for what he has done. But Braithwaite distinguishes two ways in which an offender might be 'shamed': one is that which leads to ostracism and distance, stigmatisation of the offender; the other can be the impetus for a renewed relationship between offender, victim and concerned others. Compare the kind of shaming in which someone is held up to derision, thus being treated as beneath others, to that sort of shaming that might follow a child being told off in front of the rest of the family. The child is made to listen to what is being said to them in a way that makes them unable to escape the fact that they are in the wrong; but once it has been made clear to them how things stand, and once they have

---

[18] A. Crawford, 'In the Hands of the Public?' in Johnstone, *A Restorative Justice Reader*, pp. 312–19.
[19] Braithwaite, *Crime, Shame and Reintegration*.

made appropriate acknowledgement of what they have done, they are then comforted, involved in activities again, and given a way 'back in' rather than being left out in the cold.

Braithwaite's view is that the reintegrative shaming process is more likely to lead to reform than is the use of deterrent punishment. One reason for this might be that when we are shamed by those we love and respect it strikes home in a way that it does not when it happens with strangers. But another (speculative) explanation might have to do with its appeal to the offender's *moral identity*, his self-respect as a moral being. Although Braithwaite does not make this explicit, 'reintegrative shaming' sounds like a moral process, one in which the offender is shown that he is in the wrong, admits that he was wrong and is allowed to say sorry and be forgiven. Perhaps many offenders intuitively feel that such a reaction would be the right one if the situation arose in which they could make it. There is after all something deeply intuitive about the narrative of wrongdoing ending in this way. Furthermore the restorative justice process is one in which the offender himself is given responsibility for deciding how his actions ought to be addressed. He is treated as an adult. However, when an offender is subjected to a mere deterrent regime and feels himself to be coerced, he reacts against it, lashing out and refusing as far as possible to do whatever the authorities are trying to force him to do, or treating it as a game. One explanation of this (which I do not attribute to Braithwaite) would be that – as in our criticism of the instrumentalist – the offender feels himself to be a moral being, with a certain dignity: he feels that he ought not simply to be treated as someone who can only be swayed by threats. Thus he kicks back when the criminal process tramples over or denies his moral identity. As a result all that deterrent punishment can achieve is unwilling compliance. Reintegrative shaming, on the other hand, appeals to a person's moral nature: its success in getting offenders to accept it may lie in part in the fact that it treats the offender as he feels he ought to be treated, expecting of him the reactions and the responsibility that he expects of himself. If this speculation about our moral psychology has any truth in it then it would suggest that the restorative process can bring about important ends while – and indeed because – it treats the offender as a moral being.

This description of restorative justice makes it clear that it revolves around the offender taking responsibility for what he has done. However, this focus on individual responsibility may be problematic if we recall some of the criticisms of the retributive approach to punishment. For instance, we suggested that we are all products of unchosen influences rather than our own free will, and questioned whether we could really be responsible in these circumstances. Some versions of restorative justice are just as vulnerable as retributivism to scepticism about free will because they rest on a deep belief in our moral responsibility. For instance, Zehr thinks that one of the strengths of restorative justice is that it allows for true accountability: his complaint is that often in conventional trial-and-imprisonment justice the offender never has to face her own conscience as she has to do in a meeting with her victim.[20] If it turns out that she is not really responsible, then presumably there is no urgent need for her to face her conscience. However, not all proponents of restorative justice take this line on responsibility. For others like Braithwaite and Pettit, who take a more instrumental approach on which restorative procedures are justified by their good outcomes, restorative justice could be valid even if offenders are not in any deep way responsible.[21] According to the instrumentalist approach we ascribe responsibility not because people are in some deep way responsible, but rather because holding them responsible in these ways has good consequences. While the instrumental view is insulated from the free will problem it has at least the appearance of ascribing responsibility falsely, encouraging a 'beneficial lie' so that people do believe that they are responsible even if they are not.

This consideration raises an interesting question about how close an adequate theory of restorative justice would be to an adequate theory of retributive justice. This question informs one of the major themes of this book. What form an adequate theory of restorative justice will take will partly depend on whether it is possible to give a good justification of our belief in free will and moral responsibility. We will turn to this question in chapter 3. In the next chapter we will look in more detail at some defences of retributivism in order to see what, if anything, might yet be correct in the retributive tradition.

CONCLUSION

In this chapter I have set out some fundamental criticisms of the major traditional justifications of punishment, retributive and instrumentalist. Of course, these are not the only serious criticisms that may be made of these approaches. But they do get at something that seems seriously amiss with the present state of criminal justice. Punishment is claimed to be justified in terms of retribution and deterrence, yet neither of these

---

[20] Zehr, *Changing Lenses*, e.g. pp. 196–9.   [21] Braithwaite and Pettit, *Not Just Deserts*.

goals is an obviously compelling one. Deterrence neglects the fact that offenders are moral beings, while retribution imposes suffering for reasons that seem at best dubious, if not barbaric. Swayed by these criticisms, we might find ourselves entertaining radical thoughts about how criminal justice might be done differently. An increasingly well-thought-out such alternative is restorative justice. In this chapter we have not explored restorative justice in any great detail but we have done enough to point out how this alternative can meet some of the problems that plague traditional approaches to criminal justice.

CHAPTER 2

Some retributivist themes

So far we have introduced the problem of the justification of punishment, paying particular attention to the problems associated with instrumentalist or consequentialist justifications, and have introduced restorative justice as an alternative to punishment. In this chapter we will look at some of the problems and prospects of retributive justifications. Our aim here is not so much a comprehensive overview or survey of retributivism, as an attempt to draw out some promising themes that retributivists have appealed to in attempting to explain their point of view. I will claim that there is a way of weaving these themes together that gives us a satisfying and attractive understanding of what is meant by retribution and why it is important. I will explore this approach, which leads us in the direction of an account of blame, apology and atonement, in part II of this book. What I want to do at the moment is to close this introductory part I by taking a preliminary look at some of the ideas I will be working with. Though not adequate as they stand, I will argue that each has an element of truth that bears further exploration.

THE PROBLEMS OF RETRIBUTION

As we have seen previously, what defines the retributive tradition is the idea that individual culpability is something that in itself (independently of further consequences) calls for a response, and that this response has to involve the offender undergoing hard treatment. Thus we might say that bad people deserve to suffer, and that they deserve to suffer in proportion to their badness, or to the badness of their acts. One central issue in the disagreement between retributivism and restorative justice (as in objections to retributivism in general) comes in the form of a worry about suffering. The point is a very simple one. We abhor needless suffering: this is shown for instance in our incomprehension of those who hunt animals to death for fun (and many proponents of hunting are now to be heard denying that this really is the point of it at all). Yet retribution intrinsically involves bringing about suffering as a response to wrong-doing. So what is it about punishment that makes it needful? As Bentham puts it, 'All punishment is mischief. All punishment is in itself evil unless some greater good should come of it.'[1] So the question can be raised: what is the greater good that retribution brings about that makes the infliction of suffering on someone justified?

Of course, all this objection does is to throw the ball back in the retributivist's court, asking for an explanation. Retributivists will point out that it would be begging the question against them to think that this 'greater good' has to be thought of in utilitarian terms, as Bentham does.[2] And, as we will see, retributivists are not short of explanations given in their own terms. But many have found these explanations quite uncompelling. The retributivist himself might be happy with his justi-fication, but if he cannot persuade others (others who are, let us assume, intelligent, experienced in human affairs, and who come to the issue with an open mind), might we not think that he is being a little hasty to proclaim his confidence in retribution? Why is it that, though some appear to see retributivism as obvious, others are entirely unmoved?

In the face of this seeming impasse, the subversive thought arises: is it something other than rational assent to the arguments that motivates retributivists? For in the absence of a justification that shows retribution to be necessary, it looks as if the practice of retribution is straightforward cruelty to our fellow human beings. And not just cruelty. For those disposed to retribution do not merely inflict suffering, they feel a certain righteous satisfaction about doing so. If the justifications for this satis-faction do not work, if they turn out on reflection to be implausible, will not the question be raised as to why so many have accepted these justifications? And in that case will it not be at least plausible that justifications for this practice are mere facades, a front for a cruel or even sadistic relish in the suffering of our enemies? This is certainly the view of one of the most ambivalent critics of retribution, Friedrich Nietzsche.[3] For Nietzsche, retribution is really a form of sadism; however, it is a form of sadism that he endorses. Wishing to be more humane than Nietzsche,

---

[1] J. Bentham, *Introduction to the Principles of Morals and Legislation*, ed. A. Ryan, in J. S. Mill and J. Bentham, *Utilitarianism and Other Essays* (Harmondsworth: Penguin, 1987), ch. 13.

[2] J. G. Murphy, 'Three Mistakes about Retributivism', *Analysis* 31 (1971), pp. 166–70.

[3] F. Nietzsche, *On the Genealogy of Morality*, trans. C. Diethe (Cambridge: Cambridge University Press, 1994). Nietzsche's views are discussed in M. S. Moore, 'The Moral Worth of Retribution', in F. Schoeman (ed.), *Character, Responsibility and the Emotions* (Cambridge: Cambridge University Press, 1987), pp. 189–219.

we would do better, if he is proved right, to abandon retributivism and try to reform the sadistic urges within us.

So what do retributivists say in response? For them retribution is not about cruelty but rather *desert*. The thing is, they will say, that you cannot compare the suffering of a wrongdoer with the suffering of an innocent person. Yes, to make an innocent suffer needlessly is monstrous; but to make a wrongdoer suffer in proportion to the wrongness of their acts or the badness of their character is merely to give them what they deserve; and giving them what they deserve is necessary to preserve the good of justice.

The sceptic, of course, will look at this response with a questioning eye. 'Tell us more: is it really true that people *deserve* anything at all; and even if they do, why is treating people as they deserve so necessary as to override the need not deliberately to make them suffer?' There are two problems here on which retributivism notoriously founders. The first has to do with free will and responsibility. If offenders are said to deserve their punishment, then this implies that in some way they brought it on themselves. It is not just the case that the punishment is inflicted on them for external reasons, such as policy considerations; rather they must have done something for which punishment is *intrinsically fitting*. But if this is so then they must be responsible for what they have done. And if they are responsible for the offence, then they must be in some way free *not* to have committed it. This raises the question of the nature of the free will required by retributive punishment, the coherence of the idea of such freedom, and the possibility of its compatibility with determinism. I leave this issue until the following chapter.

The present chapter is concerned with the second problem. The second problem concerns how to explicate the attractiveness, and indeed the necessity, of giving people what they deserve, where this involves making them suffer (and where it is assumed that we are indeed free in the manner required by such desert claims). We will look at a number of different ways in which recent retributivists have attempted to explain why it is important to give people what they deserve. I will look at: (1) the view that retribution involves restoring a fair balance of benefits and burdens; (2) the view that links the need for retribution with the need for censure of an offence; (3) the view that explains the supposed 'fittingness' of retributive responses in terms of the fittingness of certain emotions and their associated behaviour (e.g. resentment or indignation and their expression in harsh treatment of the wrongdoer); and (4) the view that sees punishing a wrongdoer as part of respecting him as a responsible moral agent. These different accounts are not – or certainly need not be – unrelated to each other; and it will be part of my thesis that they each express some valid insight when understood in the right way.

RESTORING THE BALANCE OF BENEFITS AND BURDENS

One well-known position is that put forward by Herbert Morris in his paper 'Persons and Punishment'.[4] This view starts by considering a society characterised by an agreement to keep to rules the purpose of which is to protect the interests and liberty of its members. Membership of this society therefore brings important benefits to its members, but they are benefits that can only be realised for the society as a whole if the members are prepared to assume a certain burden, namely the burden of restraint involved in keeping to the rules whether they want to or not. Therefore members of the society have a duty of fair play: in return for the benefits of guaranteed liberty and security that they receive they must be prepared to do their bit by not shirking the burden of self-restraint. This view of political society is notoriously prey to the problem of free-riding: a case in which a person finds that they can have the benefits of society without assuming the burdens, as long as everyone else conscientiously assumes theirs. Indeed on this picture all crime is explained as a kind of free-riding: the criminal is one who fails to keep up their side of the bargain, acting on their desires regardless of whether they are proscribed by the rules that enforce the fair distribution of benefits and burdens. Therefore the criminal gains an unfair advantage over the law-abiding members of society, who have all kept to their side of the bargain. And the thought is that punishment is necessary in order to restore fairness to the system by removing the advantage the criminal gained unfairly.

This account is initially attractive as a defence of retribution because it answers many of the questions about an 'eye for an eye'. It explains, for instance, that a punitive response to crime is necessary insofar as we care about fairness – and not simply for the sake of utility – and why such punishment would need to be proportional to the crime. If we care about maintaining fairness we will want to restore the balance of benefits and burdens. In order to do that we will have to remove from

---

[4] It has also been defended by e.g. Murphy, 'Marxism and Retribution'; J. Finnis, 'The Restoration of Retribution', *Analysis* 32 (1972), pp. 131–5; W. Sadurski, 'Theory of Punishment, Social Justice and Liberal Neutrality', *Law and Philosophy* 7 (1989), pp. 351–73; R. Dagger, 'Playing Fair With Punishment', *Ethics* 103 (1993), pp. 473–88.

the offender the advantage she unfairly took by breaking the rules by imposing a corresponding disadvantage. If we impose a disadvantage that is either greater or smaller than the original unfair advantage, then we will introduce further unfairness, so we are constrained to respond proportionately.

However, does it really show why *punishment* is necessary? The problem is that it is natural to conceive of the advantage that the offender unfairly gains, say in a tax evasion case, as a certain amount of money, as this is what they have got away with. But if this is right, would society not have done all it needed to do in redressing the balance if it took action to recover the money (plus whatever other costs it incurred in taking the action, or in loss of income in the intervening period, and so on)? This recovery does not constitute punishment. A similar question can be raised about someone who attempts to commit a crime but is unsuccessful. In such a case it seems that there was no unfair advantage gained. Why should any restorative action be necessary as a response to such failed attempts?

In order to justify punishment in such cases this interpretation has to broaden its understanding of what 'unfair advantage' is: it has to construe it as something more internal than the external (and contingent) benefit of money. As Finnis puts it, it is the failure to restrain oneself when restraint is required that is the unfair advantage;[5] it is not (or not essentially) the material benefits that may contingently be gained as a result of this failure of restraint. Therefore the society needs to act so as to take away *this* advantage from the tax evader, as well as whatever gains they made out of their attempt. This is also the way in which this account can justify taking action against failed attempts to violate rights. And it also justifies the specifically punitive part of the response. For the thought might be that taking away the unfair advantage of unrestrained willing means inflicting something specifically punitive, because it means inflicting some deprivation on the offender's will (as this is the faculty that shirked the burden of restraint) by depriving him of his liberty.

However, many have thought that the assumptions needed to back up this account of punishment are rather dubious.[6] For it looks as though the 'burden' in the fair balance of benefits and burdens is really to be thought of in terms of the burden of self-restraint. Fairness only enters the picture as the right sort of value to describe the situation on the

---

[5] See Finnis, 'The Restoration of Retribution'.
[6] See, for instance, the sustained criticism in Duff, *Trials and Punishments*, pp. 205–17.

assumption that such self-restraint really is a burden. But in this case the picture looks like a rather State of Nature one: what happens when we come into society is that we radically unsociable creatures agree to restrain our selfish and destructive urges for the sake of cooperation; and we agree that it is fair for us to do so insofar as everyone else is doing so. However, it is not clear that this picture is relevant for many of the central criminal offences, such as murder, rape, assault and so on. In actual society many (optimistically, most?) people are already socialised or civilised, and they do not need to restrain themselves in order to obey laws prohibiting such offences. They feel no burden and therefore it is not clear that someone who does have selfish or destructive urges to which they give in is really gaining an advantage over *them*. Attempting to explain the need for punishment in terms of the unfairness of failing to restrain one's will therefore raises the question (a) of the plausibility of thinking that each crime is really a case of unfairness; and (b) the question of whether its purported unfairness is really the thing that is wrong with it and that merits some sort of response taken against the offender.

Dagger has argued that, while it is not the case that Morris's account captures our intuitions about the *morality* of punishment, it is nevertheless a good *specifically political* account of punishment.[7] I will reserve consideration of this claim for chapter 8. However, the question is whether we should think of the state only as a fair system of social cooperation, and hence of our duties to the state (and to one another) simply as duties of fair play. Dagger's view might be that this is required by the liberal aspiration to neutrality, especially in conditions in which citizens differ in their substantive explanations of why precisely certain actions are wrong.[8] But I think we can expect consensus on a thicker range of values than merely those of fairness, and that the state should therefore take itself as able to criminalise and punish actions on grounds other than unfairness. It certainly seems as though we do not intuitively think of crimes just in terms of unfairness; and it is not clear that a state system of punishment can really be legitimate if it is radically divorced from its citizens' moral intuitions about the need for punishing in a particular case.

Despite the problems that afflict it as a theory of punishment, it might be that, on one interpretation, the benefits-and-burdens view is something that the restorative justice theorist could make use of. For, on some accounts, restorative justice is a view that takes restitution to be

---

[7] Dagger, 'Playing Fair with Punishment'.   [8] Cf. Sadurski, 'Theory of Punishment'.

basic.[9] The restorative justice theorist can agree that, in cases in which the offender has caused some actual damage, and is at fault in some way for having caused it, the fair outcome is that in which the offender is asked to make reparation to the victim in proportion to what was lost in the first place. Thus a joy-rider who has smashed someone's car might be asked to work in order to pay for the repairs to the car, and perhaps to give extra compensation to the victim for the inconvenience and cost of having been without the car for that period of time. This restorative response, like Morris's, might be grounded in the same way in the thought that people are entitled to certain protections, and that when offenders violate those rights or protections they ought to pay reparation and restore things to the way they were. However, this response sounds like a civil rather than a criminal one. The offender pays reparation to the victim rather than to the state: the crime is conceived of as an offence specifically against the victim rather than against the state. Further, the offender can do everything that is required of him, on this restorative interpretation, by making material reparation to the victim and without undergoing any sort of punishment.

Now, even on this 'civil restitution' interpretation, one can argue that the state has an ineradicable role in some crimes at least. For while many crimes have specific, identifiable and individual victims who can be compensated for offences, restorative justice has a problem coping with the many sorts of offences in which this is not the case. For instance, take a crime such as tax evasion. Here it seems genuinely as though the corporate body of the state is the victim. In such cases at least, someone who reads Morris's account as an account of restitution could argue that the offender would need to pay reparation to the state, rather than to a specific individual. However, this response still amounts to some sort of civil recovery scheme operated by the state rather than state punishment.

The problem with the benefits-and-burdens account as a theory of punishment is that it tries to understand all crime as a sort of free-riding. However, it might be said that the reason that this problem arises is that the theory is trying to do something too ambitious: showing that punishment literally restores the balance by imposing a burden on the offender. Perhaps, it might be said, the way forward is to keep things simpler. The fundamental thing that our criticisms of the benefits-and-burdens account show is that we need a response to wrongs that recognises them as the wrongs they are, and which is necessary because

---

[9] See e.g. Barnett, 'Restitution'.

they are those wrongs. In that case perhaps the natural thing to look at is an account on which punishment expresses moral disapproval or *censure*.

CENSURE

What underpins the censure theorist's position is the central retributivist theme that it would be a failure on our part not to react to wrongdoing in some way that recognises it *as* wrongdoing, and hence as an action that is intolerable or unacceptable.[10] Wrongdoing has to be marked in some way. It has to be marked by something that we do – directed at the wrongdoer – that acknowledges that she has acted in a way that cannot be tolerated. The retributivist strategy here is to argue that we ought to be committed to certain standards of behaviour. We ought to be committed to having a society in which people are not abused, exploited or harmed. But this means, the argument proceeds, that we ought to be committed to persons not treating one another in certain abusive, exploitative, harmful ways. Being committed to this, the retributivist can say, we have to be committed to reacting in some way that involves treating the wrong as a wrong. If there was no such reaction this would imply either that we did not think the action really wrong or that we did not think that the wrongdoer was really responsible for it. Imagine a case in which it is well known amongst his friends that a man is violently abusive to his partner, and yet nothing is said to him about it. They all continue dealing with one another as though nothing out of the ordinary were taking place. Would we not conclude that these friends are failing in some way, that they are even in some way complicit in what the man is doing? This is not to say they would also do such things, or even that they necessarily support him. But we feel that there is some duty to dissociate oneself from actions that are unacceptable and wrong, and that it is a moral weakness, perhaps a lack of courage, not to do so.

However, even if it is granted that some sort of censure is required in such a case, then the retributivist still has to answer the question why hard treatment of some sort is necessary to express censure. For instance, an influential modern version of the censure theory is given in Joel

---

[10] This theme draws out what is right in Kant's notorious remark that the members of a disbanding society would attract blood-guilt if they did not put the last murderer to death before disbanding: 'for otherwise the people can be regarded as collaborators in this public violation of justice'. I. Kant, *The Metaphysics of Morals*, trans. M. Gregor (Cambridge: Cambridge University Press, 1991), p. 142.

Feinberg's essay 'The Expressive Function of Punishment'.[11] Feinberg is concerned to point out that purely administrative accounts of the role of punishment – in which punishment is a symbolically neutral means to correct an undesirable tendency in social behaviour – miss out on something of central importance. There is a big difference between punishing crimes and, say, introducing a tax on behaviour deemed undesirable. The difference is that in punishing one implies moral disapproval or outrage. A mere tax on behaviour would simply be a way of changing the way people act in order to bring about a more desirable pattern of behaviour; but in using the criminal sanction one expresses something about the way in which the action should be viewed morally: specifically one stigmatises that action. On this view, punishment, if it is justified, expresses society's (official) disapproval of the offender's action. The state, acting on behalf of the community, makes an authoritative denunciation of the crime. However, Feinberg recognises that merely pointing out that punishment has this denunciatory function is not thereby to justify it. He argues that the denunciatory function is an important one, but asks whether there is not some less harmful way in which to carry it out. He therefore asks why moral disapproval could not be sufficiently expressed by means of symbols that do not involve the use of hard treatment.

Feinberg is interested in the issue of state punishment but the same problem can be raised if we think about the case of the violently abusive husband. Let us say that we agree that this man's friends ought to say something to him about it, that they ought not to carry on as though nothing were wrong. But should they do something that involves imposing hard treatment on this man or making him suffer? Would it not be more appropriate to say something to him, or perhaps rather *not* say something to him – cutting him off, giving him the cold shoulder, not treating him as a friend any more? Would these not be sufficient in this context if censure is the aim?

---

[11] Feinberg, 'Expressive Function of Punishment'. Feinberg's account can be seen as a (very partial) defence of the views of Lord Devlin. See P. Devlin, 'Morals and the Criminal Law', in his *The Enforcement of Morals* (Oxford: Oxford University Press, 1965), pp. 1–25. For a much earlier censure theorist, we can point out that Devlin's views echo those of Stephen, e.g. *Liberty, Equality, Fraternity* (London: Smith, Elder, 1873). Prior to Feinberg, a censure-type account had also been defended by W. Moberly, *The Ethics of Punishment* (London: Faber, 1968). See also the remarks on retributivism in R. Nozick, *Philosophical Explanations* (Cambridge, Mass.: Belknap Press, 1981), pp. 374–80.

WRONGDOING AND THE EMOTIONS

This is a criticism that we will continue to pursue through the next part of the book. However, there does seem to be a way in which the retributivist can respond. For the retributivist might worry whether, if we start to mess around with the symbols we use to express censure, we will really still be expressing censure at all.[12] Feinberg thinks that we can reinvent the symbols we use to express our disapproval. But this shows, it might be said, that he regards the symbolism as merely conventional.[13] It may be a convention that is pretty deeply rooted, but there is nothing necessary about it. However, if we regard punishment as analogous with symbolic language, it is often not the case that we can reinvent our mode of communication while keeping the message. We therefore need symbols that are adequate to the expression of what has to be said in a case of wrongdoing: symbols that will express our distaste, indignation, outrage, revulsion, or whatever is the appropriate reaction to the wrong.

The retributivist might argue that actually there is a non-contingent connection between, on the one hand, the act of censure or denunciation and, on the other hand, appropriate *expressions* of denunciation such as punishment. This is to be found in the *emotional structure* of censure. As we said above, what we need is a set of symbols that express the reactions that are appropriate to wrongdoing. The key to understanding what these symbols ought to be, this line goes, is to recognise that these reactions are emotional ones: condemnation, as human beings experience it, is and ought to be an emotional matter, since it concerns goods and values that we care deeply about. Of course, emotions can get out of control and out of proportion. But the existence of aberrant or inappropriate cases does not show that there are not emotional reactions that are quite appropriate in all sorts of situations. Say there is a situation that calls for indignation or outrage: that is, one in which we *ought* to be outraged about something. In such a case, the retributivist might say, a person cannot really be said to be outraged (or not properly) unless they are disposed to act in certain ways. If we look at the structure of the emotions of condemnation – say, resentment, indignation and blame – we find that these emotions are usually expressed in terms of some sort of

---

[12] See also J. Kleinig, 'Punishment and Moral Seriousness', *Israel Law Review* 25 (1991), pp. 401–21; I. Primoratz, 'Punishment as Language', *Philosophy* 64 (1989), pp. 187–205; R. A. Duff, 'Punishment, Communication and Community', in M. Matravers (ed.), *Punishment and Political Theory* (Oxford: Hart, 1999), pp. 48–68.

[13] See A. J. Skillen, 'How to Say Things with Walls', *Philosophy* 55 (1980), pp. 509–23.

action that is *hard* on the offender. It is not just the case that these emotions *tend* to be expressed thus, in a conventional and contingent way; rather it is *essential* to their being these emotional states that they come to be expressed in this way.

Thus it could be argued that the intrinsic fittingness that retributivists claim to find in the connection between wrongdoing and suffering is derived from the form of these emotions. It is because our perceptions of wrongdoing are essentially emotionally toned that we cannot help but feel that the behaviour by which, say, indignation is normally (and appropriately) expressed is the sort of treatment that should be directed at someone who gives us cause for indignation. Thus if we are looking for symbols that will appropriately express condemnation, we ought to look to the forms of expression of those emotions that we appropriately feel towards cases of wrongdoing. And the appropriate expression of such emotions comes in some type of action that involves hard treatment for the guilty party. As Jeffrie Murphy has written in a (qualified) defence of what he calls 'retributive hatred', '[in] a case where Jones has injured me, has taken unfair advantage of me, has brought me low, and is himself unrepentant and flourishing ... I hate him and want him brought low ... I want Jones to be hurt.'[14]

We do certainly take it that emotional reactions can be assessed as appropriate and inappropriate in particular situations.[15] Thus it is quite commonplace that we engage in arguments with one another about whether, say, the situation in Iraq is something that it is appropriate to get angry about. But such arguments take place against a common understanding of what sorts of situations it *is* appropriate to get angry in. Given our shared understanding of what anger can be about, we can say that it is inappropriate – perhaps even unintelligible – to get angry about insignificant or routine events that have no bearing on our interests: events like the appearance of snowdrops in the garden at the start of each spring. On the other hand, even in this example, we can imagine a context in which this event *is* something that it makes sense to be angry about – for instance when the appearance of snowdrops particularly early is a sign of the inexorable warming of the planet, something that will have untold consequences for us and our children. In this case we have shown how it makes sense to be angry about this event because we can

---

[14] J. G. Murphy, 'Hatred: A Qualified Defense', in J. G. Murphy and J. Hampton, *Forgiveness and Mercy* (Cambridge: Cambridge University Press, 1988), pp. 88–110, at p. 89.

[15] Cf. P. Goldie, *The Emotions: A Philosophical Exploration* (Oxford: Oxford University Press, 2000), pp. 22–3.

understand how the event does represent some important threat to our interests. Thus emotions have an internal logic of appropriateness: conditions in which it makes sense to have the emotion.

Similar things can be said about the way in which emotions are expressed. Thus if someone who claimed to be angry expressed their emotion by doing a merry dance then we would have a hard time understanding what they meant. Perhaps we could again imagine a context in which this is an expression of anger: but it would have to involve showing how the 'merry dance' really was a case of the forceful, excited, dramatic and perhaps aggressive behaviour that we associate with anger.

The crucial point here for the retributivist case is that we are not simply at liberty to invent the response that we take to be fitting to a situation, or the way in which that response ought to be expressed: we already find ourselves with a certain emotional vocabulary, a sense of what response fits which situation, and a sense of what behaviour expresses that feeling. In a way that is hard to explain, we therefore feel that there is an intimate connection between, say, a situation of loss and the action of mourning, such that the action fits the situation. Similarly, we might feel that actions that express condemnation are particularly fitting to situations of wrongdoing. This is the basis of our sense of retributive justice and, the retributivist might say, this is where questions of justification run out. Basically speaking, we have reason to condemn wrongdoing; and we have reason to perform those actions by which condemnation is appropriately expressed. If condemnation is appropriately expressed through hard treatment then by that token it is justified.

However, some readers may worry that this is rather a complacent defence of retributivism. It may be the case that human beings inescapably and appropriately experience the world through the emotions, that there is no question of expelling the emotions from our lives, and that many emotions are essential to the good human life. But it does not follow from this that we must meekly accept all of the emotions that we have. Another way of putting this is to say that although we might agree that emotions have internal conditions of appropriateness – such that, for instance, it only makes sense to experience jealousy in cases in which another person has, or threatens to take, something to which one is attached – this does not settle the question of whether those emotions are appropriate in a wider sense. Thus we can agree that jealousy is appropriate in a certain situation in the sense that we can understand why a person feels jealous. But we can still ask a further normative question about whether jealousy is a good emotion to have or give vent to. For instance, it might be claimed that jealousy is tied to a narrow-minded and competitive possessiveness or acquisitiveness, and that developing the right attitude to cooperation and sharing would mean getting rid of jealousy. Here we appeal to normative standards that (whatever one's view of their provenance) are independent of the logic of the emotion of jealousy itself.

It is in this spirit that we might criticise Michael Moore's argument that punishment can be justified by reference to the fact that the virtuous individual, were she to have committed murder, would 'feel guilty unto death'.[16] Moore's central claim is that, were one to have committed some serious wrong or crime, one's guilt would dispose one to seek out punishment. Undergoing punishment, we might say, would constitute the fulfilment of the emotion. Now this is a claim that I will defend myself in chapter 5. But I think that it needs much more argument than Moore provides. Moore's argument rests on a claim about how, if virtuous, we would feel had we committed some wrong, and how that feeling would make us want to act. However, the crucial thing here is to explain *why* we should expect the virtuous person to feel guilty and desire punishment. Talking about the virtuous person is just a way of saying that the emotion is appropriate. But we need to know *why* it is appropriate, that is, how the emotion of guilt and the desire for punishment could fit into a well-ordered life, the subject of which also pays proper attention to the demands of other goods and values. In the case of jealousy we imagined an argument for the claim that the good life would exclude such a response: could the same not be said for guilt? At the moment Moore has denied that claim but has not given us a satisfying argument against it. In order to do this we will have to get clearer about the shape of the emotion of guilt – that is, how the guilty person understands their situation, how their understanding is an appropriate one, and why it seems to them appropriate to express this through undergoing punishment. Only having articulated as favourably as we can the perspective of guilt could we be in a position to say whether it could be a component of the good human life. In order to make Moore's claim persuasive to doubters we need an understanding of the internal logic of the emotion: we need an account of why the emotion of guilt and the motivation to atone seem compelling in these situations.

Now consider Murphy's defence of resentment. As with other emotions, to experience resentment is to understand oneself to be in a

---

[16] Moore, 'The Moral Worth of Retribution'.

certain kind of situation. In order to pin down what makes resentment appropriate (that is, what it is about), Murphy asks what it is that really bothers us about wrongdoing (that is, on Murphy's first-personal focus, wrongdoing directed at oneself). He dismisses the idea that it is the actual harm that was done (which could after all have been accidental, and therefore not justification for resentment) and says:

One reason we so deeply resent moral injuries done to us is not simply that they hurt us in some tangible or sensible way; it is because such injuries are also *messages* – symbolic communications. They are ways a wrongdoer has of saying to us, 'I count but you do not,' 'I can use you for my purposes,' or 'I am here up high and you are there down below.' Intentional wrongdoing insults us and attempts (sometimes successfully) to degrade us – and thus it involves a kind of injury that is not merely tangible and sensible. It is moral injury, and we care about such injury.[17]

On Murphy's view, what is crucial to moral injuries is that they are an attack on our rights. They place in question whether we have certain rights by implying that it is all right to act in this way even though it apparently contravenes these rights. In response to such injuries, Murphy thinks, we have to defend ourselves: we have to stand up against them rather than allowing offenders to walk all over us. And, on his view, resentment is just this emotion of self-defence. Thus the situation that makes resentment appropriate, on his view, is an unjustified attack on or violation of one's rights, and the way in which this emotion is characteristically expressed is through directing some retaliatory action towards the wrongdoer. Not to experience resentment when wronged suggests a failure to care about one's rights:

I am, in short, suggesting that the primary value defended by the passion of resentment is self-respect, that proper self-respect is essentially tied to the passion of resentment, and that a person who does not resent moral injuries done to him . . . is almost necessarily a person lacking in self-respect. (p. 16)

However, the phrase in parenthesis 'almost necessarily' is an important one here. The reason Murphy includes this is to acknowledge the possibility of someone who stands up for herself in the face of attacks but without feeling resentment about being attacked. Indeed we might think of such a person as a moral exemplar, someone to be admired and, as far as possible, emulated. Murphy denies that such a person is a counter-example to his thesis because he thinks of such a character-type as saintly

---

[17] J. G. Murphy, 'Forgiveness and Resentment', in Murphy and Hampton, *Forgiveness and Mercy*, p. 25.

and unattainable for most of us. However, contrary to Murphy, it is not very difficult to think up counter-examples involving a person who (a) is a realistic type (i.e. not unattainably saintly), and (b) is concerned not to let violations of her rights or those of another pass unprotected, but (c) does not feel resentment or engaged in vindictive behaviour directed at the wrongdoer. We might point to Martin Luther King and Mahatma Gandhi as such cases.[18] Thus we would admire someone who was able to 'rise above' resentment and deal with the situation in a non-aggressive way: we can imagine someone who has been the victim of some violation finding it more constructive and more satisfying to calmly and firmly tell the offender that she is worth more than that and that he (the offender) cannot go around treating people as he has treated her. Indeed, it might be argued that restorative justice scenarios encourage precisely such a response to the offender. For they give victims and others a chance to say something to the offender, but the setting encourages these parties to remain relatively calm and precisely not to get involved in aggressive behaviour directed at the offender.

Thus, for example, we might imagine that, when it is the turn of Bryson's victim to speak at the meeting, she talks about how she remembers the accident, the impact, what it was like to go to hospital, the bewildering experience, wondering what was going to happen to her; the longer-term consequences, such as what it was like getting around in a wheelchair, the effect this has had on her ability to work, to see her friends, to get out at night and so on. (The members of the local community who are called to speak might also speak about the effect of constantly speeding cars on their neighbourhood.) But she might do all of this in an emotionally understated way. Indeed the effect would perhaps be most compelling if she does it in this way, appealing to Bryson's imagination rather than going in with all guns blazing and trying to humble him. Neither is it necessary that there be any formal structured meeting for such a response to take place: indeed the restorative justice meeting is modelled on informal processes of dispute-resolution and mediation. This non-aggressive and seemingly non-retributive appeal to conscience looks like an important alternative to Murphy's defence of resentment. Bryson's victim stands up for herself, determined to have her

---

[18] Cf. L. Stern, 'Freedom, Blame and Moral Community', *Journal of Philosophy* 71 (1974), pp. 72–84. Stern makes this claim in the context of a discussion of P. F. Strawson's defence of the 'reactive attitudes'. See P. F. Strawson, 'Freedom and Resentment', in G. Watson (ed.), *Free Will* (Oxford: Oxford University Press, 1982), pp. 59–80. I discuss Strawson's retributivism in the following chapter.

say and not let Bryson get away with it. But she does not need to 'get her own back' in a retributive way. She has full respect for her own rights, but she is not resentful.

These counter-examples provide a challenge to Murphy because they give us a way of understanding the good human life on which resentment is excluded. These lives incorporate what Murphy claims is important – self-respect and standing up for oneself – but resist the idea that it is therefore appropriate to view the perpetrator resentfully and deal with him harshly. The reasons for thinking that resentment and retaliation are not compatible with the good life are the sorts of reasons we have looked at already: that it involves needless suffering, that it escalates rather than resolves conflict, that it views human beings as responsible for matters over which they have no real control. The challenge for Murphy would be to show that the good human life does include these emotions, but this argument is lacking so far.

THE RIGHT TO BE PUNISHED

Appeal to the emotions by themselves will not settle questions of justification. There is a further issue about how or whether these emotions fit into a good human life. In order to answer this question we have to become clearer about how these emotions portray situations of wrong-doing, whether this portrayal is adequate, and whether something that involves imposing hard treatment on offenders is an appropriate way of expressing these emotions. However, while the appeal to the emotions does not settle the question, it does change the terms of the argument. We do at least have an idea of what sort of thing the retributivist's intuition that hard treatment is fitting *is*: it is an intuition about the appropriate form of expression of the appropriate emotion. The challenge to retributivism is to show that retributive emotions are appropriate in the wider sense in which they fit into a good life. The challenge is that they cause needless suffering. However, in chapter 1 I argued that as well as concerning questions of welfare, pleasure, pain and other good states of affairs, morality is also concerned with questions of respecting status or dignity. One way in which we might claim that retribution does fit into the good life is to claim that, although it involves causing suffering, such suffering is necessary in order to respect the person's status – say as a responsible moral agent or a member of the moral community.

For this reason, I want to continue by looking at another prominent theme in contemporary retributivism – that of retributive punishment as the response necessary in order to pay due respect to the wrongdoer's dignity as a moral agent. This defence of retributivism is put forward by Kant and Hegel. It is Hegel indeed who talks about punishment as the wrongdoer's right as a rational agent.[19] Their thought is something like this. Rational agents are not merely determined to act by causal factors; rather they act on reasons. But reasons exhibit a sort of universality. For instance, when we have reason to believe that the earth is round, it is implied that any rational agent in our position (that is, who forms their beliefs on the basis of evidence and who has available to them the evidence available to us) would have the same reason to believe that the earth is round. For Kant, the universality that holds for theoretical reason (that is, rationality in belief-formation) holds also in the practical case (rationality in action, or in the formation of intentions to act). Thus when I decide to act in a certain way for a reason (or a range of reasons) it is an implication of my decision that I take it that all rational agents in my position would have a like reason to act. And another way of putting this, on Kant's view (though many have doubted that this is merely another way of saying the same thing[20]), is that in acting I take myself to be legislating for all rational agents: I take myself to be saying that this action is permissible for all rational agents. I am making universal law every time I act (and it is for this reason that I am bound by the consideration of whether my action really could become a universal law).

On the Kantian view, this picture leads neatly into a defence of retribution. For the criminal has, by his action, laid down a certain law, say that murder is permissible. In order to treat him as a rational agent, that is, in order to respect the decision he has made as that of a rational agent, what we have to do is to treat him according to the law he has laid down. The criminal chooses a world in which it is permissible to murder: therefore this should be visited upon him out of respect for his rationality. This Kantian account therefore justifies treating the criminal the way he has treated others. It explains the importance of retributive punishment – which has the same importance as respecting the agent as a rational agent – and also explains the importance of proportionality in punishment (the punishment must as far as possible reflect the nature of the crime because the criminal must as far as possible be treated in accordance with the law of his own will).[21]

---

[19] Hegel, *Philosophy of Right*, §99. For reasons to do with the developmental structure of Hegel's arguments, this should not be taken as his final view, but rather as a provisional account, some aspects of which will be incorporated into, but also improved upon, in the final view.

[20] E.g. B. Williams, *Ethics and the Limits of Philosophy* (London: Fontana, 1985), ch. 4.

[21] Kant, *The Metaphysics of Morals*, pp. 140–5. Cf. Hegel, *Elements of the Philosophy of Right*, §100.

The Kantian view, if correct, suggests something like the Principle of Desert as articulated by James Rachels: people deserve to be treated in the same way as they have (voluntarily) treated others.[22] Rachels justifies his principle with reference to an example in which a person constantly relies on and takes for granted the help of others but is never willing to help others himself. Rachels' point is that we are perfectly within our rights to respond to such a person by refusing to help him when he asks for help. However, the problem with Rachels' view is that it is not clear that this refusal to help is particularly morally admirable, let alone (as Kant would have us think) morally necessary as an aspect of respecting the person's humanity. The refusal to help someone who needs it on the grounds that they have not helped others can be appropriate – but can it not also sometimes show a narrow and ungenerous insistence that everyone is responsible for themselves and has no automatic claim on anyone else? Might we not admire someone who, when the selfish person comes looking for help, overlooks their past deeds? Now it might be argued – for instance by Murphy – that the person who does so simply makes herself into a doormat for others to walk over. It might also be said – in the spirit of our earlier remarks about censure – that it is important not entirely to overlook past deeds. But it need not be the case that the person we are imagining makes *no* response whatsoever to the other's selfishness. As we have seen in the response to Murphy, she might well protest, gently but firmly, about the way he treats her and other people. But she might stop short of refusing to help. So while Rachels may be able to argue that it is *permissible* to treat others as they treat us, it is not necessary or even admirable.

This suggests that it cannot be the case that it is necessary to respecting others as moral agents that we treat them as they have treated others. However, despite these criticisms of the 'right to be punished' strategy, it is this strategy that I aim to follow in part II of this book. The crucial thing about the 'right to be punished' strategy is that it isolates an important aspect of the agent's identity – in particular, the identity of being a responsible agent – and argues (1) that this identity has to be respected, i.e. that it gives others reasons to treat the agent in a manner consistent with that identity; and (2) that seeing their suffering as appropriate when they do wrong is a necessary part of respecting this identity. In order to make this argument a success we will need to find out

[22] J. Rachels, 'Punishment and Desert', in H. LaFollette (ed.), *Ethics in Practice*, 2nd edn (Oxford: Blackwell, 2002), pp. 466–74.

what the importance of being held responsible is and why it makes suffering appropriate in the event of wrongdoing. We have seen reason to deny that being held responsible means, as for Kant, that one be treated according to the law of one's own will – at least if this implies being treated as one has treated others. The 'right to be punished' strategy as we will develop it looks rather at another element implicit in the Kantian position: that being held responsible is constitutive of being taken to be a full participant in a valuable form of social relations (on a Kantian view, the Kingdom of Ends, though we will take a more pluralistic view of valuable relationships). This requires us to find some way to bring hard treatment into the picture without relying on the principle that one should be treated as one has treated others. On my account, the justification of hard treatment will rely on issues about censure and the structure of the appropriate emotions that we have introduced in this chapter. As we saw in looking at the censure account, one important idea about retribution seems to be that it affects one's relations with one's social group or moral community, such that wrongdoing cannot go unmarked. We will look at the emotions surrounding such ruptures in good relations. And I will argue that wrongdoers need to be subjected to such emotions if they are to be treated as full members of their moral community.

PART II

Responding to wrongdoing

Responsibility, reactive attitudes and the right to be punished

In this chapter, we look at the crucial question of responsibility. The claim that criminal justice is fundamentally different from other state interventions because it is a response to *culpability* rather than mere harm rests on the assumption that individuals really are culpable for wrongful actions. Culpability, for the retributivist, is a state that in itself calls for hard treatment. This claim that some things that human beings can do *call* for hard treatment has a pivotal status in the argument between retributivists and non-retributivists. But to what extent, if any, are individuals responsible for what they do? And specifically, do we have free will in the sense that would justify retributive punishment, making it morally necessary to punish those who are culpable? In this chapter I present one of the most comprehensive sceptical arguments against moral responsibility and then consider how we might respond to it. In developing a retributivist response I start with P. F. Strawson's article, 'Freedom and Resentment'.[1] However, in this chapter I offer a novel constructive interpretation of Strawson's argument that detects in his position the basis for a 'right to be punished' strategy. I defend this strategy in this part of the book.

THE SCEPTICAL ARGUMENT FROM LUCK

We should be clear at the outset about the sense of 'freedom' that is at issue in this chapter. I will not be considering, for instance, whether the truth of determinism might mean that our sense of having free choice between future options is false; or whether all satisfactory conceptions of moral responsibility are incompatible with determinism. What I want to tackle is the specific perception that (a) a strong kind of freedom is

---

[1] P. F. Strawson, 'Freedom and Resentment'.

presupposed in the claim that failure to meet one's moral responsibilities makes one deserving of blame or punishment; and (b) that we lack that strong kind of freedom. In this section I present an argument for that sceptical conclusion. The argument begins with the thought that in order to be fully morally responsible we would have to be in full control not just of our actions but of the sources of our actions – of who we are. But, the argument proceeds, full control over who we are is impossible. Therefore ultimate moral responsibility is impossible.[2]

The central thought behind this sceptical argument is that one can be responsible for something only if one is in control of it. One is not responsible for what happens as a result of luck. For instance, we do not (except in cases of negligence and recklessness) hold people responsible for what they do by accident. Therefore control over one's actions seems to be a necessary condition of responsibility. But we need a deeper form of control than this in order to be morally responsible. For instance, we would not hold someone who is deranged or brainwashed responsible for their actions, even though those actions are deliberate. What such people lack, it might said, is the relevant ability to control their motivations. This suggests that in order to be responsible for one's actions one must be responsible for the self that produced those actions.[3] What makes us responsible for our selves? The sceptical argument gives a distinctive answer to this question. Just as one can be responsible for one's actions only if one exercises control over them, so one can only be responsible for oneself if one is able to control what sort of self one is. However, here comes the crunch. One can never exercise full control over the sort of person one is. In order to 'control' something one has to act intentionally towards it. But in order to perform an intentional action one has to express beliefs, desires and intentions. Therefore any attempt to control *some* of one's motivations will always express *other* motivations. One cannot escape from the motivations that one has in order to choose – from nowhere – a new set of motivations.

---

[2] This is the argument Galen Strawson calls 'the Basic Argument'. A version of it is to be found in T. Nagel, 'Moral Luck', in his *Mortal Questions* (Cambridge: Cambridge University Press, 1979), pp. 24–38. Cf. also B. Williams, 'Moral Luck', in his *Moral Luck* (Cambridge: Cambridge University Press, 1981), pp. 20–39. For a recent restatement, see G. Strawson, 'The Impossibility of Moral Responsibility', *Philosophical Studies* 75 (1994), pp. 5–24.

[3] See e.g. H. Frankfurt, 'Freedom of the Will and the Concept of a Person', *Journal of Philosophy* 68 (1971), pp. 5–20; G. Watson, 'Free Agency', *Journal of Philosophy* 72 (1975), pp. 205–20; C. Taylor, 'Responsibility for Self', in Watson, *Free Will*, pp. 111–26; S. Wolf, 'Sanity and the Metaphysics of Responsibility', in Schoeman, *Responsibility, Character and the Emotions*, pp. 46–62.

On the terms of this sceptical argument what we are fully responsible for has to be that which is not down to luck. And yet, when we look at it, everything about us is dependent on luck in some way; nothing is left to pure autonomous agency. The point is not that agents are really automata, incapable of making real decisions. People do deliberate, and act on the basis of their deliberations; they ask themselves whether their motivations are the motivations that they ought to have. But the nature of our deliberations depends on the materials we bring to them: the beliefs and desires, character strengths and defects, sensitivities and insensitivities that are given to us by our upbringing and heredity. Even our ability to reflect on our desires is in part a matter of luck: some people are better at it than others. This view does not need to deny that human beings can change through their lives: perhaps no one is stuck with their initial endowments. But even the most optimistic perspective on our abilities to change has to allow that the ways in which we are able to think about changing, and our success in doing so, *depend* on our initial endowment. Thus even this is tainted by luck: it is not something over which we have full control. And hence, the argument goes, we are not really (fully, properly) morally responsible for it.

This argument rests on a normative claim about what we would have to be like if it were to be fair to hold us morally responsible. The claim is that this could only be fair if (impossibly) we had ultimate control over who we are.[4] The target of this argument is the idea that people can be blameworthy or deserving of hard treatment. When we make a judgement of blameworthiness we are making a judgement about the appropriateness of treating someone in a certain way – in particular about the justice of treating bad people badly: we think that there is something *for which* they should be blamed, castigated, held to account. The sceptical argument from luck attacks these judgements of blameworthiness. The sceptical argument seeks to show that it could never be the case that a person really deserves to be blamed or punished. In order to deserve to be ill treated for wrongdoing, the argument goes, one would have to be responsible not just for those particular actions, but for being the sort of person who performs those actions. If it is not really her own fault that she does not care about other people's happiness then how can she really be responsible for acts in which she fails to give others due care? Yet how

---

[4] Cf. the analysis of this type of argument and the centrality given to fairness in R. Jay Wallace, *Responsibility and the Moral Sentiments* (London: Harvard University Press, 1994). See also R. Clarke, 'On an Argument for the Impossibility of Moral Responsibility', *Midwest Studies in Philosophy* 24 (2005), pp. 13–24, at pp. 20–3.

can she be responsible for being that sort of person when she could not possibly have chosen to be that sort of person? If there is any sense in which she does choose to be such a person, she chooses it in part because of who she already is. Her choices are conditioned by who she is. There is no choice entirely free of one's antecedent character. Therefore, the argument goes, one cannot be blamed or justly punished for being a bad person, or being the kind of person who performs wrongful actions.

The sceptical argument from luck poses a challenge to those who would defend the retributive idea that people who have done wrong in some sense deserve hard treatment. And the challenge is an ethical one. It says that only if we had ultimate control over ourselves could it be just or morally appropriate to treat us in that way: the presence of luck makes such treatment unjust. The theorist who seeks to defend the retributive idea has to find some way of showing why hard treatment after wrong-doing is 'fitting' in such cases, even though we are only ever partly in control of who we are. In this book I seek to respond to the sceptical argument from luck by developing a 'right to be punished' strategy. This strategy argues that blame is appropriate because it is essential to a valuable form of social relations. Not to blame someone would be to fail to treat them as a full member of such a relationship. Given that we have reason to respect a person's status as a full member of such a relationship we have reason to blame. Therefore the fact that a person has no ultimate control over who they are is irrelevant to the importance of holding them responsible. In this chapter we introduce this strategy. Now, as I proposed in the previous chapter, accounts of the supposed right to be punished depend heavily on an account of what is going on in punishment, and we considered a Kantian account on which we have a right to be punished as universal legislators. A more promising account, I claimed, would combine the claim about the right to be punished with one of the other strategies for retributivism that we looked at, namely by arguing for the importance of censure or moral criticism. As we saw, a promising way to get punishment into an account of censure is to provide some link between censure and the moral emotions. Therefore, a picture in which censure, the moral emotions and the right to be punished are linked is a good place to start in providing an account of blameworthiness that does not involve an impossible notion of autonomy. Just such a picture, I will argue, can be derived from the well-known account offered by P. F. Strawson.[5]

---

[5] Strawson, 'Freedom and Resentment'.

STRAWSON ON THE REACTIVE ATTITUDES

Before we begin to look at Strawson's account I should anticipate some criticism by admitting that the reading I provide here is an unorthodox one that, while hopefully in the spirit of his position, goes beyond what Strawson himself says in four important ways. First of all, I will take it that we can say more about the *content* of emotional reactions than Strawson himself says. Strawson does not do much to distinguish different types of 'reactive attitudes', or precisely how we must think of a person if we are to think of her as the proper object of such attitudes. Yet a more detailed account of what makes these emotions 'fitting' to their objects is needed if Strawson's view is to avoid some of the objections that can be made to it. Secondly, Strawson's argument aims to show how moral responsibility can be seen as compatible with determinism. However, the question of determinism will not be our main concern here, since our target is rather the claim that true moral responsibility requires full control over who one is. Nevertheless, Strawson's argument about the actual basis of responsibility will be of relevance to us here: his claim that the actual basis of moral responsibility is compatible with our being determined can be straightforwardly transposed into the claim that the actual basis of moral responsibility is compatible with our lacking full control over who we are. Thirdly, I will present a Strawsonian argument, the main thrust of which is a normative argument in favour of retributivism, or at least in favour of certain emotional attitudes that we can see as the basis of our sense of retributive justice. I am not claiming that it is Strawson's intention to present this normative argument: though he does make some assertions to this effect toward the end of 'Freedom and Resentment', these are not really backed up with argument. Nevertheless I will argue that the normative argument can be constructed from distinctively Strawsonian materials, that it makes sense of some otherwise puzzling claims at the end of his paper, and that one who accepts Strawson's overt argument will be not too far away from accepting the normative argument I make in his name. And, fourthly, the normative argument that I offer is more Kantian than Strawson allows himself to be. While Strawson distinguishes an 'interpersonal' from an 'objective' perspective, he is non-committal about their relative moral value. Central to my position, on the other hand, is the claim that where a person is one with whom one could engage in some form of interpersonal relations, this affects how one ought to treat them. Therefore I take more seriously the

Kantian view that our capacity for interpersonal relations gives us a status that ought to be respected.

The basic structure of Strawson's position is as follows. He argues that we can identify two distinct, mutually exclusive but nevertheless compatible 'perspectives' on human behaviour. From one perspective we are seen as potential participants in human relationships who are subject to certain normative expectations (call this the involved attitude), while from the other we are seen from the perspective of natural science as systems whose outputs (such as behaviour) are causally determined by inputs (call this the objective attitude). Essential to the involved perspective are a set of emotions Strawson calls the reactive attitudes, and amongst these reactive attitudes are the emotions of resentment, indignation, guilt and so on (call these the retributive attitudes) that he thinks form the basis of our sense of the need for deserved punishment. On the involved attitude we can be seen as being properly subject to retributive attitudes when we do wrong. By contrast, the objective attitude leads us to see the wrongdoing as the inevitable outcome of certain antecedent influences, and can inform us about how to control or manage a person in order to prevent such actions being repeated. Strawson wants us to see that both perspectives can be valid and coexisting ways of understanding human behaviour. Thus he does not want to deny that human behaviour can be understood in causal terms, but he does deny that it follows from this that human beings ought only to be regarded as objects to be controlled and managed rather than subject to reactive attitudes and claims of responsibility. He asks whether the possibility of determinism should lead us to abandon the reactive attitudes. His answer is negative, and comes in two parts. First of all he argues that the truth of determinism is not a good reason to excuse or exempt someone from responsibility, judged by the standards internal to our practices.[6] Secondly, he argues that there is no genuine possibility of judging the value of our practices from some point of view wholly external to them: if there could be such a way, it could only be a point of view based on the gains and losses to the value of human life, and on this point it would be

---

[6] Strawson, 'Freedom and Resentment', pp. 67–8. This involves denying that the fact that a person 'could not have done otherwise' (in the sense that her action was determined) is sufficient to exempt her from responsibility. Strawson's view seems to be that as long as a person could have done otherwise in *another* sense – that is, in the sense that she had the moral capacities necessary to engage in ordinary adult interpersonal relationships (and hence, presumably, to recognise the demands of those relationships) – it is irrelevant to the issue of responsibility whether her action was determined.

irrational to abandon the reactive attitudes and the rich set of relationships they entail.[7]

This is the barest sketch of the argument for the compatibility of
moral responsibility and determinism on which commentators usually
concentrate. However, towards the end of the paper Strawson makes an
explicit defence of the retributive attitudes and the hard treatment of the
offender that by their nature they involve. This is a normative aspect of
Strawson's view that has received less attention:

> Indignation, disapprobation, like resentment, tend to inhibit or at least to limit
> our goodwill towards the object of these attitudes, tend to promote an at least
> partial and temporary withdrawal of goodwill; they do so in proportion as they
> are strong; and their strength is in general proportioned to what is felt to be the
> magnitude of the injury and to the degree to which the agent's will is identified
> with, or indifferent to, it. (These, of course, are not contingent connections.) But
> these attitudes of disapprobation and indignation are precisely the correlates of
> the moral demand in the case where the demand is felt to be disregarded. The
> making of the demand *is* the proneness to such attitudes. The holding of them
> does not, as the holding of the objective attitude does, involve as part of itself
> viewing their object other than as a member of the moral community. The
> partial withdrawal of goodwill which these attitudes entail, the modification they
> entail of the general demand that another should, if possible, be spared suffering,
> is, rather, the consequence of *continuing* to view him as a member of the moral
> community; only as one who has offended against its demands. So the pre-
> paredness to acquiesce in the suffering of the offender which is an essential part
> of punishment is all of a piece with this whole range of attitudes of which I have
> been speaking.[8]

In this passage Strawson presents a version of the retributivist strategy that
I have been calling the right to be punished. Strawson's claim is that the
retributive attitudes are essential to a perspective in which we see people
as subject to certain demands: the demands of some interpersonal relationship or moral community. But the retributive attitudes dispose us to
a partial and temporary withdrawal of goodwill from the offender: a
withdrawal that is bound to cause a certain suffering or to be experienced
as hard treatment. Therefore seeing someone as subject to this withdrawal
in the event of their offending is just the same as seeing them as subject to
these demands in the first place. A necessary part of seeing someone as a
participant in characteristically adult interpersonal relationships, therefore, is that we see the withdrawal of goodwill as a fitting response to
them when they fail to meet the demands of those relationships. This part

---

[7] Strawson, 'Freedom and Resentment', p. 68. [8] Strawson, 'Freedom and Resentment', p. 77.

of the book is devoted to understanding, developing and defending the ideas presented in this passage.

RESPONSIBILITY AND THE LOGIC OF EXCUSES

Strawson begins his paper by taking a detailed look at the involved attitude and the structure of moral responsibility as it appears therein. The involved attitude can be thought of as the attitude appropriate to our engagement with others in what Strawson calls 'ordinary, adult interpersonal relationships'. The objective attitude, by contrast, excludes such relationships. Now it might be argued that we have a relationship of some sort even with the person with whom we adopt the objective perspective.[9] But Strawson clearly has something different in mind. As examples he gives us the kinds of relationship we have with people 'as sharers of a common interest; as members of the same family; as colleagues; as friends; as lovers; as chance parties to an enormous range of transactions and encounters'.[10] Strawson points out that in each of these sorts of relationship we attach great importance to how the other parties to the relationship deal with us: what their attitudes towards us are. This is most obviously true in loving relationships. But, Strawson can argue, it is also true in the other examples. For instance, when I find my local shopkeeper regularly short-changing me I might be angry about it in a way that does not simply reflect the loss of that (perhaps trifling) amount of money. The object of my (indignant) anger is not so much the loss itself, but the shoddy way I have been treated: in other words, what makes me angry is the contemptuous attitude towards me that this action displays. As this example brings out, it is natural for us to care about the attitudes others have towards us; and it is natural for us to react emotionally to such attitudes: in my example, a form of anger is the response to contempt; but if it was instead the case that the shopkeeper ran after me as I was leaving the shop with the goods that I had forgotten to pick up from the counter, then I would be grateful at this display of goodwill. Similarly, one does not just have this care for how others treat *oneself*: in many situations it can be equally appropriate for us to feel indignant when another person is slighted or taken advantage of as it can be to feel indignant on our own part. These reactive attitudes, such as resentment,

---

[9] Cf. J. Bennett, 'Accountability', in Z. van Straaten (ed.), *Philosophical Subjects: Essays Presented to P. F. Strawson* (Oxford: Clarendon Press, 1980), pp. 14–47.
[10] Strawson, 'Freedom and Resentment', p. 63.

indignation and gratitude, reflect the interest we take in the attitudes people display towards one another, ourselves included.

Thus what is distinctive about the reactive attitudes is that they are attitudes towards the attitudes others adopt and express towards one another. They are attitudes towards attitudes.[11] Now it is part of Strawson's naturalism that he tends to underplay the cognitive elements of the reactive attitudes. For instance, apart from the fact that the reactive attitudes are attitudes to the goodwill we show towards one another, he has nothing explicit to say about what we would now call the *intentional content* of the reactive attitudes: the object to which such attitudes are directed. However, we can explicate this content by saying that another aspect of what is distinctive about the reactive attitudes is that they are conditioned by (what the reactor takes to be) *reasonable expectations* of goodwill. This is particularly clear in the case of the retributive attitudes. Thus it is not the case that I expect unlimited goodwill from my shopkeeper: rather I expect a degree of goodwill appropriate to the relationship. I experience resentment or indignation when the shopkeeper fails to show me the goodwill appropriate to our relationship. (We might also say that we experience gratitude when someone shows more than the goodwill minimally appropriate to the relationship: when they go beyond obligation and do something that shows they are better disposed to me than is strictly called for by the relationship.)

Furthermore, when we talk about 'expectations' in this context we do not mean simply predictive expectation. Rather we are talking about having an expectation of someone in the sense of ascribing a responsibility (in the sense that we might 'hold' someone to an expectation[12]). Thus I might have such a low opinion of a person that I have no expectation – in the predictive sense – that they will be straight with me; but I might still appropriately feel indignation when they again attempt to deceive me – showing that I continue to have an expectation of them in the normative sense. In this case I continue to act as though I 'expect more of them'. Strawson does not explicate matters in quite this way, writing simply of the expectations of goodwill that we tend to have of one another. But I take it that this distinction is in the spirit of his position. What is at its root is a model of social relations or community in which

---

[11] Cf. the reading of Kojeve/Hegel on a 'desire for a desire' in Francis Fukuyama's *The End of History and the Last Man* (London: Penguin, 1992), pp. 143–52. For the original iconoclastic reading of Hegel's master/slave dialectic, see A. Kojeve, *Introduction to the Reading of Hegel* (New York: Basic Books, 1969).

[12] Cf. Wallace, *Responsibility and the Moral Sentiments*, ch. 2.

agents participate in relationships that involve (normative) expectations that each will observe certain standards of goodwill or respect towards one another.

It is also worth pointing out (a point that we will come back to in later chapters) that Strawson's account helps us to explain what it is that is important to us about wrongdoing over and above the material harm it causes. He gives this example:

> If someone treads on my hand accidentally, while trying to help me, the pain may be no less acute than if he treads on it in contemptuous disregard of my existence or with a malevolent wish to injure me. But I shall generally feel in the second a kind and a degree of resentment that I shall not feel in the first.[13]

Now conventional legal theory marks a fundamental distinction between causing harm, perhaps quite serious harm, on the one hand, and being culpable and thus punishable on the other (between harming someone and committing some wrong).[14] It is characteristic of much writing on restorative justice to place the importance of this distinction in doubt, arguing that it is really the harm caused that needs to be addressed. However, an account of what we are doing in criminal justice that is based on something like Strawson's position gives us a reason to make the distinction between harm and wrong. A person commits a wrong, and thus becomes culpable, when she displays some reprehensible attitude towards another, because it is then that she fails to meet some normative expectation to which we can reasonably hold her.[15] It makes sense, if Strawson's view is correct, to insist that there is more to crime than harm: crime is the violation of obligation or normative expectation and not just the causing of harm.

Strawson argues that from this understanding of the reactive attitudes we can explain the logic of excusing conditions. He separates excuses into

---

[13] Strawson, 'Freedom and Resentment', p. 63.

[14] J. Gardner, 'Rationality and the Rule of Law in Offences against the Person', in J. Gardner, *Offences and Defences* (Oxford: Oxford University Press, 2007), pp. 33–55 at pp. 36–9.

[15] If the critic presses the point and asks why we need an institution that exhibits such a concern with the attitudes citizens display towards each other, then perhaps we can give some sort of Strawsonian response, that such a concern is constitutive of adopting the involved attitude. The details of this response will have to be worked out across further chapters. In particular the relevance for a political community of the sort of concern for its citizens' attitudes towards one another that Strawson claims is characteristic of more informal relationships will be a major issue. But the more that the political community can be shown to be a common project in which citizens are engaged, the more it might be shown to be like the sort of thing that Strawson has in mind. On the distinction between harm and wrong in criminal justice, see e.g. J. Hampton, 'Correcting Harms Versus Righting Wrongs: The Goal of Retribution', *UCLA Law Review* 39 (1992), pp. 1659–702.

two different categories. In one case, we continue to see a person as the proper object of the reactive attitudes, though we come to understand a particular action as one that does not merit resentment or indignation. This would be the case, for instance, for unintentional action, or non-culpable ignorance. When someone treads on my hand, I might immediately feel indignant anger towards them. But when I realise that it was a genuine accident my anger abates, and ought to abate. What is going on here, Strawson might say, is that I recognise that their hurting me, because unintentional, is quite consistent with their displaying the appropriate attitude of goodwill towards me. Because it is the presence or absence of goodwill towards me that is the object of the reactive attitudes, in this case indignant anger has no ground. Thus when I recognise a good excuse my anger ought to abate, for it has no justification. In this case, I continue to recognise the agent as someone to whom I correctly have reactive attitudes, but I no longer see her action as expressing her attitude towards me. Thus Strawson's account offers an explanation of why we should recognise unintentional action as a good excuse: if the point of the criminal sanction is to punish displays of reprehensible attitude, unintentional action does not give us such a display.

The other type of excusing condition to which Strawson draws our attention is where we no longer see the agent as the proper object of the reactive attitudes at all. We can take this attitude towards the agent either on a temporary or a permanent basis. (We might also argue that we can take this attitude towards them on a local or a global basis, recognising that they are the proper object of reactive attitudes on certain topics but not on others.) Thus we might say that while the first type of condition excuses certain actions from evaluation by the reactive attitudes, the second type of condition exempts the agent from such evaluation altogether.[16] The clearest case is that of permanent exemption, and for ease of exposition we will concentrate on this. This sort of condition 'presents the agent as psychologically abnormal – or as morally undeveloped. The agent was himself [i.e. was not acting strangely out of character]; but he is warped or deranged, neurotic or just a child.'[17] In other words, when we make such an exemption we deny that we can really be concerned with the agent's attitudes towards others in the way that we are generally concerned with such attitudes. We are saying that we cannot expect of this agent what we can expect of others and that it is therefore not reasonable to have reactive

[16] Following the distinction made in Wallace, *Responsibility and the Moral Sentiments*.
[17] Strawson, 'Freedom and Resentment', p. 66.

attitudes towards him. But this is because we are denying that this person is really the sort of person with whom we can properly form the sorts of interpersonal relationships in which we expect things of one another in the normative sense: it does not really make sense to hold this person to those demands. This suggests that for Strawson a necessary condition of moral responsibility is some sort of responsiveness to the normative demands of one's relationships, the expectations that people can reasonably have of one another; it is because the psychologically abnormal or morally undeveloped lack the appropriate capacity to respond to those demands that they cannot be held to them.

Now we are in a position to understand Strawson's vindication of responsibility. Rather than looking at the question of determinism, as Strawson does, let us look at the sceptical argument from luck. Strawson's response in either case will be essentially the same. The sceptic believes that full autonomy (however impossible) would be necessary for us to be truly morally responsible in the sense of deserving to be treated badly when we have done wrong. To this Strawson will first of all say that what being treated badly consists in is being subject to the reactive attitudes. So what we have to look at is the justice of the reactive attitudes. He then asks whether the fact of our lack of ultimate control is a good reason for excusing or exempting us from the reactive attitudes. And his argument will be that this lack of ultimate control could not be the sort of thing that counts as a good reason for such an excuse or exemption: the sorts of cases in which we excuse people are when their (apparent) actions do not really express their will: the sorts of things that give us reason to exempt people from responsibility are psychological abnormality or moral underdevelopment. Therefore moral responsibility does not require ultimate control. It requires psychological normality, a certain level of moral development and the freedom of action to express one's intentions in action. And lack of ultimate control does not preclude any of these things.

Furthermore, we can see why moral responsibility should require moral development rather than ultimate control. On Strawson's view, what we are doing in holding someone responsible is holding them to the demands of some relationship. The conditions for responsibility have to do with one's capacity to participate in such relationships – where this centrally involves having the moral capacity to recognise and respond appropriately to what can reasonably be expected of one within those relationships – rather than a capacity for radical self-determination. As long as this moral capacity is not undermined by a lack of ultimate control, neither is our appropriateness as objects of the reactive attitudes.

Thus Strawson's response to scepticism about moral responsibility is to look more closely than the sceptic does at the logic of our practice of holding people responsible, based on the reactive attitudes. He starts with a model of social relations in which we have responsibilities to treat one another with a reasonable degree of respect or goodwill. He then argues that the reactive attitudes are a product of our concern that these responsibilities are met. Given this picture it will be fair to hold a person responsible as long as the initial expectations we had of them were not overly demanding, and as long as they were capable of meeting those demands. Where these conditions are met there is nothing unfair about holding someone to account for a failure to meet those demands.

THE REACTIVE ATTITUDES AS EVALUATIONS OF CHARACTER

Nevertheless, critics of Strawson have sometimes found this argument worryingly uncritical.[18] It is worrying, they might say, because it leaves our practices of ascribing responsibility unquestioned. Strawson's strategy is to claim that lack of ultimate control is not the sort of thing that counts as a good excuse in our practice of holding people responsible. And his attitude to our practices is not merely descriptive, since he goes some way to explaining why it should not count as a good excuse. But his strategy assumes that *as long as there is no excuse*, holding a person responsible (and subjecting them to the reactive attitudes) is justified. And this, the critic might say, is simply to assume that holding people responsible is the default position. Strawson assumes (without argument) the justifiability of a practice in which people have responsibilities to which they can be held in the event of a failure to comply: his only argument is about when we should exempt people from this practice. But, the critic might claim, the sceptical argument from luck shows this very practice to be problematic. Let us see what can be said for this latter claim.

Strawson's position is that where a person has the capacity to recognise and respond appropriately to moral demands (that is, the demand – in the context of some relationship – that they show others respect and goodwill) we are justified in holding them accountable to those demands. But what is involved in being 'capable' of meeting the demands to which one is being held? Evidently one can be capable of meeting these demands even though one does not actually meet them. So we might say that a person is capable in the sense that they *would have* grasped the force of

---

[18] See e.g. E. Kelly, 'Doing Without Desert', *Pacific Philosophical Quarterly* 83 (2002), pp. 180–205.

those demands if they had thought about it hard enough, and that if they had grasped the force of the demands they would have been motivated to comply with them.[19] (Thus the problem with the 'psychologically abnormal and the morally underdeveloped' is that this is not true of them: no matter how hard they thought about the matter they could never have grasped the force of the demands.) However, while it might be true that *if* someone thought about the matter hard enough they would see why they should not act like that, it might nevertheless also be the case that *being the kind of person they are* they never *will* think that hard about such a thing. The person in question might just be too self-centred or insensitive for the thought to occur to them. This will not undermine their responsibility in Strawson's terms. This person will still be the object of reactive attitudes, having nothing that will count as an excuse. But if we understood them fully then we would see that really they were unable to comply with the demands of the relationship. And given this, the critic might argue, why should we make such a big deal about holding people responsible?[20]

The thing is that there are two different senses of 'could have recognised and responded appropriately' at work here. The person we are imagining 'could have' in the sense that *if* they thought hard enough they would. But at the same time they 'could not have' in the sense that in reality thinking about it hard enough is not something that fits with their habitual psychological make-up. But in that case we are in a strange position. For given our practice of responsibility we hold this person to have an obligation to comply, an obligation to which we will hold him. But if we knew all that there was to know about him we would see that we could predict that he would not comply. There is a certain inevitability about his non-compliance. Given this, is it really fair to hold him responsible? Is our temptation not to react retributively undermined by greater knowledge of why the person acts as he does? *Tout comprendre est-ce tout pardonner?*[21]

However in response to this restatement of the sceptical argument, Strawson's position has the resources to explain why, even if there is a certain inevitability about a person's non-compliance (and even if we

[19] See e.g. J. O'Leary-Hawthorne and P. Pettit, 'Strategies for Free-Will Compatibilists', *Analysis* 56 (1996), pp. 191–201.

[20] An argument to this effect might also be extracted from M. Nussbaum, 'Equity and Mercy', *Philosophy and Public Affairs* 22 (1993), pp. 83–125.

[21] Cf. e.g. G. Watson, 'Responsibility and the Reactive Attitudes: Variations on a Strawsonian Theme', in Schoeman, *Responsibility, Character and the Emotions*, pp. 256–86.

could predict their non-compliance if we knew everything that there is to know about their history), this is irrelevant to whether they are responsible. In order to make these points we will have to develop Strawson's position rather than stick religiously to what he says. But again I take it that my interpretation remains in the spirit of his position. Basically the response is that what we do when we have reactive attitudes towards wrongdoers is to evaluate those wrongdoers as members of a relationship, and that in order for such evaluation to be appropriate we do not require ultimate control, we only require moral capacities (such that, for instance, if we thought about our responsibilities hard enough we would understand their significance).

Let me explain these points in more detail. Strawson thinks that what motivates the practice of moral judgement is our concern that people treat one another with basic standards of respect and goodwill. He does not think that the reactive attitudes have an essentially instrumental role, where we aim to encourage compliance with these standards by blaming those who do not comply. But neither is it enough to see reactive attitudes as a mere 'bite-back' response to a perceived threat.[22] Rather his view seems to be that in our moral judgements we evaluate a person's compliance with these standards, assessing the extent to which their actions express adequate respect or goodwill.[23] What we are doing is assessing the extent to which a person has or exhibits a certain trait of character – or virtue or excellence – namely that of responding well to the demands of the relationship. Now consider how we evaluate people in other contexts and for other excellences. For instance, we evaluate people for their intelligence or beauty, we evaluate how good their essays are, how well they do their job, how well they deal with a difficult situation. In each case we grade a person's qualities, or their responses to the demands of a situation, against a notional scale of better and worse responses. But we do

---

[22] J. L. Mackie, 'Morality and the Retributive Emotions', *Criminal Justice Ethics* 1 (1982), pp. 3–9.
[23] These remarks locate Strawson in a broadly Humean tradition on which the role of moral judgements is to evaluate character: see D. Hume, *Treatise of Human Nature*, ed. L. A. Selby-Bigge and P. H. Nidditch (Oxford: Oxford University Press, 1978), pp. 606–13. On this view, as long as actions really do reflect one's character they are germane to moral assessment (see Hume, *Treatise*, p. 349). For discussion of this approach, see S. Wolf, *Freedom Within Reason* (Oxford: Oxford University Press, 1990), ch. 3, on the 'real self' view. Such judgements have also been called *aretaic*. See M. Slote, *From Morality to Virtue* (Oxford: Oxford University Press, 1992); G. Watson, 'Two Faces of Responsibility', *Philosophical Topics* 24 (1996), pp. 227–48. Since 'character' is a very wide category (particularly on Hume's account) my reading of Strawson sees moral judgements as evaluations only of a particular aspect of one's character, namely, one's commitment to moral demands. For another example of this type of view, see R. M. Adams, 'Involuntary Sins', *Philosophical Review* 94 (1985), pp. 3–31.

so without worrying about whether such judgements are ultimately fair in the sense that we have ruled out the influence of luck. If I say that one person is a better footballer or musician than another, my judgement is not undermined by the fact that luck may have played a significant role in this outcome: the fact is just that one person does the activity better than the other. The evaluation can be correct (if the scale is determinate and my judgement good) even though it is not ultimately the agent's fault that they are worse. Strawson can say the same thing about moral judgement. The reactive attitudes, he could say, function as evaluations of a person's responses to moral demands. Some people are better at responding to moral demands than others. There might be a certain inevitability about any given person failing to comply in a particular situation, or given a particular competing attraction. This is a matter of bad luck, since it means that some people will be subjected to the reactive attitudes more than others. But it is not radically unfair in such a way as to undermine the correctness of the judgements.

So the way to understand Strawson's claim here is to see that the judgements that underpin the reactive attitudes have the same basic evaluative or grading structure as many other judgements that we make quite innocently, and that take little account of luck. Of course, our moral judgements of a person need to take some account of luck. We need to discount accidental action, action from ignorance and so on. We also need to discount cases in which a person is unlucky enough to lack the capacities necessary for full engagement in interpersonal relationships. However, we discount luck in these cases because the features conditioned by luck are irrelevant to the assessment we are trying to make: an assessment of the quality of a person's will. It is illegitimate to generalise – as the sceptical argument from luck does – from these cases to a general 'control condition', according to which one can only be morally judged for that which is ultimately within one's control.[24]

'THE RIGHT TO BE EVALUATED AS A MEMBER OF MORAL RELATIONSHIPS'

This aspect of my interpretation of Strawson establishes the possibility of such evaluative judgements of a person's excellence in a certain field. These judgements are appropriate ones to make of persons when we look at them from the involved perspective. However, even though they are in

[24] As in Nagel, 'Moral Luck'.

some sense appropriate, it might be claimed that we need a further argument to show that these judgements should determine how we treat wrongdoers. The thing is that we are still left with two ways of seeing wrongdoers. On the one hand, we can evaluate them as participants in interpersonal relationships. On this perspective retributive attitudes follow on from negative assessments of a person's will: we withdraw goodwill from such persons. But we can always switch to the equally valid 'objective perspective', on which we understand their actions as being the result of antecedent factors. And it might be suggested that by switching back and forth between the involved and the objective perspectives, we can defuse the temptation to treat wrongdoers harshly by reminding ourselves that the involved perspective on which we see them as deserving such treatment is, after all, only one way of looking at their behaviour.[25] Of course, we might say, she is uncaring, insensitive, selfish. This is a correct judgement on her. But she is also the product of a particular history of which she was not the author. Given this, might we not hold that the negative evaluation of her is correct but that we are not bound – and perhaps, given the obligation to avoid unnecessary suffering, not permitted – to treat her harshly on the basis of the negative evaluation? Strawson's defence of reactive attitudes assumes that the involved perspective takes *priority*, perhaps even that the objective attitude is sometimes inappropriate. But his official position seems to be that both perspectives are equally valid. In order fully to justify the retributive attitudes we need to explain why we should not allow the objective perspective to undermine them.[26]

Strawson does go some way to meeting this point. He claims that it would impoverish human life if we only adopted the objective perspective. Therefore there has to be a place in human life for that perspective in which we see persons as participating in relationships that place normative demands on them and evaluate those persons according to how well they respond to those demands. However, while we may accept the conclusion that it would impoverish human life if there was no place for holding people responsible or evaluating them as participants in these relationships, it nevertheless seems that for any particular case Strawson will acknowledge that there is always the possibility that we should view the person through the objective perspective or the involved perspective (or indeed both). Both

---

[25] Watson, 'Responsibility and the Reactive Attitudes'.
[26] Cf. also R. Wasserstrom, 'Why Punish the Guilty?' in G. Ezorsky (ed.), *Philosophical Perspectives on Punishment* (Albany, N.Y.: SUNY Press, 1972), pp. 328–41.

perspectives are after all valid. However, if we acknowledge this it seems that there might be something arbitrary about our choice, in any particular case, to react to wrongdoing with the reactive attitudes rather than the objective attitude. It will simply be a matter of the responder's psychology at the time as to which perspective takes precedence.

What the defence of the reactive attitudes requires is therefore some argument to explain why it is sometimes appropriate to adopt one perspective rather than another. The heart of this response – and what brings us to the idea of a 'right to be punished' – is the idea that it is somehow important to be subjected to the demands of relationships. We can argue that it is important to be subjected to the demands of relationships by seeing why not being treated as though one were subject to the demands of relationships would be intolerable. We can see this by looking at what Strawson presents as the alternative to the reactive attitudes: the objective perspective.

The traditional compatibilist approach to the free will problem seeks to solve the apparent conflict between moral responsibility and determinism by arguing that responsibility requires far less in the way of freedom than sceptics assume. But – in the simple version that Strawson attacks – the compatibilist makes this argument by adopting an instrumentalist approach to the practices of blame and punishment, an approach that can be characterised as the 'economy of threats' approach.[27] To be free or responsible on the instrumentalist line does not mean 'was in full control of their actions and therefore deserving of punishment'; rather it means 'can be punished effectively: punishment is likely to deter them from further misdemeanour'. This compatibilist line makes it plausible that we are responsible *in this sense* – we are sufficiently rational to be swayed by incentives. The instrumentalist view of our blaming reaction is that these reactions are a productive way of controlling that person, and getting them to change the way they behave.

Strawson presents the 'economy of threats' approach as a morally intolerable one. He assumes that in order for compatibilism to be plausible we would have to improve upon it. This is because the 'economy of threats' approach exemplifies what Strawson calls the *objective attitude*. In the objective attitude, we look at others as forces to be controlled and managed, the objects of some sort of social control.

---

[27] For this terminology, see H. L. A. Hart, 'Legal Responsibility and Excuses', in *Punishment and Responsibility* (Oxford: Oxford University Press, 1968). For an example of the approach, see J. J. C. Smart, 'Freewill, Praise and Blame', *Mind* 52 (1961), pp. 291–306. For critical discussion, see Wallace, *Responsibility and the Moral Sentiments*, pp. 54–9.

To adopt the objective attitude to another human being is to see him, perhaps, as an object of social policy; as a subject for what, in a wide range of sense, might be called treatment; as something certainly to be taken account, perhaps precautionary account, of; to be managed or handled or cured or trained; perhaps simply to be avoided . . . The objectivity of attitude may be emotionally toned in many ways, but not in all ways: it may include repulsion and fear, it may include pity or even love, though not all kinds of love. But it cannot include the range of reactive feelings and attitudes which belong to involvement or participation with others in inter-personal human relationships; it cannot include resentment, gratitude, forgiveness, anger, or the sort of love which two adults can sometimes be said to feel reciprocally, for each other. If your attitude towards someone is wholly objective, then though you may fight with him, you cannot quarrel with him, and though you may talk to him, even negotiate with him, you cannot reason with him, you can at most pretend to quarrel, or to reason, with him.[28]

Thus when we adopt the objective perspective towards someone, we see him as a 'factor' that has to be taken account of and dealt with in some way, by management or treatment. The objective attitude is not an emotionless attitude; but Strawson thinks of it as an attitude from which the emotions most characteristic of dealings between human beings have been removed. In the objective attitude, seeing people as 'factors', we do not see in them the features characteristic of human beings: it might be said that we do not see them specially as people at all. We might say that because in the objective perspective we do not see people as the kinds of beings with whom we could have those sorts of interactions characteristic of human intercourse. For instance, the objective attitude is a perspective that excludes reasoning with the other party (we can negotiate, in some sense, but we cannot reason). When we adopt the objective attitude towards someone the question of whether they can reason or not becomes irrelevant.

Thus Strawson makes an important distinction between two different ways of understanding human behaviour: on the one hand, the categories of understanding and the mode of engagement used when we are dealing with other human beings as fellow participants in relationships; and, on the other, this external, objective perspective that we adopt when seeking to understand the causes of human behaviour and the ways in which we might change social conditions in order to achieve different behavioural outcomes. Now Strawson agrees that the objective perspective is *true* to the facts of human behaviour: it gives us knowledge of how human behaviour is produced. Thus if we want to know how to get certain results in a certain social situation – say, how to reduce obesity; how to

---

[28] Strawson, 'Freedom and Resentment', p. 66.

reduce reoffending – then knowledge gained in the objective perspective might help. But if this perspective is true to the facts, what can be wrong with it?

What we might say at this point is that the objective attitude is lacking as a *mode of interaction* with other people. And this seems to be the Kantian moral heart of Strawson's approach. Though he does not state this point explicitly, his approach seems to be motivated by the understanding that, when we come to thinking about how we should treat one another – when we are thinking about our modes of interaction – there is more to think about than merely how to get people to behave in desirable ways. Although the information we get from the objective perspective reveals many truths that we could deploy in devising strategies for bringing about desirable results, this perspective provides at best a partial answer to the question of how we should act, or how we should treat one another. For it has no room for the idea that we should treat one another as members of relationships, that we have responsibilities to one another as members of such relationships, that – to recall my criticism of instrumentalism in chapter 1 – when it comes to thinking about how to treat one another, there are relevant considerations other than simply those of desirable ends and the most efficient means of realising them. We have already seen another source of what Strawson thinks of as normative demands: the demands that we are under to show one another a certain standard of goodwill or regard given the relationships in which we stand to them. We saw that different sorts of relationships bring with them different sets of normative expectations that participants can have of one another. These relationships may be actually existing social relationships, but they may not be. A person's status as a member of a relationship can give us responsibilities to treat her in a way appropriate to the relationship. If these are genuine responsibilities then they would be neglected if we simply adopted the objective perspective. Kantians tend to talk as though it is only a person's status as a rational agent that gives us reasons for respect.[29] But – despite the undeniable Kantian heritage of his view – Strawson's approach holds out the possibility of a richer set of

---

[29] The Kantian position picks up on one aspect of this point, or one type of relationship. Two rational agents are in a certain relationship with one another by virtue of their shared rationality. Certain modes of interaction are open to them – those like dialogue, debate and reasoning, that use their shared rationality – and because of the (intrinsic) importance of our rationality and those modes of interaction based on rationality, we ought to respect another person's ability to reason rather than treat them simply as a means by which we could bring about a desirable end. Elements of this interpretation of Kant can be found in T. Nagel, 'War and Massacre', in his *Mortal Questions*, pp. 53–74; and in Korsgaard, 'The Right to Lie'.

'associative obligations' (that is, relationships we have by virtue of different sorts of community or relationship with others).[30] For instance, by virtue of our relationship, my shopkeeper owes it to me to give me the correct change; by virtue of our relationship I owe it to my friend to help him out when he is in need; by virtue of our relationship I owe my daughter more in the way of detailed concern and attention than I owe to other seven-year-olds. Participating in some valuable relationship or mode of human interaction brings with it certain responsibilities. If I value the relationship (as in some cases presumably I ought to) then I ought to comply with the responsibilities it involves.[31]

On this reconstruction of Strawson's account, then, we have some responsibility to treat one another in a manner appropriate to our relationship with them (to treat them with the goodwill or regard that can reasonably be expected of us). These relationships may be actually existing social relationships, but they may not be. We said earlier that what seems wrong with the objective perspective is that in it we do not see people as capable of the kinds of interaction characteristic of human beings. If we are drawn by the thought that in some cases we have an obligation not to adopt the objective attitude, then this suggests that we take ourselves to be in a relationship that might be structured simply by the *potential* for a certain valuable form of interaction. But if this is the case then it cannot be appropriate simply to adopt the objective attitude towards others. For on the objective attitude one does not see any such thing as responsibilities to another person by virtue of her status in a valuable form of interaction. One only sees efficient causes and probabilities. These are relevant if one wants to know how to get a person to behave in a certain way. But there is something else one might want to know – something else that it is important to know – and this is what one owes to the other person as a participant in a certain relationship. Thus the reason why we should not give up the involved attitude, why we should attend to the demands of these various relationships, is simply that these relationships consist in forms of human interaction that are valuable in their own right: they have a claim on those who are in them because they are important forms of human activity. The normative basis I am suggesting for my development of Strawson's position is wider than Kantianism, since it includes claims about the inherent value of relationships other than the relationship

---

[30] For the use of this term, see e.g. R. Dworkin, *Law's Empire* (London: Fontana, 1986), pp. 195–202.
[31] Cf. S. Scheffler, 'Relationships and Responsibilities', *Philosophy and Public Affairs* 26 (1997), pp. 189–209, at pp. 200–1.

between rational agents (the claim, that is, that we may reasonably be expected to treat someone with a degree of goodwill or regard that is not just the respect they are owed qua rational agent), and of activities other than rational activity as such. But the position shares with Kant a non-consequentialist pluralism about morality: the claim that the moral life does not just involve thinking about ends and means; that we must also think about whether we are treating one another in a manner appropriate to the relation in which we stand to them.

This provides us with a subtle and pluralistic argument against the 'economy of threats' approach. For it acknowledges that the 'economy of threats' approach is motivated by something important, namely, the wish to bring about desirable ends. But in pointing out that the 'economy of threats' approach exemplifies the objective attitude, this Strawsonian argument lets us see that the 'economy of threats' approach is based on an impoverished view of the normative demands that our relationships make of us. The person who adopts the objective attitude thinks that the only consideration determining how she should treat another person is what she can do to bring about the best result: the other person's status as a fellow member of some relationship is not seen as affecting the deliberator's normative situation at all. What our argument points out, however, is that our relationships bring different sorts of demands on us, and that in general we owe a certain goodwill or respect to our fellow participants. We owe our fellow participants something as individuals – each by virtue of their status – namely that we treat them in a manner appropriate to the relationship we have with them; we do not just have a general duty to bring about good results, hence the conclusion that the 'economy of threats' approach, with its reductive 'objective' attitude, is morally intolerable: it neglects too much of what is ethically important.

So far the argument against the 'economy of threats' approach has had nothing positive to say about moral responsibility, or why we should hold one another responsible. It has simply pointed out what is problematic about treating one another simply as objects to be controlled by threats and incentives. But the Strawsonian approach can establish a stronger conclusion than this. For if it is true that we owe a certain goodwill to people, what this means is that we should – as I have glossed it – 'treat them in a manner appropriate to the relationship'. We should treat them with the respect due to the status they have as someone with whom we have some valuable relationship, or with whom some valuable form of interaction is possible. However, this status, in the sort of relationships Strawson has in mind, has two faces. On the one hand, it concerns what we should *do for* the person – say, in the way of non-interference and positive treatment – but on the other hand it concerns what we should *expect from* them. For being subject to certain expectations is another aspect of being treated as a participant in a relationship. If our general duty – in this non-consequentialist aspect of morality – is to treat others in a manner appropriate to the relationships we have with them, to do justice to their status as participants within those relationships, then it is also the case that we ought to hold people to the expectations that one has of such a participant. Not to treat someone as though one had those expectations of them would not be to treat them as a full member of that relationship.

This idea can be spelled out by an example. Say one has a relationship with a friend that verges on the abusive. This friend has a very busy, high-flying job and he is often under a lot of pressure. However, the way in which he deals with this pressure has the result that the arrangements he makes with his friends always take second place to his job and its demands. He often fails to turn up when you have arranged to meet; and when he does turn up he always seems to have something else on his mind: he spends half his time on his mobile phone talking to someone else. Furthermore, the pressure he is constantly under makes him short-tempered and he lashes out at people (oneself included) when things do not quite go his way. Now in this situation one might quite rightly, as a good friend, give such a person a certain amount of leeway, on the assumption that their behaviour, charitably interpreted, could be compatible with their continuing to have one's interests at heart. One might therefore not find cause for complaint immediately. However, after a certain point, there is surely a question of what sort of relationship one has with this person. Now one thing that one might do in such a situation is to bite one's lip and to let the relationship die, letting one's friend go his own way. However, another thing that one might do, if one values the relationship, is to speak out, to complain, to try to get one's friend to see what he is doing. In other words, one might hold one's friend to the demands of the relationship, and doing so can be a necessary part of taking him seriously as a member of that relationship. In this situation it is not just humanity or compassion to hold one's tongue: not holding the person to the demands of the relationship would be a signal that one does not really regard him as a friend anymore.

If the above argument is plausible, then we finally have an explanation of why our awareness that a person is not the sole author of their personal history does not count as a reason not to hold them to the demands of the relationship – unless, that is, their personal history is such that they lack the capacity fully to respond to the demands of that relationship. For holding a person to the demands of a relationship is a necessary part of treating her as a participant in such a relationship. If we are to respect her status as a member of that relationship we have to hold her to its demands. The only reason not to hold a person to the demands of the relationship would be that she was incapable of responding to its demands. Therefore taking one's lack of 'full' autonomy as a reason not to hold a person responsible would be the same as not treating her as a proper member of that relationship in the first place. The fact that we are unable ultimately to choose the kinds of people we are is irrelevant to our responsibility; not treating us as responsible would be to fail to treat us as members of that relationship who are capable of responding to its demands. This is the final part of our Strawsonian vindication of moral responsibility against the criticisms of the sceptical argument from luck. It also completes the initial statement of the 'right to be punished' strategy: the right to be punished is really a 'right to be evaluated as a member of moral relationships'.

HARD TREATMENT AND HOLDING SOMEONE RESPONSIBLE

Nevertheless, the critic may have another go at saying what it is that bothers her about our retributive practice. Let us assume that the critic accepts the ideas given so far: that we have duties to treat one another in a manner appropriate to the valuable relationships we stand in to one another; that this involves not just treating one another with goodwill but of holding one another to the demands of the relationship when appropriate. Let us say the critic accepts that one would not be treating one's friend as a friend unless one made it clear to him that he was acting in a way that was incompatible with friendship. Nevertheless, the critic might say, there are different ways of holding people responsible. What we have imagined in the case of the friend is saying something to him, pointing something out to him, trying to get him to realise what he is doing. However, this is a long way from hard treatment, from 'acquiescing in his suffering' in the way that Strawson thinks is involved with the reactive attitudes. Strawson may give us the basis for a novel defence of holding a person responsible, but why does holding a person responsible have to involve something distinctively retributive? Why can it not simply involve a non-retributive appeal to conscience?[32]

---

[32] This point is made in Stern, 'Freedom, Blame and Moral Community'; Watson, 'Responsibility and the Reactive Attitudes', pp. 285–6; and Wallace, *Responsibility and the Moral Sentiments*, pp. 72–3.

Furthermore, the critic might say, surely this non-retributive appeal to conscience is quite compatible with Strawson's argument. The way in which 'right to be punished' strategies work is to isolate some important identity of the agent and to argue that this identity can only properly be respected by something that amounts to punishment. Thus Strawson's argument isolates the offender's identity as an agent who can participate in interpersonal relationships, a member of the moral community, and argues that it is constitutive of treating him as such that we see him as the appropriate object of a range of reactive and retributive attitudes. Not to see him as subject to these retributive attitudes is to adopt the objective attitude and therefore not to treat him in a manner appropriate to the relationship we have with him. But in appealing to one's friend's conscience, in trying to get him to see that he is violating the demands of friendship, one is plainly treating him as psychologically normal and morally developed: if he were not, it would not make sense to appeal to his conscience at all. It would rather be a case, if any moral communication were possible at all, of attempting to develop a conscience in him. But that is not what is going on in this example. Therefore appealing to a person's conscience is compatible with treating him as a morally capable agent but it does not involve retributive treatment.

This objection allows that Strawson is right to say that adopting the objective attitude can be demeaning to the wrongdoer in that it fails to treat him with the respect due to his status as a member of the relationship. But Strawson appears to assume – the critic might continue – that we have only two ways of dealing with deviant behaviour: retributive attitudes or objective attitude. However, as Lawrence Stern puts it:

The lives of men like King and Gandhi seem to furnish evidence to the contrary. They publicly rebuked others for doing wrong. We have every reason to believe that the rebuke was a sincere expression of a sentiment. Therefore, in some important sense they blamed others for wrongdoing. Yet it is not clear that they wished those they blamed to suffer. Nor did they exclude them from the moral community. For their method of action was to appeal to the conscience of their adversaries.[33]

The approach taken by King and Gandhi is what we might call non-retributive dialogue: the attempt to change someone's behaviour through moral argument. As they saw it, the crucial thing was to persuade the wrongdoer of her wrong. Their aim was reform, but they did not pursue this aim in disregard of the offender's identity as a moral agent. Rather, as

---

[33] Stern, 'Freedom, Blame and Moral Community', p. 78.

Stern puts it, they appealed to the offender's conscience. But they did so in ways that seemingly did not involve the distinctive retributive desire that the offender should suffer. Their example seems to be entirely admirable, and widely agreed to be so. It respects wrongdoers as morally capable but does not involve 'acquiescing in suffering'. The idea of non-retributive dialogue therefore represents an important ideal for the progressive critic of retribution. It points out a false dichotomy underpinning the Strawsonian 'right to be punished' strategy. In the face of this example, the retributivist now needs to show either that King and Gandhi are morally deficient in some way as a result of their non-retributivism; or that, contrary to appearances, their behaviour is compatible with an appropriate commitment to retributivism. But neither of these options looks particularly hopeful at this stage.

However, there remains a possibility for the retributive 'right to be punished' strategy, a possibility that I explore in more depth in the next chapter. The non-retributivist concentrates on dialogue because he takes it that dialogue is both a necessary and a sufficient mode of respecting what is valuable about someone's identity (that is, their identity as a rational agent). However, the way forward for the retributivist might be to argue that, while dialogue is what we owe to people when we consider their relationship with us as one between rational agents, rational agency is a rather bare aspect of our identity. Our actual practical identity is a far richer matter: we are members of families, friendships, voluntary associations, political parties, universities, churches, nations, polities. As well as duties to respect others as rational agents we may have a range of associative obligations to respect others as members of other forms of valuable relationship, to treat them in a manner appropriate to the relationship we have with them. The retributivist might explore the possibility that, while non-retributive dialogue is sufficient to respect a person's identity as a rational agent, retributive responses are necessary in order to respect their identity as members of richer forms of association.

This is the strategy that I will begin to explore at the end of chapter 4 and that will culminate in chapter 5. However, the bulk of the next chapter will be taken up with working out an adequate model of non-retributive dialogue. In doing so I am thinking about a model for how we ought to deal with offenders in a way that respects their identity as members of the moral community. Such a model could underpin an attractive form of non-retributive restorative justice. The idea that we should engage offenders in a sort of dialogue that involves holding them accountable – holding them to the demands of their relationship with the victim – but from which retributive reactions have been expunged is one that sits well with some accounts of what restorative justice should look like.[34] Having developed what I will claim is the strongest form of non-retributive justice we will begin to assess whether we do need certain distinctively retributive responses.

[34] I am thinking of those accounts (discussed at the end of chapter 1) that take holding the offender accountable to be something important in its own right (something we owe to the offender and her victim) rather than something that is only a contingent means to a further end. An example of this tradition is H. Zehr, *Changing Lenses*.

CHAPTER 4

Non-retributive dialogue

In the last chapter I developed a Strawsonian defence of individual responsibility. The idea I defended was that holding someone responsible in cases of violation was a necessary part of treating them as a fellow member of some valuable relationship. However, our inquiry in this book concerns the basis of retribution, and the criticism that we encountered at the end of the last chapter was that holding someone responsible is not the same as retribution. The retributive attitudes, we pointed out, require some further justification. Furthermore, we pointed out that it was by no means clear where such a justification could come from, at least if we are thinking in terms of the 'right to be punished' strategy that we are pursuing here. We respect someone's identity by engaging them in dialogue, not by making them suffer. Therefore if we are swayed by the arguments in favour of individual responsibility that we developed in the last chapter then non-retributive dialogue could be an attractive basis for some form of justice.

In this chapter I want to develop two models of non-retributive restorative justice. Restorative justice is a kind of 'deliberative justice': it centres on a kind of conversation between the offender and other interested parties, often including the victim. Over the next two chapters we will be trying to work out an adequate conception of this conversation. In doing so we will be pursuing the same strategy as in the last chapter: we will be trying to work out what an adequate mode of interaction with wrongdoers is, given who they are and what they have done. At the moment we are not concerned with the question of *who* interacts with the wrongdoer, whether it is the business of the state or private individuals to do so. We are just trying to develop a model that represents an adequate response to offenders given their status.

I will contrast two types of dialogue: *negotiation* and *shared inquiry*. In the latter, the idea is that the dialogue is a process in which the parties collectively assess the merits of, say, a belief, an action or an attitude by considering what can be said in its favour. It aims to get the parties to agree that the considerations relevant to this assessment point to some compelling conclusion about its merits, with the result that all parties become persuaded of that conclusion. In the former the aim is rather through bargaining to find some compromise between the parties to the debate, a balance that may depend on what the parties' interests are in the first place and what power they are able to exert over the proceedings. The question is, which of these is the most adequate response to someone like Bryson? If we take the shared inquiry model, I will argue, we end up with some sense in which the offender is responsible for what she has done, and on the basis of which she ought to be subject either to moral criticism or moral (re-)education. If we take the latter, on the other hand, we need not invoke responsibility, but end up instead with a model of conflict-resolution. The strategy of this chapter will be first of all to argue for the shared inquiry model over the negotiation model. However, I will then raise a concern about the shared inquiry model that will lead us back to a further consideration of the retributive attitudes in the next chapter.

SHARED INQUIRY

Let me begin first of all by giving a deeper characterisation of shared inquiry, with which the account of negotiation can then usefully be contrasted. My account of shared inquiry draws on the description of the 'conversational stance' provided by Michael Smith and Philip Pettit in their 'Freedom in Belief and Desire'.[1] Like Strawson, Pettit and Smith seek to describe the assumptions implicit in a certain perspective on human beings and their behaviour, a perspective that is embedded in certain forms of interaction. Their proposal is to describe the perspective we adopt when we engage in *conversation* with other people, in particular those conversations in which we aim to find out the truth on a given matter. What they call 'intellectual conversation' I term 'shared inquiry'. Pettit and Smith's argument starts from the mundane but, they think, striking observation that, in the types of conversation the authors are interested in (focusing on questions of what to do or what to believe), we tend to *listen* to each other and take seriously what others have to say. We tend not to simply make up our minds in a solipsistic bubble.

[1] P. Pettit and M. Smith, 'Freedom in Belief and Desire', *Journal of Philosophy* 93 (1996), pp. 429–49. In what follows I provide a reading of Pettit and Smith that aims to explain and not merely to describe their view. For instance, the term 'shared inquiry' is mine rather than theirs.

We invest one another with a certain kind of authority or status; we accept one another as conversational partners.

Let me give a very ordinary example. Say at a gathering of friends the topic of conversation veers unaccountably on to a discussion of Mongolia, and the group fall into disagreement about the name of its capital. Most of the party have no idea; two or three come up with the correct answer, Ulan Bator, while one says Tashkent and another Kathmandu. At this point one party pipes up that Tashkent is the capital of Kazakhstan, at which there is a murmur of recognition from some and the suggestion is withdrawn, while another goes off to get the atlas. When the atlas is produced, all parties come to the same conclusion and form the same belief: that the capital of Mongolia is Ulan Bator (while Tashkent is the capital of Uzbekistan and Kathmandu of Nepal). The question is conclusively settled for all members of the party.

In this situation, each person at the table is a participant in the conversation. They are all invested with authority in the sense that they are acknowledged within the interaction as a person who has the right actively to contribute, and whose contributions will be taken at face value and will merit some sort of response. None of these people is regarded by the others as merely passive, uncomprehending observers, locked in their own worlds: they are active participants in the common world. In shared inquiry, we examine and criticise one another's beliefs and actions (and our own), engaging one another in argument, considering and assessing the validity of the different points of view presented, and deliberating together about what we ought to believe or do.

To explain this feature of our conversational practice, Pettit and Smith argue that we must be making certain rather significant assumptions: these assumptions make sense of our engaging in this practice. First of all, it is not simply the case that everyone has their own subjective view of the matter under discussion, a view that is unconstrained by any standards of correctness or adequacy. Rather we take it that a discrepancy between participants signals that someone is in the wrong. Secondly, in investing one another with authority and applying the status of conversational partner, we must be assuming that each party to the conversation is in some way worth listening to. This is a matter of assuming their capability of following and contributing intelligibly to the discussion. While there are experts and apprentices in any realm of inquiry, no conversational partner gets dismissed out of hand and no one gets universal deference: each expert is considered accountable to the evidence, and each person invested with conversational authority is considered to have an at least minimal ability to grasp the evidence and bring their beliefs into line with it. And, thirdly, we must be assuming that where there is disagreement in beliefs, a review of the available evidence can usually reveal who is in the wrong and thereby establish agreement. If the parties are properly responsive to the evidence, therefore, *inquiry tends towards agreement.* In entering into some shared inquiry with other people we think of ourselves as being engaged in some common project with them: the project of finding out what we ought to believe. Because we take it that what we are trying to find out together is what we ought to believe in the light of whatever evidence there is, we must take it that the evidence requires the same responses from each of us.

Of course, it is naïve to think that agreement will always be the result in the actual practice of shared inquiry. But Pettit and Smith point out that the way we react to failures to reach agreement *reinforces* their claim that the assumptions given above are central. For, they say, where stubborn disagreement exists, we do not treat this as the expected or natural result but rather feel bound to give a special explanation for it. Either we postulate (a) that one party lacks the ability to grasp the evidence that is necessary to gain authorisation (and hence that it is of no significance if *they* do not agree with us); (b) that the available evidence leaves the question unsettled; (c) that, though all parties are authorised and there is conclusive evidence available, one party does not have access to all the evidence; or (d) that one party is not attending properly to the evidence (through wilfulness, carelessness or laziness, etc.). In other words, we either explain stubborn disagreement by saying that the evidence available to both parties is not conclusive (either because it really is not conclusive, or because it has not been made apparent to both parties that it is conclusive); or we say that, although the evidence is conclusive and apparent, one party is at fault through not giving the matter due thought and attention. By explaining disagreement in this way, Pettit and Smith point out, we save our assumption that, were the evidence conclusive and the parties attending to it properly, they would reach agreement.

The scenario of the atlas illustrates Pettit and Smith's point as follows. The fact that this group bothers to discuss the question and goes through the process of reviewing the evidence shows that (1) they think that there is a single answer to the question, not that each person is entitled to her own opinion; (2) that each person is equally capable of responding appropriately to the evidence, when it is made available; and (3) that a review of all the available evidence will bring the group to an agreement. At the initial stage of disagreement, the group assumes (that is, they all assume together) that the disagreement exists because the evidence is not fully available to all: this is why the atlas is brought in to settle the issue. And settling the issue involves bringing all parties to the same conclusion. All this is so obvious as to pass unremarked when we are actually engaged in shared inquiry.

Now although there is something democratic or egalitarian in the notion of our sharing authority and being partners in inquiry, we should remember that this model is compatible with one partner being an expert and the other a novice. Thus the model is quite compatible with the shared inquiry really being a context in which one party is educating the other: in this context (and this is one thing that distinguishes education from indoctrination) the educator takes it that there is evidence about what one ought to believe, and believes that the student is capable of grasping the evidence and coming to the appropriate belief. In that case, she invests the student with authority in the inquiry: the authority, for instance, to ask questions that will be treated as valid and to have them answered in a way that she can grasp as satisfying. What being an authority means, in Pettit and Smith's sense, is being able to grasp the evidence and apply it to one's beliefs. But this is an ability one can have by degrees. What the apprentice is learning is how to grasp the significance of the evidence; but in order to be an apprentice one has to already see that there is such a thing as shared evidence and that it bears on one's beliefs. On this model, students have to be active in understanding because they are being taught how to see the evidence in the correct light: they have to learn how to do something for themselves. But the assumptions of the conversational stance do not imply that the student's perspective is just as valid as that of the expert. An expert will typically have a far firmer grasp of the evidence and what it signifies than the student. The educator does not take the student's views at face value, therefore, but has to believe that the student is capable of grasping the evidence and latching on to what they are being taught. Thus the notion of an *authority* in shared inquiry is a continuum. At one end it encapsulates the educable agent; and at the other it covers the expert.

I have introduced this model by concentrating on examples of inquiry into straightforward matters of empirical fact. But we might think that we can extend this model to moral inquiry, or inquiry into other questions about values. Of course, there is widespread scepticism about this possibility, scepticism that I will go some way towards addressing below. But let us consider its possibility. For it to be possible we would have to assume, for instance, that there is such a thing as evidence in questions of value, evidence that we can articulate and assess in inquiry; and that human beings are or can become responsive to such evidence. Furthermore, it seems appropriate to assume that what being responsive to any such evidence consists in is not merely updating one's beliefs, as when one is convinced of some matter of empirical fact. If there is evidence about what one morally ought to do, then being fully responsive to that evidence will involve not just believing that one ought to do this thing but actually *doing* it. Now this is to make a controversial assumption of internalism about moral motivation.[2] It assumes, in other words, that were there to be moral evidence it would be not merely belief- but also action-guiding. However, this is what we would intuitively expect. For instance, the same goes for other value-laden attitudes: if there is evidence about what one ought to admire or deplore or feel ashamed of then being properly responsive to such evidence will involve not just believing this to be the case but actually forming the attitudes in question.

Of course, it is not usual to talk of there being evidence for moral claims. If it sounds odd, we could equally well talk about morality as providing us with reasons for action, reasons that we can discover through deliberation, reasoning or the exercise of the imagination, and to which we can be responsive by coming to act accordingly. By and large the nature of my project here will involve my assuming rather than arguing for this traditional picture of moral reasons. However, further on in this chapter I will attempt to rebut some scepticism about this picture by considering the range of meta-ethical positions that could be compatible with the model of shared moral inquiry.

For now, however, we will assume that there can indeed be such a thing as evidence for moral claims, evidence to which we are or can be responsive. Now consider what moral wrongdoing amounts to on this picture. It can be conceived of as a kind of *disagreement*, disagreement about whether the action is permissible or not. If we take the example of Bryson's speeding, we might say that his action expresses the view that his driving at a certain speed in a busy built-up area was permissible, while his victim and other members of the local community believe that there are considerations that conclusively demonstrate that it is not permissible. Now on the model of shared inquiry we have said that we can either explain disagreement in terms of (a) one party to the dispute lacking the authority to engage in the dispute; (b) the question not having a

---

[2] For this debate contrast e.g. the internalist position of C. Korsgaard, 'Skepticism about Practical Reason', *Journal of Philosophy* 83 (1986), pp. 5–25, with the externalism of David Brink, 'Externalist Moral Realism', in M. Smith (ed.), *Meta-Ethics* (Aldershot: Dartmouth, 1995). Also useful is the discussion in M. Smith, *The Moral Problem* (Oxford: Blackwell, 1994), ch. 3.

conclusive answer to which the evidence points; (c) the conclusiveness of the evidence not being available – or cognitively accessible – to one of the parties; or (d) one party to the dispute, though authorised, having failed to pay proper attention to evidence that is conclusive and available to them. If we take it that there is indeed such a thing as evidence relating to this question, and that all parties to the dispute can be responsive to the evidence, then we can rule out (a) and (b). In which case the appropriate response to the situation might be thought to be to engage the wrongdoer in a kind of shared moral inquiry, an inquiry aimed at leading him to see that what he did was wrong.

Engaging wrongdoers in shared moral inquiry has a number of virtues. In the first place, it demonstrates respect for the offender as a moral agent, that is, as an agent authorised in moral inquiry. It does not treat him as an agent simply to be controlled or treated: it treats him as someone who has a conscience, who can be reasoned with and who can be expected to respond when the considerations relevant to his action are made clear to him. (In Bryson's case, this involves making clear what the accident might already have made clear to him – the risks he was taking with other people's welfare.) The idea that we ought to respect an agent's status as authorised in shared inquiry – and that this will rule out merely coercing them or manipulating them – is one way of understanding the Kantian dictum that we ought to treat agents as ends and never as mere means. In the terms we employed in the last chapter, we might say that shared inquiry is an intrinsically valuable, characteristically human activity, and that those who can engage in such inquiry – the authorised – derive moral status from being potential participants in it. Treating someone as a participant in shared inquiry is the opposite of adopting the objective attitude towards him. However, the model of shared inquiry also has some of the forward-looking aims of rehabilitation and deterrence: it aims to change the wrongdoer's behaviour, make him less dangerous, deter him from crime. It is forward-looking but does not involve excluding the offender from the community of agents of whom we can have certain normative expectations (specifically whom we can expect to understand and respond appropriately to moral claims).

The model of shared inquiry represents the assumptions underpinning those views on which we ought to respond to wrongdoing with some form of *moral communication*.[3] The type of interaction with the wrongdoer that

---

[3] As we saw in chapter 2, this includes those who take punishment to be justified as censure as well as those who would defend non-retributive forms of communication. See, for example, Moberly, *The*

we are imagining is that in which the parties reason together about whether the wrongdoer was right to act as she did, and in which they attempt to get the wrongdoer to understand and accept that what she did was wrong. Through collective discussion the parties aim, not just to get the wrongdoer to back down or to agree for the sake of a quiet life, but to recognise *why* what she did was wrong. Furthermore, these views can be seen as invoking some conception of responsibility: what it means to be morally responsible on this view involves aptness to be called to account, to be asked to defend – or if they are indefensible, to repudiate – one's reasons for the action in question. Because the offender has done something genuinely wrong, and because she is capable of understanding it as wrong (either by giving the evidence due attention as she should have done in the first place; or else by undergoing a process of moral education), it makes sense to *call her to account for it*, by which I mean to engage her in a process in which she is called to justify her action and assess the justification that she offers for it. The shared inquiry model therefore provides us with a conception of moral responsibility as rational accountability.[4] Rather than presupposing ultimate control over one's actions to the exclusion of all contingency, this conception of responsibility simply presupposes *normative competence*: the capacity to understand and respond appropriately to moral reasons.[5]

The shared inquiry model aims at moral agreement and rational persuasion of the offender, and holds the offender to be morally responsible insofar as she can be expected to see the force of moral claims. However, to repeat, this does not mean that agreement will always actually come about, or that the offender ought not to have been held responsible if it does not come about. As I said above, many disagreements persist as a result of stubbornness, prejudice or wilful refusal to be open to the evidence. Yet we do not take such disagreements to show either that there is no right answer to these questions, or that the person in question is pathologically incapable of appreciating it. There is an important difference, on this model, between agents who could *in principle* be brought to see the force of the evidence and those who are barred from grasping it because of some incapacity. The difference is hard to pin down in the abstract. But when we say of someone who does not see the force of certain considerations

---

Ethics of Punishment; Hampton, 'The Moral Education Theory of Punishment', *Philosophy and Public Affairs* 13 (1984), pp. 208–38; Duff, *Trials and Punishments*; von Hirsch, *Censure and Sanctions*; Kleinig, 'Punishment and Moral Seriousness'; Primoratz, 'Punishment as Language'.
[4] Duff, *Trials and Punishments*, ch. 2, on blame and moral criticism.
[5] See Wolf, *Freedom within Reason*, ch. 4 (on the 'reason' view); Watson, 'Two Faces of Responsibility'; T. M. Scanlon, *What We Owe To Each Other* (London: Belknap Press, 1998), pp. 267–90.

that she nevertheless could, we mean something like this: that she would understand if she could be brought to see it correctly – if it could be presented to her in the right way – and that she could be brought to see it correctly without a complete change in her nature.[6] For instance, if we found the right way of putting it, if we explained it correctly – and perhaps if we explained a few other things first; or if we got her in the right situation, in which she felt comfortable and open and not on the defensive, etc.; in other words, if the situation and the mode of presentation were right, then she would find the evidence persuasive. We think that her inability to recognise the reasons we are putting to her is pathological if we think that in no such situation would she be persuaded of what we are saying, for, with regard to those sorts of considerations at least, she is not responsive to reasons. In other words, what being responsible comes down to in the end is that one would actually respond to such evidence as might be presented in the conversational stance in ideal circumstances.

However, one might also take a more sceptical and radical view, which is that disagreement is all that we can reasonably expect from shared moral inquiry, either because, as in (b), there is no such thing as evidence in moral questions, which simply do not have objective and conclusive answers; or because, as in (a), human beings are just not the sorts of beings who are capable of understanding and responding to moral requirements, even if there are any. If one is tempted by either of these views then one might reject shared inquiry as a model for interacting with the wrongdoer, along with its associated conception of responsibility. What shared inquiry aims for – namely, the acceptance by the defendant of certain considerations as counting conclusively against performing an action – is a goal that, on this argument, cannot be achieved in the moral case. In which case, the theorist who is tempted by this sceptical view, but who wishes to hold on to some form of dialogue, will be led rather towards a type of interaction that involves debate with the defendant but in which there is no attempt to hold the defendant to account. This is the mode of interaction that I will characterise as *negotiation*.

NEGOTIATION

In shared inquiry we assume that discussion will tend to lead towards agreement on some matter, given that all parties have the evidence to

---

[6] This draws on Pettit and Smith's own formulation of what this capacity amounts to: see 'Freedom in Belief and Desire', p. 446.

hand and that they are assessing it conscientiously and in good faith. The model outcome here is unforced agreement on what the available evidence calls one to believe or do. In negotiation, by contrast, we are attempting to reach a compromise of interests. We are bargaining.[7] In bargaining, the aim is also to reach an agreement. Furthermore, in bargaining the parties do not necessarily view one another from the objective stance, as 'factors' to be managed. Rather the assumption might be that each party is independent, and that it would be wrong to simply invade their independence and to attempt to change their behaviour. It is also assumed that at least some goodwill can be expected from all parties, at least such goodwill as is shown in a determination to resolve the issue by discussion and agreement rather than sheer force (though of course it might be the case that the parties have come to this determination simply because force has not worked). However, while the aim of inquiry might be to reach an agreement informed by evidence, the validity of which is independent of the parties, the aim of bargaining is simply to strike a deal that all are willing to accept given their particular starting points, given the leverage each can exert over the proceedings, and given the consequences for each of failing to reach agreement. The point of agreement in negotiation is not independent of the parties' interests and control over the negotiation. There is no point to impartiality. Each party approaches the negotiation seeking to further their individual interest as far as possible. Thus the outcome of the bargaining may reflect the relative power of the participants. Although bargaining or negotiation aims at agreement, it may in the end be an agreement that some parties accept only unwillingly.

Applying the negotiation model to the case of wrongdoing, we end up with a view in which victim and offender are not really viewed as such but are rather seen as two parties to an interpersonal conflict or dispute. This way of regarding them refuses to take sides, remaining neutral on the question of who is in the wrong. It is this model that is often espoused by

---

[7] In the argument here I am concentrating on the issue of how we should best understand our interactions with wrongdoers, but obviously the debate between the moral inquiry and the negotiation model raises deeper issues about the nature of morality. For instance, some theorists put forward a contractarian view of morality as rules, the validity of which is settled by a process of bargaining. See D. Gauthier, *Morals by Agreement* (Oxford: Oxford University Press, 1986). This view is meant to be an alternative to what these theorists see as the failed idea that morality could be discovered by shared inquiry. For a theory of punishment that begins from this starting point, and argues that it has significant consequences for the way we understand punishment and political theory, see M. Matravers, *Justice and Punishment: The Rationale of Coercion* (Oxford: Oxford University Press, 2000). I briefly discuss some reasons for keeping faith with the shared inquiry model – and hence for rejecting Matravers' starting point – below.

those proponents of restorative justice who think that criminal justice should be genuinely informal.[8] On such views there is a refusal to deal with predetermined roles such as 'defendant' and 'plaintiff'. The discussion is not seen as having to do with working out and ascribing responsibility but rather with solving the concrete problem of what to do next. There need be no moral element to the discourse at all, certainly none that involves claiming that one person was definitively in the wrong. Perhaps the very idea that the truth of the matter is something that we ought to be aiming at is viewed with suspicion.

Now one initial problem with the model of negotiation is that the parties bring with them different degrees of leverage over the process. Sometimes in negotiation it might be that one party is able to exercise unfair and undue power over the process by threatening the other with some bad consequences should they fail to agree with what is being proposed. Therefore it seems that even if we are attracted by the idea that we ought not to impose our moral views on the offender, and ought to leave the field as open as possible for parties to make their own agreements, we ought still to distinguish between fair and unfair bargaining strategies. We might want to distinguish, in other words, between legitimate offers and illegitimate threats.[9] We might want to construct the bargaining position in such a way that no party can bring their position of power to bear on the proceedings so as to make another party accept something that they would not otherwise freely accept. Therefore there has to be some role for constructing the negotiating meeting as a somewhat artificial situation in which the parties can be allowed to negotiate from a position of rough equality. For this reason it seems that negotiation will have to involve a facilitator or arbitrator to whom the parties agree to give the power to enforce certain ground rules. These rules may consist in, for instance, a rule about speaking in turn, a rule allowing the offender to opt out of the meeting should she desire, but also rules that characterise certain bargaining strategies as illegitimate.

This concession is important because it means that even on the model of negotiation the interaction with the offender cannot be entirely informal. Because the very least we want is fair negotiation with the

---

[8] I am thinking here in particular of Christie, 'Conflicts as Property', who makes this explicit. However, many formulations of restorative justice as the attempt to get parties to agree on a way to address the consequences of some action do not distinguish between my models of negotiation and shared inquiry.

[9] This is a point made by Philip Pettit in his discussion of 'discourse-friendly relationships'. See his *A Theory of Freedom* (Cambridge: Polity, 2001), ch. 4 at pp. 73–5.

offender – negotiation in which the offender is not allowed to bring illegitimate bargaining strategies such as threats of violence or recrimination to bear on the proceedings – there has to be some agency with the power to enforce these ground rules and to compel the offender to submit to them. Perhaps the most obvious such agency is the state, but it need not be. Perhaps there are or could be a variety of neutral community or voluntary organisations that could take this role. However, because we need to construct a level playing field on which some sorts of strategies (e.g. 'Keep your mouth shut if you want to stay safe') are ruled out, the interaction with the offender has to take place under the auspices of some wider organisation that has the power to enforce ground rules and is not swayed by threats or illegitimate offers from one or more of the parties.

The mediator or facilitator has a pivotal role in either model of non-retributive dialogue. The difference between my models of inquiry and negotiation can be thought of as differences in the role they give to facilitators, and the conception of impartiality involved. On the model of negotiation, the facilitator is thought of as having a responsibility to remain neutral as to the morality of the situation, simply enforcing some ground rules that ensure the two parties resolve their dispute fairly and without threats, intimidation or violence, and perhaps having a responsibility to dissuade the parties from engaging in moral recrimination. As long as the parties negotiate fairly, there is nothing the facilitator should say about whether the compromise reached is an appropriate one. On the shared inquiry model, however, while the facilitator does not take the victim's side, she should make it clear, say, that the evidence points to the defendant's culpability (if it does) and that he therefore has some case to answer. In this case the role of facilitator might be thought of as like that of a tutor in a student seminar. In a seminar, certain points of view can be ruled out as irrelevant or unhelpful to the main issue under discussion, for there is a definite issue that the tutor wishes the group to grasp. However, a seminar differs from a lecture because in the former the tutor wishes the group, under her guidance, to discover the points at issue for themselves: the discussion is student-led, though the tutor has a crucial role in keeping it on the right topic and in asking pertinent questions if they have not been raised by the group themselves. While encouraging the group to discuss the matter for themselves the facilitator retains an important guiding role missing in the model of negotiation.

The moral neutrality of negotiation is appropriate when we think either that there is no conclusive answer to the moral question or when we do not think that the parties to the discussion are capable of grasping and adhering to the moral conclusion. However, this suggests a criticism of negotiation as a response to many of those sorts of actions we classify as crimes.[10] The criticism is that negotiation fails either to take the wrong seriously, and therefore to stand up for the victim's rights as someone who ought not to have been violated in this way, or it fails to take the wrongdoer seriously as a responsible agent who ought to have seen that this action was a wrong one. To take the first half of the criticism, the claim that negotiation fails to take the wrong seriously is that it involves regarding matters as open to bargaining that ought really to be non-negotiable. Bryson's victim is not merely in dispute with Bryson, as if they differ on some matter about which one could agree to disagree. Some disagreements take place because one party is in the wrong, as in our atlas example. It seems important to recognise that this is the case with Bryson. It is not just that he has done something that his victims and others object to, and where there is a need to find a reasonable compromise between his view and theirs. He has done something *objectionable*, something they *rightly* object to. He is in the wrong in his thinking about what conduct towards others is justifiable – and this salient fact has to be built in to the process.

To take the second half of the criticism, it might be that opting for negotiation suggests not so much that there is no truth of the matter, but rather that Bryson is unable to grasp it. But Bryson is no psychopath: he is not the kind of agent who is beyond appreciating the force of moral considerations. His misdemeanour was carried out accidentally (though recklessly) and under the influence of alcohol: there is no suggestion that he would ever have been motivated to harm the cyclist deliberately and in cold blood. Further, he feels sorry for what he has done. Bryson, as I have tried to portray him, is an averagely moral, impulsive, but in the end reasonably sensitive, responsible young man. It would be insulting and dismissive of him if it were suggested that the only way to treat him was to enter into negotiations with him on the grounds that he was not capable of understanding his action as wrong. Treating his case as one for negotiation would deal with him as someone it would be inappropriate to engage in shared inquiry; yet this would be insulting given his evident remorse when he realised what he had done.

If these considerations are valid, then we can say that if we are to take the wrong seriously – if, that is, we are to take the victim and the offender seriously – then we owe it to the victim to adopt an attitude towards the

---

[10] Duff, *Punishment, Communication and Community*, pp. 92–3.

wrongdoer on which his action is objectively and conclusively wrong. Furthermore, if we are to take the offender seriously as an agent with whom we could engage in certain sorts of relationships – for instance, those sorts of reciprocal relationships that involve counting on the other person to take one's interests into account – then we owe it to him to treat him as an agent who is capable of seeing that the action is wrong.

A BRIEF EXCURSION INTO META-ETHICS AND THE PHILOSOPHY OF PRACTICAL REASON

Now someone might object to the criticism of the model of negotiation presented here. The critic I am imagining agrees with my diagnosis that the model of negotiation is appropriate when – and therefore implies that – moral agreement will not be forthcoming, but sees this as a *good* reason to adopt the model of negotiation. This critic wishes to put forward some sceptical position about moral requirements. For instance, this critic might say, the model of shared inquiry assumes that morality is such that it demands a certain response from us, and that we are set up to be able to recognise this demand and respond accordingly, adjusting our motivations in obedience. In other words, the view that makes sense of moral inquiry is one on which the world is in some sense morally ordered and in which agents have a faculty through which to apprehend this moral order and conform to it. But many people doubt the validity of this realist and rationalist picture.[11] Many people doubt that the world is morally ordered: for them, the world is a 'disenchanted', essentially physical place, with no room for mysterious moral requirements. Furthermore, many people take the Humean view that 'reason is the slave of the passions': they deny that reason would have the capacity to discern moral requirements even if there were any, as the only capacity that reason has is the instrumental one of discovering effective means to satisfy our desires. For them, morality is something we project on to the world on the basis of our contingent desires rather than a law that we read off the face of reality.

Now I do not have the space to do justice to the increasingly complex arguments about the pros and cons of moral cognitivism and non-cognitivism. The arguments over these positions quickly become so sophisticated and subtle that it makes them hard to summarise quickly.

---

[11] For instance, the model of shared inquiry seems to invoke the view of moral requirements as 'objectively prescriptive' that is rejected in J. L. Mackie, *Ethics: Inventing Right and Wrong* (Harmondsworth: Penguin, 1977), ch. 1.

However, I am not sure that I need to, for the point on which I wish to insist can be made briefly. It is a point about the phenomenology of moral experience. This is that *moral argument works*. In other words, people have genuine experiences of being convinced by moral claims, where this involves coming to see something that they had not previously appreciated, and to see a person or a thing as having a certain claim on them that they had not previously been fully aware of. Such experiences are different from merely acquiring one prejudice in exchange for another: they authentically appear to the person who has them as a form of learning, a deepening of one's awareness and appreciation of the world. It seems unsatisfying, to say the least, to describe these experiences simply as illusions or to see those who undergo them as being caught up in some mystifying ideology, by explaining them in terms of some other motivation (the desire to please the person one is arguing with; the desire to be like the person one is arguing with; etc.). This is an aspect of the phenomenology of moral experience that any account of what moral properties are has to explain.[12] If a particular meta-ethical account explains it in a way that is not consistent with the authority of moral claims, then we have some reason at least to doubt the validity of the account. After all, which do we have more reason to give up, the sceptical account or the understanding of moral requirements as something we discover that seems a perfectly good explanation of our experience and behaviour?

However, the critic might insist (a) that we have very good reason to think that the view of moral properties as objectively prescriptive is inconsistent with the scientific view of the world; and (b) that we have little reason to give up the scientific view of the world. Therefore there is some onus on the theorist who wishes to defend the view that moral requirements are the sort of thing that we can argue about. In response to this, one way in which this might be done is to draw an analogy between values and colours.[13] Colour is an example of a *response-dependent* property: that is, a property the specification of which has to make some reference to the way it is experienced by a normally

---

[12] For instance, the task for sophisticated expressivist theories is to show how the theory that moral claims are just expressions of our desires is *compatible* with the phenomenology of moral argument rather than how it undermines it. See e.g. A. Gibbard, *Thinking How to Live* (Cambridge, Mass.: Harvard University Press, 2003).

[13] See e.g. C. Taylor, 'Self-interpreting Animals', in his *Philosophical Papers*, vol. I (Cambridge: Cambridge University Press, 1985), pp. 45–76; D. Wiggins, 'Truth, Invention and the Meaning of Life', in G. Sayre-McCord (ed.), *Essays on Moral Realism* (London: Cornell University Press, 1988), pp. 127–65, esp. pp. 142–3; J. McDowell, 'Values and Secondary Qualities', in his *Mind, Value and Reality* (London: Harvard University Press, 1998), pp. 131–50.

constituted human observer.[14] For something to be red, in other words, is for it to *appear* red to a well-situated and normally constituted human observer. On one view, therefore, colour does not really exist in the world; there are only light rays of varying wavelengths that to the human visual apparatus appear to be coloured. Nevertheless this irrealism about colours at the metaphysical level does not undermine the model of shared inquiry.[15] For with colours there can still be evidence about what colour something is, evidence about which we can be right or wrong. There are standards of correctness and inappropriateness that regulate our judgements about colour. Similarly, it might be said, what it is for there to be a moral property that calls for a certain response (an act that is not to be done, or a goal that is to be pursued, a person who is to be admired) is for such a response to appear compelling to an ideally situated and constituted human observer. This is roughly what J. S. Mill argued about 'higher pleasures': that the standard by which we should judge whether there are such pleasures is that of the person who has been able to properly experience them and compare them with their 'lower' counterparts.[16] As with the case of colour there can be evidence about what moral properties something has that has to do with how human beings ought to be affected by the property.[17] However, the validity of this evidence assumes that we are the sorts of creatures who have certain moral sensibilities: it is not possible for someone with no such sensibilities to appreciate the evidence, any more than someone who is blind can appreciate colours. But just because those with no moral sensibility fail to see the force of moral evidence does not mean that we should doubt the authority of our moral judgements, any more than the existence of the blind gives us reason to doubt our colour judgements. Of course, it might be pointed out that this view does rely on a notion of normal or ideal human response or moral sensibility. How do we know what the ideal observer thinks or how she would react? This is a fair point. But it is one thing to recognise that our judgements are fallible, quite another to claim, as the sceptic does, that there is nothing about which we can really make judgements in this area.

---

[14] See e.g. P. Pettit, 'Realism and Response-Dependence', *Mind* 100 (1991), pp. 587–626.
[15] Essentially the same point is made by Dworkin in *Law's Empire*: see pp. 78–85.
[16] J. S. Mill, *Utilitarianism*, in J. S. Mill and J. Bentham, *Utilitarianism and Other Essays*, ed. A. Ryan (Harmondsworth: Penguin, 1987), ch. 2.
[17] This approach is sometimes taken to suggest an Aristotelian concern with appropriate emotion: see e.g. L. A. Kosman, 'Being Properly Affected: Virtues and Feelings in Aristotle's Ethics', in A. O. Rorty (ed.), *Essays on Aristotle's Ethics* (Berkeley, Calif.: University of California Press, 1980), pp. 103–16.

Even if this argument – which I cannot defend here in any depth – is on the right lines, however, the sceptic has another card to play. If we accept that there is a rough analogy between moral requirements and redness, the critic will say, there is also an important disanalogy.[18] For while it may be true that *any* human being with a properly functioning visual apparatus sees light of a certain wavelength as red, it is not the case that all human beings have a moral sense that is sensitive to moral behaviour and moral demands. Rather our moral consciousness is a product of culture, and of the specific culture into which we are inculcated: it is our education into a certain form of life that brings it about that we share a sense of what the fitting response to certain events or actions is. While within a specific culture there are standards of correctness about the application of moral terms and the making of moral judgements – just as there are standards of correctness about the use of language in general – these judgements do not hold across cultures. While the 'moral sense' view gives us a form of objectivism about moral judgements, it also brings with it a form of relativism. And this is problematic for the model of shared inquiry in our increasingly multicultural societies. It suggests that there may not be moral demands that are objective, conclusive and accessible to all members of modern society. In which case it suggests that, while for one party to an offence, the offence may look conclusively like a moral wrong, to another it may not – and there may be no evidence that both parties could come to see as conclusive.

The effect of this argument would be that, while we can indeed talk about moral reasons and their force and conclusiveness, while we can indeed see human beings as responsive to such reasons and properly engaging in shared inquiry, the force of these reasons is relative to cultures, or perhaps relative to the culturally conditioned sensibilities that human beings bring to moral deliberation. Whether an issue is conclusively resolvable in moral inquiry – the kind of issue on which agreement can really be expected amongst authorised inquirers – would depend on the agents involved, their cultural heritage and prior commitments. It may be that something like this relativism about moral debate is

---

[18] As well as this disanalogy, there might be another one. In perception of colour, we have a clear idea of the faculty involved (sight) and the causal processes by which perceptions are produced. Do we have the same in the case of value? In the case of value, I want to argue, the relevant faculty is that of the emotions: it is through the emotions of guilt, indignation, admiration, awe, etc. that we become aware of the evaluative aspects of situations. This role for the emotions is quite central to the outlook of the book and might need to be made more explicit. What of the causal processes involved? Do the emotions pick up on values that are really 'out there' independently of us, or do we rather project our emotions on to reality? I do not think I need to choose between these two possibilities for the purposes of the argument here.

inescapable: I am not sure that we can even understand the notion of a reason (for action or belief or whatever) that is conclusive *as such*, rather than conclusive *given* certain sensibilities, commitments or convictions the nature of which changes and develops over time and culture.[19] However, it is hard to see why these deep speculations should affect our willingness to engage with others in shared moral inquiry. After all, it is impossible to say in advance of actually trying whether, with any particular interlocutor, one will share enough to make a mutual exploration and assessment of views worthwhile. Where fundamental disagreement might be more threatening is when we are thinking about moral responsibility. On the shared inquiry model it seems a necessary condition of being responsible that one should be able to understand the conclusiveness of certain moral reasons. If this is made impossible by a person's cultural heritage then it may be that moral responsibility is something that varies across cultures.[20]

The fundamental point that I want to draw from this brief rebuttal of scepticism is that we have no meta-ethical reason to give up on the authority of our moral judgements or the possibility of shared moral inquiry. From this point of view, the idea of responsibility as rational accountability is a strong one and we have no reason to abandon it – either as the basis for our interactions with wrongdoers or as a conception of moral theorising – in favour of the bargaining model.

ACKNOWLEDGING RESPONSIBILITY

So far I have argued in favour of engaging wrongdoers in moral inquiry, inquiry that is aimed at getting them to see their action as wrong. However, in what follows I wish to argue against the shared inquiry model as the standard response to wrongdoing. Or, rather, I want to argue that it is insufficient by itself for central cases of wrongdoing. The notion of shared inquiry developed by Pettit and Smith contains two importantly different ways of explaining the sort of disagreement that we might have in a case of wrongdoing, both of which are consistent with assuming that (a) there is a determinate answer to the question raised by the disagreement, and (b) that all of the parties are able to appreciate this answer when presented with the evidence in favourable conditions. On

---

[19] J. McDowell, 'Aesthetic Value, Objectivity and the Fabric of the World', in his *Mind, Value and Reality*, pp. 112–30.
[20] On this point see N. Levy, 'Cultural Membership and Moral Responsibility', *Monist* 86 (2003), pp. 145–63.

the one hand, we might say that one of the parties did not have the evidence available to them; on the other, that one of the parties failed to appreciate the available evidence through lack of attention, laziness, wilfulness, negligence, etc. The idea of shared inquiry as moral education takes the first option: it operates on the assumption that the offender had not grasped the moral significance of the action, though once it is pointed out to him (in favourable conditions) then he probably will grasp it (in principle he will). However, the moral education strategy is not so obviously appropriate for agents who *could* legitimately have been expected to understand *by themselves* that what they were doing was wrong and to conform their behaviour to that understanding. Such agents may have done wrong through what we might call some internal moral weakness that it was their responsibility to overcome: laziness; selfishness; lack of due care and attention; weakness of will; stubbornness and pride; wilfulness; etc. The question is how we ought to treat these agents in light of this salient difference. In what follows I try to bring out why exactly this is such a salient difference and in the next chapter I will argue that a retributive response – of a certain sort – is the appropriate response to such agents.

The argument that moral education is inappropriate in such cases and that the retributive response is the fitting one is a pivotal point in the 'right to be punished' strategy being developed in this part of the book. The general strategy is to show that a retributive response to wrongdoing is necessary to fully acknowledge the wrongdoer's status as a responsible agent. At the end of the last chapter this strategy was seemingly halted by the objection that non-retributive moral criticism is a form of response that adequately respects the wrongdoer as a responsible moral agent: subjecting the wrongdoer to moral criticism authorises and engages her as an agent who can grasp and apply moral reasons. This suggests that the retributive attitudes are not necessary – as our strategy would claim – simply in order to treat the wrongdoer as she ought to be treated. But now I want to suggest a problem with the idea that wrongdoers should be given moral criticism. We start with an objection to moral education as a response to wrongdoing. This objection rests on the thought that it is disrespectful to do for a person, without her consent, what it is her responsibility to do for herself. When one does so, the thought is, one treats her as if she were not capable of doing it herself. If this principle is valid, it will have repercussions for moral edu- cation accounts of criminal justice.[21] For, on such accounts, the offender is

---

[21] See e.g. Hampton, 'Moral Education Theory of Punishment'.

put into a position in which the reasons why certain actions are wrong are presented to her, on the assumption that she does not fully understand them.[22] However, whether or not she does fully understand them – whether her position is one of doing something she knew to be wrong or doing something that she was unaware was wrong because she had not given the matter sufficient attention – it can be the case that it was nevertheless *her responsibility* to give the matter sufficient attention and to discover its moral dimensions. When we give an adult with certain moral capabilities (we come on to a more definite specification of such a person below) moral education in the basic matters that make up the core concerns of the criminal law, then it can be the case, according to the argument I am proposing, that we fail to respect her by doing what it is her responsibility to do for herself.

Now even if this objection is successful the proponent of the non-retributive moral criticism response to wrongdoing may be unswayed. For moral criticism is not moral education. As we said earlier, the model of shared inquiry is a continuum from cases of moral education to cases of mutual criticism carried out by experts. There is nothing patronising in the latter, no failure of respect in one expert pointing out errors or inadequacies in another's views. Therefore even if there is a problem with moral education there is no such problem with moral criticism, at least when it is made clear that it is addressed to an equal. However, we will suggest reasons for thinking that there *is* something inadequate in the non-retributive response. And the reason has to do with our 'right to be punished' strategy: non-retributive moral criticism fails to do justice to an important aspect of the wrongdoer's status.

In order to illustrate this point, consider the following example. Jane is a teacher. As part of her position she has certain responsibilities that require certain abilities. She has to be on top of her material; she has to be able to put it across in a way that the students will understand; and in addition she has to be able to deal with the students in an engaging manner. Now let us say that she does not discharge these responsibilities very well. Students complain that the material often goes over their heads, and Jane skates over fundamental and complex issues with little or no

---

[22] Thus Hampton: 'The state is justified in punishing rapists and murderers because their choices about what to do betray a serious inability to make decisions about immoral and moral actions, which has resulted in substantial harm to some members of that community' ('Moral Education Theory of Punishment', p. 181). On the view I am proposing we need some further response that recognises that, even if it was true that a wrongdoer was unable to make the right choices, it was nevertheless her responsibility to make sure that she acquired the ability. Mere moral education would not recognise this difference between culpable and non-culpable ignorance.

explanation, as if she does not understand them very well herself; this impression is reinforced when students dare to ask a question, which is either brushed aside or answered in a manner that only serves to make the issues more opaque. At other times, the opposite occurs, and Jane labours very trivial points to the point of boredom. She does not appear to be in control of the material that she is supposed to be teaching or to have much idea of how to put these issues across in ways that are conducive to students' understanding. Let me make this aspect of the example clear. It is not just that Jane's teaching is out-dated, or not quite as good as it ought to be. It is not that, although she is a decent teacher, she lacks an awareness of what is now considered 'good practice'. Rather she is failing to meet the most basic responsibilities she has towards her students.

Now as a teacher Jane is a member of a wider organisation such as a school or a university. More generally, she is a participant in what Alasdair MacIntyre has called a practice.[23] Practices, for MacIntyre, are those cooperative human activities participation in which can be characterised as the pursuit of goods internal to (non-instrumentally related to) the activity and the development of standards of excellence associated with the activity. In other words, practices are activities that are worth doing in their own right; they are non-instrumentally valuable. The kinds of things to which we might refer in explaining what it is about the activity that makes it valuable in this way are the goods internal to the activity. And in becoming good at the activity, in developing the skills and modes of understanding associated with a good practitioner of the activity, we are developing what can be thought of as standards of human excellence.

Now there is some tendency in MacIntyre's exposition of this notion to suggest that practices are in some way self-contained. For instance, two of his central examples – chess and portrait-painting – are activities we have no further reason for engaging in than the enjoyment of the activities and their standards of excellence themselves. However, it is clear that activities that are worth pursuing in their own right – in the sense that they generate standards of excellence – can also have a further purpose.[24] Education is an example of such a purposive practice. A teacher may wish above all to transmit knowledge and to teach people to think for

---

[23] A. MacIntyre, *After Virtue*, 2nd edn (London: Duckworth, 1985), p. 187.
[24] See the distinction between *self-contained* and *purposive* practices in D. Miller, 'Virtues, Practices and Justice', in J. Horton and S. Mendus (eds.), *After MacIntyre* (Cambridge: Polity, 1994), pp. 245–64.

themselves. But in the development of her skill in doing so she can also see herself as developing an expertise and an authority that is an excellence, a justified source of self-respect. In other words, the practitioner can see her professional development as an important form of achievement: something that makes her life more worthwhile than it would otherwise have been.

This suggests that in the practice of education participants stand in an intrinsically valuable relationship to one another: they participate together in an intrinsically valuable activity. If this is the case then being a participant in the practice of providing education will, by the terms of my Strawsonian strategy from the last chapter, provide agents with a valuable form of *status*. The type of status I am interested in at the moment is an intra-practice form of status: the fact that someone is a participant in an intrinsically valuable practice gives other members of that practice reason to treat him differently from non-members: members can expect a certain respect or goodwill from one another by virtue of their membership of the relationship. Participation in the practice – the status of fellow cooperator in some non-instrumentally important activity – is therefore a valuable identity that ought to be marked or recognised in the way other members treat the agent, just as we ought to treat our friends in a way that marks them out by virtue of our participating together in the valuable relationship of friendship. However, now note that this status within a practice can come in two broad categories: that of *qualified* member of the practice and that of *apprentice*. By a qualified member of the practice I do not mean someone who has no more to learn. Rather the qualified member of a practice is one whose participation in the practice is in an important sense self-governing or independent. The qualified member of the practice knows how to go on in the practice by himself, without further intervention or training from superiors. As I say, this does not mean that the qualified participant does not continue to learn how to engage better in the practice, or that he does not learn from others. But the qualified practitioner has a grasp on the activity such that he can identify opportunities for further learning for himself. His learning can be autonomous and self-directed in a way that the learning of an apprentice cannot. Therefore we can distinguish two different forms of status of participant. Being a qualified participant is a particular reason for respect because it stems from a mastery of some valuable activity.

When I am friends with someone I mark this by certain special sorts of treatment appropriate to the relationship. How do we mark the special status of being a qualified agent? Education is a purposive practice and in the end can be assessed, not just by how well its practitioners meet the standards of excellence vouchsafed by tradition, but also by how well it meets its fundamental purposes of imparting knowledge and the ability to learn. For this reason in a practice like education we can talk of practitioners having *responsibilities* in a way that sounds metaphorical in the case of activities like portrait-painting. Teachers have responsibilities to their students, and to their fellow practitioners with whom they are engaged in a collective enterprise. But it is the qualified rather than the apprentice practitioners who have such responsibilities. Or, rather, when apprentices are given such responsibilities they are supervised in a comprehensive way that would be inappropriate for a qualified practitioner. The qualified practitioner can be allowed a greater measure of independence in thinking for himself about how to discharge the duties of his role. And giving someone such freedom or autonomy in discharging their role is the way we respect him as a qualified practitioner. He can be left alone to get on with things – and can *expect* as a matter of right to be left alone to get on with things – in a way that the apprentice cannot. Becoming qualified therefore entitles a participant to a sphere of autonomy or independence in a cooperative endeavour: if he is qualified to make the decisions then as a matter of status it should be left up to him how to discharge the duties of his role.

Let us now return to the model of shared inquiry. As with the case of Bryson discussed earlier, we can say that Jane's teaching puts her at odds with the organisation (or with those who are committed to the proper goals of the organisation) in the sense that it can be understood as a source of disagreement between people who are engaged in a practice of shared inquiry. It will not be appropriate for the organisation to treat Jane's case as one on which there is inconclusive evidence. If it were to do so it would undermine its commitment to standards of good teaching. Therefore that has to be regarded as non-negotiable. But, unless this is a particularly extreme case, it is probably also inappropriate for the organisation to treat Jane as one who is in principle incapable of ever being a good teacher. It is probably inappropriate to deny that she could be authorised as a participant in a shared inquiry into the nature of good teaching. If this is right then there remain two explanations of her problems. The first is that, although there are very good grounds for thinking that her teaching was unacceptable, those grounds were not accessible to her: in other words they are grounds that she could not really have been expected to understand. The second is that she *could* reasonably have been expected to understand that her practice was unacceptable and that her failure to reach an acceptable standard is down to her failure to give the matter due care and attention.[25]

Under the first explanation, Jane is incompetent. Either she does not really know the topic she is meant to be teaching or she has no real idea how to teach it to students. In the other case, she is not just incompetent but negligent. The charge of negligence assumes that there was a legitimate expectation that Jane would be able to sort matters out for herself or seek the help she needed: in other words that it was Jane's responsibility to ensure that she had the abilities necessary to fill her role properly. Taking the first explanation leads one to the assumption that what the situation requires is that Jane be given training in what her duties and roles are, and in how to discharge them: she requires *rehabilitation*, or re-education in what it means to be a teacher. Now the first point that I want to make is that in a case in which Jane's failure *is* a case of *negligence* rather than incompetence – that is, where she is a genuinely qualified practitioner rather than an apprentice (where this is a matter of ability rather than just certification) – it would be *disrespectful* for the organisation to treat her as though she simply needs retraining. It would be to treat her as an apprentice rather than a qualified participant in the practice. For then it would be treating her as though it were not her responsibility in the first place to determine for herself how to discharge the duties of her role.

This suggests a general criticism of accounts that hold that we should respond to wrongdoers with *moral education*. Moral education is the analogy of retraining. If it makes sense to think of wrongdoers as engaged with us in an intrinsically valuable activity or set of activities (more on this in the next chapter) and it makes sense to think of there being qualified practitioners and apprentices in such activities, then we can say that it would be disrespectful of the status of qualified, independent, self-governing moral agents if we were to respond to their wrongs with an attempt at moral education. For moral education would suggest that it was not the wrongdoer's responsibility to discover and decide for themselves how to meet their responsibilities within the practice. Moral education suggests that the person could not reasonably have been

---

[25] In order to simplify matters I am leaving out another plausible explanation of Jane's failure, namely that she is temporarily incapacitated by depression or some other affliction. In many real-life cases this diagnosis of Jane's failure will be more plausible, perhaps, than either straight incompetence or wilful negligence. However, for the purposes of my argument it will be enough if I can show that retributive attitudes are necessary in a clear case of responsible wrongdoing. It will then be a further and interesting question how we ought to deal with less clear-cut cases. I am grateful to Linda Radzik for pointing out this further possibility.

expected to do better. Yet in the case of the qualified practitioner it is part of their status within the fabric of social relations that they are the kind of person who *could* have been expected to do better.

But now it might look as though we can at last revive the 'right to be punished' strategy from the last chapter. These considerations suggest that we need something other than an educative response in the case of the qualified practitioner. We need a response that recognises that their status is that of the disgraced expert rather than the apprentice. The kind of response we need is one that recognises that Jane is capable of seeing for herself the mess she has made. Condemnation is such a response. Condemnation is a response that is communicative: it calls for an answer. But what is being communicated is not supposed to be news to the person at whom it is directed. It is something it was his responsibility to know – or to ensure that he knew. It is more an expression of anger or blame or outrage than an attempt to show someone something he does not already know. Condemnation is a response to someone's failure to do something it was reasonably held to be his responsibility to do. Therefore official censure of Jane is a response that is consistent with her professional status in a way that simple retraining is not.

The point I am making now relates to the Strawsonian strategy we developed in the last chapter. In the last chapter I suggested that when we are in a valuable relationship with someone it means that we have special responsibilities towards him, specifically duties to treat him in a manner consistent with his being in that relationship with us. But I pointed out that sometimes, say, treating a friend as a real friend means holding him to the demands of the relationship, rather than allowing him to treat you abusively. The same argument is being made here. The other members of the organisation are in a valuable relationship with Jane since they participate together in the shared project of exercising and developing certain valuable skills, the possession of which is a special reason for respect. In this case, in which someone seriously or persistently fails to meet the demands of that relationship, then taking her seriously as a participant means holding her to its demands. At the end of the last chapter we considered the criticism that entering into moral criticism of the wrongdoer might be sufficient as a way of holding her to these demands, since it recognises her as a rational agent. But the response now is that while the shared inquiry model does treat her as a rational agent it does not treat her adequately as a qualified member of the shared project.

Could it be argued, then, that Jane has a 'right to be condemned'? The critic of retribution might allow this and yet argue that such condemnation of Jane as is legitimate, while it should not just be moral education, should also not involve the suffering involved in retributive responses.[26] Thus the non-retributivist might suggest that there is a kind of condemnation that lies in between these two types: moral criticism. Moral criticism, it might be suggested, involves holding someone to account for their actions in a way that moral education does not. Consider, for instance, the examples of Gandhi and King that we considered in the last chapter: the non-retributive appeal to conscience. An 'appeal to conscience' sounds like an appeal to something the person already knows, or could have known if they had 'listened to their conscience'. So perhaps there is a kind of non-retributive moral criticism that can be directed at qualified wrongdoers without the patronising overtones of moral education.

However, it remains the case that the shared inquiry model treats cases of wilful wrongdoing and culpable ignorance (i.e. involving a qualified practitioner) in the same way as cases of non-culpable ignorance (involving an apprentice). In both the response to the wrongdoer is to point out that the offender neglected to take salient issues into consideration in acting, and that he ought to give these issues due weight and hence revise his attitudes or patterns of behaviour. In the case of incompetence we call this response moral education, while in the case of negligence we call it moral criticism. But the basis of the response is the same. On the model of non-retributive dialogue all that the offender need do in response to criticism is to reform what has been shown to him to be inadequate to the evidence. But if this is the case then the moral criticism approach would treat the offender *in the same way* whether he was an apprentice or a qualified practitioner. However, as we have seen, the distinction between these two forms of status is an important one that ought to be marked. The qualified practitioner ought to be respected by being expected to (that is being given the freedom to) comply with responsibilities by himself, without further external intervention or supervision. But this opens the way for the suggestion that where the type of failure expressed in an action is quite different, depending on whether the perpetrator is an apprentice or a qualified practitioner, then this also ought to be marked: merely morally criticising a person for wrongdoing would, on this view, involve a failure of respect because it does not make

---

[26] Cf. T. M. Scanlon's defence of a moral criticism approach to moral appraisal but rejection of the 'Desert Thesis' on which negative criticism implies the Strawsonian 'acquiescence in suffering': Scanlon, *What We Owe to Each Other*, ch. 5.

enough of a difference to how the person is treated. If this objection were correct then the shared inquiry model by itself would be inadequate to cases of culpable wrongdoing: that is, cases that involve a culpable lack of due care and attention to responsibilities on the part of a qualified agent. Someone who appropriately values this status ought to find it unsatisfactory when this is not recognised: that is, where this identity does not make a difference to the way in which he is treated. The shared inquiry model would therefore fail to give proper respect to the offender's identity as one who was responsible for what he failed to do.

Now whether this objection to the moral criticism model is successful depends on there being a defensible and indeed attractive way of marking the distinction between responsible wrongdoing and the failures of the apprentice. Where there is such an alternative it will look as though we are not taking the wrongdoer seriously as a qualified agent when this reaction is not forthcoming. And there is an obvious contender. Thus consider that, in response to the charge that I have made, the proponent of moral criticism may point to the fact that the qualified moral agent whose conscience is awakened may *feel bad* about what she has done in a way that would not be appropriate for an apprentice. An apprentice may be able to excuse herself from such pangs of conscience or feelings of guilt by saying that she could not reasonably have been expected to know better, but a qualified practitioner cannot. Therefore it *is* the case that the qualified practitioner ought to react differently to the apprentice when faced with moral criticism. This is a point on which I agree. Guilt is the feeling of having failed as a qualified moral agent. However with this response we leave behind the non-retributive dialogue model, since guilt is one of the retributive attitudes. The retributive attitudes are the alternative to mere moral criticism that marks out qualified wrongdoers as such. Once the critic has admitted that feelings of guilt are appropriate for the qualified wrongdoer, then she has admitted the truth of some interpretation of retributivism.[27] In the next chapter I will give an account of why retributive reactions are particularly suited to mark the failures of qualified practitioners.

---

[27] Of course, the critic might deny that guilt *is* appropriate. See e.g. R. Bittner, 'Is it Reasonable to Regret the Things One Did?' *Journal of Philosophy* 89 (1992), pp. 262–73. See also the discussion of the critics of guilt in H. Morris, 'The Decline of Guilt', *Ethics* 99 (1988), pp. 62–76. For some discussion of these themes see W. Neblett, 'The Ethics of Guilt', *Journal of Philosophy* 71 (1974), pp. 652–63.

CHAPTER 5

The cycle of blame and apology

RETRIBUTION AND THE 'RIGHT TO BE PUNISHED' STRATEGY

The overall strategy that I seek to defend in this chapter derives from our discussion of Strawson in chapter 3. There we identified the idea that as agents we participate in relationships that are partly constituted by the responsibilities – to show respect and goodwill – that we have towards one another as members of such relationships. These relationships can in many cases be non-instrumentally valuable, as in the case of friendship, collegiality, shared participation in a MacIntyrean practice, and so on. I argued that part of the responsibility one can have to a fellow participant in such a relationship is to hold her to the responsibilities of that role in the event that she should violate them. Our 'right to be punished' strategy argues further that retributive reactions are a necessary part of holding a person responsible and hence necessary in order fully to respect her as a member of the relationship. However, the question with which we ended chapter 3 was whether engaging a wrongdoer in non-retributive dialogue was not a perfectly adequate way of holding members of relationships responsible.

The argument of the last chapter developed our 'right to be punished' strategy, again putting forward the claim that various possible modes of interaction with a wrongdoer would not do justice to her identity as a moral agent. Thus I claimed that merely negotiating with wrongdoers fails to take the wrong seriously and fails to take the wrongdoer seriously as someone who can understand the action as wrong. A better mode of interaction is the moral criticism or shared inquiry approach. However, we also saw reason to doubt the adequacy of non-retributive moral criticism. Subjecting all wrongdoers only to (strictly non-retributive) moral criticism makes no distinction between two importantly different sorts of cases: one in which the agent is non-culpably ignorant of the wrongness of her act; and another in which she did or could have been expected to know better. For the moral criticism approach the response in both of these cases is essentially the same: present the wrongdoer with the reasons why what she did was wrong, seek to get her to grasp the full force of these reasons, and thus to determine to reform her attitudes and conduct for the future. But, I argued, this approach therefore makes no distinction between the treatment of *qualified* members of an ethical practice or relationship (those who are self-governing[1] or independent in the sense that they can be expected to see for themselves, without further intervention, what their responsibilities are and how to meet them) and those who are in some way not self-governing (for instance, *apprentices*). Given that this is a distinction by which we rightly set some store, regarding it as a matter of pride or self-respect when we are qualified in such practices, a self-governing wrongdoer could appropriately feel demeaned by being merely criticised for what she had done. This suggests the need for a further layer of moral response that will do justice to the case of wrongdoing by self-governing moral agents. In this chapter I will argue that when we get clear about the nature of this response we will see the truth in the retributivist's claim that there is something intrinsically fitting about the suffering of the wrongdoer. This chapter therefore brings the 'right to be punished' strategy to a conclusion, the claim being that when one's identity as a self-governing moral agent is fully respected it has to be seen as appropriate that one suffer in certain ways.

Having said that in this chapter we will defend retributive reactions, however, it will become clear that the defence I will offer has much in common with the insights offered by writers on restorative justice. Hence this chapter could also be read as an attempt to put forward an ideal model of restorative justice that adequately respects the status of wrongdoers as moral agents. I will argue that central to a successful defence of retributive or restorative justice is the idea that by committing a wrong one accrues certain further responsibilities – responsibilities to repair the bad effects of one's action. As Howard Zehr puts it, 'violations create obligations': 'The primary obligation, of course, is on the part of the one who has caused the violation. When someone wrongs another, he or she has an obligation to make things right. This is what justice should be about.'[2]

---

[1] For the sense of self-government in which I am interested, see e.g. J. Skorupski, 'Welfare and Self-Governance', *Ethical Theory and Moral Practice* 9 (2006), pp. 289–309, especially the statement of the 'insight principle' at pp. 292–3.

[2] Zehr, *Changing Lenses*, p. 197. Cf. R. Swinburne, *Responsibility and Atonement* (Oxford: Clarendon Press, 1985), p. 81.

Wrongdoing creates responsibilities, and it is a central insight of the retributive tradition that if we are properly to acknowledge the seriousness of the wrong (rather than condoning it or overlooking it[3]) we ought not to deal with wrongdoers on normal terms until they have recognised and taken steps to discharge these obligations. In this chapter we will defend this idea and look at what an offender has a responsibility to do by way of making things right. My account of these obligations will draw on a notion of what we might call the *virtuous offender*.[4] I derive an account of the offender's responsibilities to make things right by looking at what someone would do if they were properly affected by the fact that they have done wrong. To see what we ought to do in such a situation, we look at how someone would act if they had the reactions to the situation that we think are appropriate. And to see why suffering is necessary we have to see how it is built in to these reactions.

STATUS IN QUESTION: THE STORY OF BLAME

It will turn out that the central aspect of an adequate defence of retributivism is the normative claim that we should not treat those who have done wrong in just the same way as we would treat those who have not. We will therefore start our discussion by looking at the nature of *blame*, which I will argue is the reaction that most fundamentally embodies this normative claim.[5] Consider a situation in which Bryson and Brewster are neighbours. Bryson, being the carefree young man that he is, likes to have parties: loud parties that often last well into the night. This happens even on week nights, but it happens especially on weekends. Now Brewster has been to talk to Bryson about this because it has an effect on all those living in close proximity. No doubt he is partly motivated by the annoyance it causes him personally. But he is particularly concerned with its effect on a neighbouring family: Brewster knows that the single mother in this family works many weekends, and

---

[3] On these possibilities, see the discussion of 'condonation' in A. Kolnai, 'Forgiveness', *Proceedings of the Aristotelian Society* 74 (1973/4), pp. 91–106.

[4] I have also developed this account in C. Bennett, 'The Varieties of Retributive Experience', *Philosophical Quarterly* 52 (2002), pp. 145–63; and in 'Personal and Redemptive Forgiveness', *European Journal of Philosophy* 11 (2003), pp. 127–44. The term 'virtuous offender' may seem a contradiction in terms. For some further discussion, see P. Greenspan, 'Guilt and Virtue', *Journal of Philosophy* 91 (1994), pp. 57–70.

[5] The argument of this section defends and develops the account of blame as 'withdrawal of recognition' put forward in J. Skorupski, 'The Definition of Morality', in *Ethical Explorations* (Oxford: Oxford University Press, 1999), pp. 137–59; and 'Freedom, Morality and Recognition: Some Theses of Kant and Hegel', also in *Ethical Explorations*, pp. 160–89.

has to get up early. She needs to sleep during the night, as Brewster has told Bryson – though she would never confront Bryson about the noise herself. Bryson, being not entirely insensitive, sympathises and promises to keep things under control. But the next weekend there comes a point, once the drink has been flowing long enough, when he forgets about this promise, forgets about his neighbours (or thinks, 'Sod it!'), and whacks up the volume on the stereo so that he and his friends can sing along at the tops of their voices.

Brewster is not on good terms with Bryson. It is not that he is sulking: he simply thinks that Bryson is not taking his neighbour's need to sleep seriously enough. So now, when Brewster passes Bryson in the street, and Bryson breezily (or sometimes, after a particularly loud night, sheepishly) says 'Hello!' Brewster walks straight past. It is not that Brewster wants Bryson to think that he has not heard him. Perhaps he even looks straight at Bryson, staring or glaring while he walks past saying nothing. So it is not that he is merely avoiding Bryson. Rather there is something important being communicated by his silence. By ignoring him (what used to be called 'cutting him dead') Brewster is trying to make Bryson *understand* that he is being ignored. Furthermore, he is trying to make him understand that they are not on friendly or even civil terms, and that Bryson cannot expect to be treated with civility by Brewster.

Why does Brewster think that this reaction is appropriate? That is, if Brewster were to try to spell out fully why it seems to him that this is the right way to treat Bryson, what would he say? Perhaps this: if Bryson will behave so inconsiderately to those who live nearby – as such a bad neighbour – then he cannot expect others to behave in a neighbourly way towards him. However, as I imagine his reaction, it is not that Brewster is simply seeking to inflict the same treatment on Bryson as his neighbours have had to suffer from him: it is not this 'eye for an eye' form of retributivism that motivates him. Rather his point is something like the following. Brewster takes it that Bryson and his neighbours are in a certain kind of relationship (call it 'neighbourliness'?) in which they have some sort of cooperative common project. This is not a grand affair: it is simply that they participate together in maintaining the kind of good relations that are necessary amongst people who live together in close proximity and therefore have business in common. But it is enough to provide us with an example of the sort of relationship we discussed in the last chapter: a relationship whose value for its participants is not merely instrumental. Being a good neighbour can be, for them, some small part of the good life. This relationship of neighbourliness is a simple kind of common good. Furthermore, although the demands of neighbourliness are not particularly demanding, it is a practice that allows of a distinction between apprentices and qualified practitioners. The distinction here is not necessarily a matter of having been trained in a craft (as with teaching): rather it is a matter of competence or mastery of a set of responsibilities. The qualified practitioner is simply one who can be expected to recognise and comply with the responsibilities of her place in the practice autonomously, without external supervision. Brewster takes it that – perhaps unlike some of the neighbouring children who are also noisy at various times of day and night – Bryson is a qualified member of the relationship. Now Brewster might recognise that people have different conceptions of the responsibilities that neighbours have to one another, and he may shrink from any demanding notion of 'community' that would conflict with the relative anonymity that he enjoys in urban living. But he takes it that what Bryson is up to violates even the most minimal reasonable conception of the responsibilities of neighbourliness. Because he cares about what Bryson is doing and the lack of consideration it shows for those around him Brewster feels that this has to make a difference to the way in which he treats Bryson.

And the difference is this. With the rest of his neighbours, Brewster acts in a certain way in virtue of the fact that they are his neighbours: he hails them when he passes them in the street; he stops to discuss the weather when he has time; he makes polite though non-intrusive enquiries about their welfare. These are forms of behaviour that he does not adopt with just anyone: rather they are marks that show he recognises that they are in a way members of a common enterprise; they are a kind of respect that he takes to be due to these people by virtue of the special relation they stand in to him.[6] They are aspects of the responsibility he has to show respect and goodwill to those who are engaged in this relationship with him by virtue of their status as co-members of the relationship.[7] Now we can understand how Brewster acts towards Bryson as the *withdrawal of the respect specific to the relationship*. It is not that he thinks Bryson has forfeited all right to respect, or even forfeited his right not to have music played loudly when he wishes to sleep. Rather he thinks that, because Bryson's conduct violates even the most minimal

---

[6] They are marks of *recognition*: a person is treated in a certain way because of their status. On the Hegelian notion of recognition, see A. Honneth, *The Struggle for Recognition: The Moral Grammar of Social Conflicts*, trans. Joel Anderson (Cambridge: Polity, 1995).

[7] I argued for a responsibility to respect this status both in our development of Strawson's position in chapter 3 and in our discussion of Jane in chapter 4.

conception of his responsibilities within that relationship, he can no longer treat him with the respect due to someone with whom he has that relationship of neighbourliness. However, it is not that Brewster thinks that no such relationship exists any more between Bryson and his neighbours. For that would be like saying that Bryson no longer owed his neighbours anything. And he clearly does not think *that*. Thus his ignoring of Bryson precisely does *not* imply that Bryson is no longer a neighbour who has to be acknowledged as such. Rather the withdrawal of the socially required respect *is* Brewster's way of dealing with Bryson *as a* neighbour (who therefore has certain responsibilities) – but as a neighbour who has culpably failed to meet the responsibilities of that role.

The set-up in this example is similar in relevant respects to that in the example of Jane from the last chapter. We have a person being regarded as a qualified member of some valuable relationship, membership of which gives him a status that, other things being equal, ought to be respected by other members (it gives other members of the relationship reason to treat him in a distinctive way as a member of that relationship). Yet this person has failed to meet those minimal responsibilities that can reasonably be expected of him as a qualified member. There are three points that I want to make about this example. The first is that those who are engaged with the wrongdoer in a such a cooperative relationship and who subscribe to the values of the relationship – in our examples, being a good neighbour or a good teacher – have reason to regard the wrongdoing as affecting the agent's status in the relationship. When one cares about the fact that a wrong has been committed in such a context one (appropriately) feels bound to acknowledge it by treating the person who has committed it differently as a result. If one had no motivation whatsoever to react negatively to wrongdoing this would imply either that one did not take the act to be really wrong (that one did not think it mattered) or that one did not see the agent as fully responsible. The second point is that whatever acknowledgement one makes has to be symbolically adequate: that is to say, it has to use symbols that express what needs to be expressed in the situation. And my third claim is that the story about the withdrawal of respect or recognition that I have used to elucidate Brewster's reaction to Bryson is what gives us the fitting retributive symbols to express our disapproval of the wrongdoer as a self-governing moral agent within a certain relationship.

This last point is important by way of distinguishing the retributive account offered in this chapter from the moral criticism approach of the last. The idea is that when someone has the capabilities necessary to assume certain responsibilities within a relationship – she is able to govern herself in such a way as to meet these responsibilities without external guidance or supervision – we are able to include her in certain relationships that can only exist between such self-governing agents: relationships like that between friends or good neighbours, or between teachers (as in the example of the last chapter) or between citizens. Specifically, she can be included as a qualified participant in a shared enterprise, which can legitimately be regarded as a status worthy of respect by fellow participants. The retributive reaction of withdrawing respect is one we have towards self-governing agents in such a relationship or enterprise who fail to meet responsibilities with which it is reasonable to expect them to comply. It is only possible to have this reaction towards someone to whom one would otherwise give the respect due to a self-governing and independent member of the relationship. Hence the class of agents who can be subject to these reactions is narrower than the class who can be properly subject to moral criticism. The conditions of moral responsibility are more demanding when we are considering these retributive reactions than if we are considering moral criticism. For these retributive reactions the requirement is not just the capacity to engage in moral discussion or inquiry, but rather the capacity to meet a set of responsibilities by oneself independently of external guidance or supervision.

This withdrawal of respect or recognition is our most basic response to wrongdoing and thus can correctly be described as the expressive form of *blame*. It is the most basic response to wrongdoing because it essentially involves the recognition that our relationship has changed in some way as a result of wrongdoing. Perhaps we can even say that wrongdoing – that is, the failure to do what it is one has a moral obligation to do – is just whatever properly motivates us to this withdrawal of recognition.[8] What blame expresses, through its symbolic withdrawal of recognition, is a deterioration in relationships: it expresses the view that things have changed for the worse between 'us'. A natural metaphor to reach for in explaining this is to talk about distance, or a rupture in relationships;[9] we might even talk in more grandiose fashion about the alienation of the wrongdoer from the moral community. This is a metaphor that we *act*

[8] Cf. Mill, *Utilitarianism*, pp. 321–2. Mill's view is developed and defended in these terms by Skorupski, 'Definition of Morality'.

[9] See e.g. H. Morris, 'A Paternalistic Theory of Punishment', *American Philosophical Quarterly* 18 (1981), pp. 263–71; Duff, *Trials and Punishments*, pp. 256–7.

out in withdrawing from the wrongdoer: through our behaviour we give expression to this metaphorical distance. It is because the metaphor is a fitting way to capture our understanding of the situation that this (retributive) behaviour is a particularly fitting response to wrongdoing.

Now it might be said that when we withdraw from someone, we *cause* a breakdown in our relationship. This is certainly the case. In deciding to make a point of cutting Bryson off, Brewster brings it about that the two are no longer on speaking terms. Thus in some sense it is Brewster who is the cause of the rupture. But Brewster thinks that acting in this way is only appropriate. In fact he might say that it is appropriate because the deterioration in the relationship had already happened as a result of Bryson's action, and that his action in distancing himself is really no more than a recognition of this fact. The way we behave in blaming the wrongdoer simply reflects the fact that a wrongdoer has changed our relationship with her.[10] The relationship ruptured when this agent failed to live up to what could minimally be expected of her as a party to the relationship: therefore all that blaming behaviour does is to give others a way of expressing this evaluation of the situation to the wrongdoer.

In my example Brewster blames Bryson by giving him the cold shoulder. This is one way of expressing blame, but it need not be the only one. The crucial thing about blaming behaviour is that it has to express a recognition of deterioration in relationships in a way that is consistent with the gravity of the wrong and the degree of the wrongdoer's responsibility. But this can be done in other ways too – sometimes by angrily confronting the wrongdoer; sometimes by more gentle confrontation; sometimes even perhaps by doing something like turning the other cheek (for instance, in a situation in which it is clear to both parties – if unspoken and maybe unacknowledged – that one has wronged the other). In order to sort out which behaviour is symbolically appropriate for expressing blame we have to pay attention to the details of the situation. The basic thing is that we are bound to treat the wrongdoer as though our relationship with her has changed, and changed in proportion to the gravity of the wrong.

This is why the moral criticism approach to Jane – which we considered in the last chapter – is inadequate. The moral criticism approach does not recognise that in inexcusably failing to meet her responsibilities as a teacher Jane damages her relations with those who are in the teaching enterprise with her in such a way as to affect how they ought to treat her.

---

[10] Duff, 'Restorative Punishment and Punitive Restoration', in L. Walgrave (ed.), *Restorative Justice and the Law* (Cullompton: Willan, 2002), pp. 82–100, at p. 87.

Although of course one aspect of what Jane has done is the way she damages her relations with her students, the case we are particularly interested in is the damage she does to her relations with her fellow teachers. As with Brewster's view of 'neighbourliness', Jane is involved in a shared cooperative enterprise with her fellow teachers in which each shoulders certain responsibilities – responsibilities that might be expressed in a conception of the good teacher or the good neighbour (or if that sounds too virtuous, call it the minimally decent teacher or neighbour). Jane violates the minimal reasonable conception of her responsibilities within this enterprise and insofar as she continues to be treated as a qualified member of the enterprise at all, she has to be treated in a way that recognises what she has done. She has to be blamed – in the sense in which this term is being used here, i.e. subjected to a (temporary) withdrawal of the respect specific to her place in the shared enterprise. Those who do wrong – who violate the minimal responsibilities of their role as a qualified practitioner – cannot be treated just as those who have not. The way in which we should mark this change in relations is by some withdrawal of the treatment they could otherwise expect as a qualified practitioner.

This leads us to a response to those who think that Martin Luther King and Gandhi present us with examples of conduct that is non-retributive. Can we really say that these figures lacked the retributive sense that what was being done to them and their social group affected their relationship with their oppressors – and indeed the relationship between the oppressors and all right-thinking people? If they did, then – given that it does not make sense to say that they did not see the oppression as wrong – it could only be because they thought that their oppressors were not fully responsible: perhaps that they were not qualified, self-governing, independent moral agents. However, this would suggest that King and Gandhi thought that they were morally superior to their oppressors in the sense that they could not expect their oppressors to come up to the same moral standards to which they would hold themselves. It seems unlikely that either of these figures saw themselves as part of a moral elite in this way.[11] But if they did take their oppressors to be (in my jargon) qualified

---

[11] Of course, the important issue is not about what these historical figures actually thought. The figures of King and Gandhi are invoked in discussions of the retributive emotions in order to substantiate a certain moral claim, namely, that the good human life need not involve retributive emotions. In this chapter I am questioning this claim. So the way to interpret my point here is that it would be *inappropriate* not to take one's oppressors to be fully responsible, regardless of what the historical King and Gandhi actually thought.

members of some shared moral relationship, then their response to their oppressors was retributive in the minimal sense I am discussing at the moment. Hence, in my terms, they did blame their oppressors for what they were doing. Granted they used imaginative ways to draw attention to the oppression that was occurring, but their reaction was a blaming one nevertheless, in the sense that the way in which they treated their oppressors was imbued with the recognition that they were in a relationship of mutual responsibility that one party was abusing and violating.

MAKING THINGS RIGHT

Another reason for thinking that King and Gandhi did blame their oppressors would be if they thought that their oppressors had a responsibility to put things right, and in particular if their understanding of the obligation to put things right relied on a retributive conception of what needed to be addressed. First of all, start by considering a non-retributive conception of the obligations created by wrongdoing. Even the staunchest non-retributivist can accept that when one responsibly harms another person's interests one has a duty to make restitution or pay compensation.[12] For instance, if one were simply interested in fairness (as in the benefits-and-burdens conception considered in chapter 2) as opposed to retribution one might think it a good idea to have a rule that where interests are unfairly damaged or appropriated the party who has caused the damage should repair or return.

However, the retributivist will insist that our moral relations would be far poorer if restitution were all that we thought we owed in cases of genuine wrongdoing (that is, for example, in criminal rather than civil cases). The retributivist thinks that the wrongdoer has damaged her relations with those with whom she has a certain relationship, and hence merits blame (the withdrawal of the respect specific to that relationship). She has to be treated in a way that reflects what she has done (not just by the victim but by a certain community of people who care that some specified standards of behaviour are met – hence it makes sense for Brewster to blame Bryson for what he is doing to the young family). As well as the obligation of restitution arising from fairness there is also an obligation on the wrongdoer to do certain things in order that others can treat her normally again. In other words, for the retributivist the counterpart to the distance that the wrongdoing creates is a question of

---

[12] See e.g. the explicit non-retributivism of Barnett, 'Restitution'.

redemption and restoring the wrongdoer's place in the relationship. This is an irreducible aspect of Zehr's obligation to 'make things right'. King and Gandhi are retributivists if they think that their oppressors have this sort of obligation to make things right and redeem themselves – for this would be a sign that, however they expressed it, they did blame their enemies in the sense of seeing distance between them that had to be made up before they could treat one another normally. But how is this redemption to be brought about?

This sounds like a strange question and its strangeness is no doubt one reason why writers on restorative justice have concentrated on restitution and repairing harm rather than 'righting the wrong' (material rather than symbolic reparation). When we discuss harm, we have some idea of what might need to be done to repair it. We understand, for instance, what it is for a car or a vase to be harmed, and what its repair consists in. Even if it is psychological harm that is at issue, although it might be far more difficult to see how to repair it, the difficulty lies in our contingent lack of knowledge: if we knew more about the workings of the mind then perhaps we could fix psychological harm too. 'Righting wrongs', on the other hand, sounds precisely like the unhelpfully metaphorical kind of thing that retributivists are wont to say, which it turns out is impossible to express clearly. Thinking perhaps of the model of repairing harm, people often complain that once an action is done it can never be undone – for instance, once an insult has been issued we cannot put time back and dismiss the whole idea.[13]

However, we actually have a clear and intuitive understanding of how to right wrongs, something without which our social relations would be unrecognisable. This is by saying sorry.[14] It seems strange that retributivists have appealed to metaphorical notions like paying debts – thus incurring the responsibility to explain how wrongdoing is like incurring a debt – when they had at hand such an intuitive part of our sense of justice. Writers on apology sometimes refer to the almost magical power that apology seems to have to restore relationships.[15] However,

---

[13] See C. Bennett, 'Satisfying the Needs and Interests of Victims', in G. Johnstone and D. Van Ness (eds.), *The Handbook of Restorative Justice* (Cullompton: Willan, 2007), 247–64.

[14] See e.g. E. Goffman, *Relations in Public* (London: Penguin, 1971), pp. 108–18 on 'remedial interchanges'; N. Tavuchis, *Mea Culpa: A Sociology of Apology and Reconciliation* (Stanford, Calif.: Stanford University Press, 1991); Bottoms, 'Some Sociological Reflections on Restorative Justice', pp. 93–9; Duff, 'Restorative Punishment', pp. 87–91. For a discussion that links apology to the issues of repentance, atonement and penance that I go on to discuss, see Swinburne, *Responsibility and Atonement*, ch. 5.

[15] See Tavuchis, *Mea Culpa*; and Bottoms, 'Some Sociological Reflections'.

I will argue that we can understand how apology works if we try to make sense of it in the way we have tried to make sense of Brewster's reaction to Bryson: that is, by trying to articulate what someone who performs the action might ideally say was their purpose. But in order to do so we need to see how apology is linked to reparative or more properly penitential behaviour, and how such behaviour is linked to the emotions appropriate to wrongdoing. On my account apology restores relationships and redeems wrongdoers because it expresses the emotions that are appropriate to wrongdoing. Thus apology and penance are what one is motivated to do when one experiences emotions like guilt; and guilt is what one feels when one fully understands oneself to have done wrong. It is the fact that the wrongdoer fully understands that what they have done is wrong that achieves reconciliation and the restoration of relationships. It is this that allows them to be reaccepted as a member of the relationship from which their action removed them.

Now often this link between repentance and penance is simply asserted rather than justified. Thus, as we saw in chapter 2, Michael Moore argues for a retributive theory of punishment from the claim that, if one were to feel as guilty as one might if one had committed murder – and (to use the terms given in my account) were fully aware of the wrongness of what one had done – then one would wish to 'suffer unto death'.[16] On the line presented here, this claim is certainly not unintelligible; but it does raise rather than answer all the important sceptical questions.[17] It draws on a theme of the redemptive power of suffering[18] rather than explaining or defending this theme to those who find it hard to understand or even barbaric.

However, when writers do attempt to explain why making reparation is necessary they sometimes fail to do justice to its expressive power. For instance, in rejecting Moore's account as an endorsement of suffering for its own sake, Linda Radzik has argued instead that atonement and penance are necessary in order to bring about the wrongdoer's reconciliation with those whose relationships with her have been damaged as a result of the wrongdoing.[19] The offender, on her view, has damaged her relationship with the victim, but also with a wider community and with

---

[16] Moore, 'The Moral Worth of Retribution'.

[17] Cf. the critical remarks in Matravers, *Justice and Punishment*, p. 86. See also the references at ch. 4 n. 21.

[18] Also invoked in the context of a discussion of apology by Murphy, 'Forgiveness and Resentment', pp. 27–8.

[19] L. Radzik, 'Making Amends', *American Philosophical Quarterly* 41 (2004), pp. 141–54.

her own self (since she may have lost confidence in and respect for her own moral agency as a result of what she has done). She argues that mere repentance and a determination to reform could not be enough to achieve reconciliation because this would not be enough publicly to demonstrate renewed trustworthiness. A full account of making amends would thus need to show what must be done to repair all of these relationships. In order to demonstrate to these various parties that she has turned the corner and can be accepted again, Radzik argues, the wrongdoer has to take responsibility for making right what was damaged. She needs to repair what was materially damaged but also repair the relationships in question. In order to repair the relationships in question she has to feel bad about what she has done (since only then will she be able to show that what she has harmed matters to her), she has to say sorry and she has to do penance. Undertaking penance shows one is serious about the relationship because one is prepared to do something onerous in order to save or restore it. While I agree with much of Radzik's account, I do not think that it gets to the heart of why penitential action is necessary to the process of repentance. We can imagine someone who does something that he finds perfectly unobjectionable but which offends a person who is very important to him. In such a case this person might, as Radzik imagines, find himself undertaking a penance in order to demonstrate how serious he is about keeping up the relationship. Yet we would normally think of this as an unusual case of penance, or not a proper case, because the person's penance does not express the fact that he thinks that what he did was wrong. Although it expresses his view that he is sorry that what he did offended his friend and that he wants to make things better, we normally think that penance is something one does in an attempt to *expiate* wrongdoing. Of course, it may be that we can make no sense of this notion of expiation or the redemptive power of penance, in which case we may find Radzik's notion a useful reconstruction of the practice of penance. However, I think that we can do more to articulate the point behind the idea of expiation through considering why penance might be something the virtuous offender finds it appropriate to do.

Something closer to the explanation we are looking for is given by R. A. Duff. Duff argues that penance has to involve hard treatment for two reasons. One is that it 'forces the offender's attention' on to the crime and its implications, making it harder for her to ignore than some less punitive response. The second is that undertaking such hard treatment can be an 'appropriate vehicle for the expression of remorse' that the offender ought to feel about the crime.[20] Now these two reasons give us quite different explanations for the use of hard treatment. Whether the first is a good reason for hard treatment would seem to depend on its efficacy in evoking remorse in offenders. The point of forcing an offender's attention on to the implications of their crime is, on Duff's view, to induce in them the appropriate response. On the assumption that the appropriate response is remorse, we could assess whether this technique was working by looking at how well it does bring these responses about. Duff's argument for this point therefore seems to rely on the commonsense (though empirical) hypothesis that this technique is indeed likely to bring these results about. Nevertheless it seems that this ground for hard treatment cannot be the central one.[21] It cannot give us the reason a person might feel it appropriate to undertake penance because it gets the order of explanation the wrong way round. When one has done some wrong one feels motivated to undertake penance (if one does) *because* one feels bad about what one has done, not *in order that* one feel bad. It is Duff's second type of reason that gives the type of explanation that we need. For on that explanation whether we have good reason to endorse hard treatment would depend on whether undertaking hard treatment really is an adequate or satisfying *expression* of remorse. This raises the question of the symbolic adequacy of hard treatment rather than its empirical efficacy. If we could explain why penance or hard treatment is symbolically adequate as an expression of guilt or remorse, then we could explain why it is that a person might undertake it because they feel bad. However, it is not clear that Duff has a fully articulated account of why undertaking hard treatment should be the characteristic or most adequate expression of remorse.[22] And this leaves him open to sceptics who claim that the notion of penance is a throwback to religious conceptions of sin and atonement that we are better off without. However, I would now like to argue that this scepticism is unjustified and that we can give a good defence of the expressive connection between moral change of heart and penance.

---

[20] See e.g. Duff, *Trials and Punishments*, pp. 260–1. For a penetrating sceptical discussion, see A. von Hirsch and A. Ashworth, *Proportionate Sentencing* (Oxford: Oxford University Press, 2005), pp. 93–4.

[21] Though discussions of Duff often take this justification to be central. See N. Walker, *Why Punish? Theories of Punishment Reassessed* (Oxford: Oxford University Press, 1991), pp. 79–80.

[22] Though the account I offer below has been importantly influenced by what Duff has to say e.g. at *Trials and Punishments*, pp. 246–7.

THE REDEMPTIVE POWER OF SUFFERING?

The key to understanding how apology works on the retributivist conception put forward here – why it has to express guilt and be backed up by penance; how it redeems – is to start with the idea of blame. The sorts of apologies that we are interested in are those that someone who is rightly blamed ought to make. (This is not to deny that there are other cases in which apology is appropriate. For instance, when one accidentally – though not negligently – treads on someone's toe one can owe the person an apology even though one is not blameworthy.[23]) The wrongdoer has done something that has damaged his standing in a relationship with other people. Those committed to the values underpinning that relationship have reason to treat him differently. Now what has caused this rift is the fact that in performing the action the wrongdoer expressed an inappropriate disregard of the interests or status of others. Thus even though Bryson will disturb his neighbours when he plays his music too loud late at night, at the point of action that nevertheless seems to him an OK thing to do (and the fact that he is drunk when he does so does not fully negate the fact that it is one of his own attitudes that he expresses in doing so). Jane presents her students with drastically under-prepared material and, at the point of decision, this seems all right to her. Of course the attitudes expressed in these actions may well be ones these agents would disown on reflection. But it is nevertheless these attitudes that they express in their action.

To see how such wrongdoers can restore their place in a set of relationships we have to see what is involved in their rejecting the attitude the expression of which caused the rift. An apology works when it is sincere: that is, when it expresses the wrongdoer's acceptance that what she did was wrong and her repudiation of it. In other words, the apology has to express the fact that the wrongdoer understands her action as wrong, that it matters to her. Now when the wrongdoer understands her action as wrong, and it matters to her, she will feel bad about it. She feels bad in part because she now understands that she has damaged something precious or important: Jane now thinks about the damage she did to the education of so many students. And it pains her that something valuable has been damaged. But she also feels bad because *she did it*: she

---

[23] I am grateful to John Skorupski, Suzanne Uniacke and others for making sure that I acknowledge the force of this point. It is an interesting question why apology seems necessary in such cases (since the apology seems more than just the compensation one might owe, on grounds of fairness, to someone one has non-culpably harmed) and more should be written about it (though not here).

feels *guilty*.[24] Guilt is what one feels when one turns blame upon oneself. If blame is a case of withdrawing from the wrongdoer, guilt is a case of withdrawing or dissociating oneself from (a part of) oneself. It is a painful splitting of oneself in two: rejecting or repudiating that aspect of oneself (one's greed, laziness, insensitivity, selfishness, pride, etc.) that brought the wrong about; and yet recognising that it is nevertheless part of oneself.[25] Now feeling bad about oneself like this, though painful, is an essential part of 'making things right'. If the retributivist is right that we ought to blame wrongdoers, then it must also be the case that wrongdoers should be subject to the pain of guilt. For the pain of guilt and what we might call self-dissociation will be an essential part of understanding that one has done something that merits blame and withdrawal.

When one feels guilty it affects the way one feels able to present oneself to others. Just as when one blames another person it affects the way one feels one can treat them, so when one blames oneself and hence feels rightly blamed by others it affects how one feels one can act towards them. When one feels guilty one is motivated to do something that would otherwise be servile or masochistic: something penitential. Now on the face of it this seems intensely problematic. It looks like precisely the sort of repressive, self-denigrating mechanism that a normally healthy and self-confident person might wish to be without. However, we can explain why in some form such penance is the fitting expression of feeling guilty if we see guilt as self-blame. Self-blame is withdrawal of that respect for oneself that one would have been due as a member of that relationship. In other words, one is usually justified in drawing a certain pride or self-respect from one's identity as a self-governing member of a valuable relationship, but when one comes to see oneself as having contravened some of the most basic responsibilities that come with being a member of that relationship one can no longer fully have that self-respect. Nevertheless, just as with the case of blame, it is not that one repudiates that identity, for that would be to deny responsibility. Rather one sees oneself in the problematic position of having certain responsibilities and hence a certain status (which is normally grounds for self-respect) but having behaved in such a way as no person with that status ought to behave. The way this recognition of one's position is expressed in action is that one puts oneself in a position that would otherwise be inconsistent

---

[24] I. Dilman, *Morality and the Inner Life* (London: Macmillan, 1979), p. 73.
[25] Cf. Goffman, *Relations in Public*, p. 113; Skorupski, 'Freedom, Morality and Recognition', pp. 182–4.

with one's dignity or status as a member of that relationship. That is why penitential behaviour can look servile or masochistic: it contravenes one's dignity. But this is precisely the point. It puts into behaviour one's recognition that one no longer fully has such dignity as a result of one's troubled status within the relationship.

Thus, for instance, if Jane were to feel truly sorry about teaching such ill-prepared courses would this not affect the way in which she sees herself? I have said that seeing oneself as a qualified member of a practice or relationship can be a source of self-respect. It would not be right for Jane to think that she was no longer a qualified teacher and to lose this source of self-respect entirely. She still is a qualified teacher. But she is a teacher who is in the uncomfortable position of having to admit that she has not lived up even to the minimum of what that role demands. Thus she withdraws respect from herself, putting herself in a position that shows that she does not see herself as due the respect that might otherwise come to her from other participants in that shared enterprise. She has to find a good way to symbolise that sense in her behaviour. The result is penance, which is the undertaking of something arduous or demanding that could not normally be asked of you as a matter of duty. The reason that this is fitting is therefore that it is the expression in behaviour of the way one sees one's relations with those in the relevant shared enterprise or relationship.

Thinking about the matter in this way can shed light on what sorts of things it might makes sense for Jane to choose to do by way of penance. The traditional bogey-man of penitential self-mortification has no place here. Jane's penance has to recognise her status as a teacher as well as the fact that she has acted in a manner inconsistent with that status. Furthermore it has to recognise her penitential understanding of the importance of the interests that she has harmed. Thus she might do penance by undertaking unpaid remedial work for students who are in difficulty (particularly, though perhaps not exclusively, those who are in difficulty as a result of her negligence). She might also do some voluntary teaching outside of the university, say in schools or as an evening class. She might even take a teaching development course to ensure that she is able to meet, not just the minimal responsibilities of her role, but the demands of being a genuinely inspiring teacher. However, if she does take this latter option it will be very different in significance from the case (considered in the last chapter) where such retraining is imposed on her as re-education in her role. The problem with her being sent on the course because her conduct shows that she needs it is that it suggests that Jane was not responsible for and capable of meeting the demands of her role independently. However, if she undertakes it as a kind of penance then what she does *is* being acknowledged as an aspect of her identity as a self-governing and autonomous participant in the enterprise.

Whatever she decides to undertake, however, it should express, in its duration and onerousness, her sense of the gravity of her offence. Thus in the case of minor wrongs a simple verbal apology is often enough. However, in more serious cases merely *saying* sorry can be a sign that one has failed properly to appreciate what one has done. This makes sense if we think that apology and penance put into behaviour one's sense of how one stands vis-à-vis one's fellows, and the degree of one's self-blame. If one's sense is that there is a large issue between oneself and one's colleagues then one will present oneself with corresponding humility; if on the other hand one thinks that what has happened is a minor wrinkle then one will shrug it off with an apology (though of course the loss of face that can be involved in apologising and admitting that one is wrong should not be underestimated). Hence where one wrongly thinks that an apology is enough this will fail to earn redemption in the eyes of others, because it will simply be a further sign that one does not really see why what one did was so bad.

Thus we arrive at an important general conclusion: that the amount of penance that we expect someone to do in order to redeem herself (its duration and onerousness) is the way in which we express our sense of the seriousness of the action. The penance therefore has to be *proportional* to the offence. This takes us into the realm of the symbolic, but it is not thereby merely conventional. No doubt it is a matter of cultural variation how much penance we think is enough for which crimes (and indeed which crimes we feel are the most serious). But this does not mean that it is simply up to us to choose the symbols. If we accept the articulation I have given here of the purpose of blame, apology and penance then we have to accept that there is good reason why we have certain symbols for the expression of condemnation and why these symbols have to have something to do with hard treatment and suffering. What I have told is a story in which certain specific types of suffering are necessary for wrongdoers to experience in the context of their coming fully to understand the significance of what they have done.

CONCLUSION

The defence of the 'right to be punished' strategy that we began by looking at Strawson in chapter 3 culminates here. What we have been seeking to defend is the idea that being subject to retributive reactions (of blame and guilt, withdrawal of goodwill) is an essential part of being treated as a 'member of the moral community': that is, an essential part of being included in an attractive form of social relations. We have now come to an interpretation of what Strawson means in talking of 'ordinary, adult, interpersonal relationships'; we have an account of why it is important to be treated as a member of such relationships; and we have explained why the retributive attitudes might be said to be 'all of a piece' with such relationships. Let us recap the main features of this account, starting with the model of relationships that we have developed. This form of social relations centres on a conception of human relationships as a union of independent, qualified agents in cooperative activity. These activities are ones in which participants bear certain responsibilities: that is, they can reasonably be expected to meet certain standards of behaviour. Furthermore, this conception of social relations sees participants as by and large capable of understanding the normative force of their responsibilities and complying with them without further external guidance. The status of being a qualified member of such a relationship is something that merits a certain amount of respect – and self-respect – even in the case of mundane examples like that of 'neighbourliness'. This conception of social relations is also an attractive one since the status of being qualified or independent in this sense allows participants autonomy, freedom or discretion in the way they discharge their responsibilities: being a qualified practitioner is a status that gives one a right to be 'left alone' compatible with membership of a shared endeavour.

This part of the argument aims to show that this is a model of social relations, of status, respect and responsibility, that we would not want to get rid of. Even if it is true that people are – when we look at them from Strawson's objective perspective – the product of myriad external influences, and not (impossibly) creatures of their own making, we still have reason to treat one another as qualified members of the cooperative endeavours in which we are engaged. It would be morally inappropriate to treat the ubiquity of luck as a reason not to treat a person as having the responsibilities attached to her place in those endeavours. If we can then show that retributive reactions are the most appropriate response to someone who fails to meet the responsibilities of her role then we will have shown that, contrary to the sceptical argument of chapter 3, luck does not undermine retribution.

However, it might be suggested that, given what we know about the influence of luck, we have reason not to respond to one another with the characteristically harsh retributive reactions. Why would moral criticism not be an equally valid moral response, one that did not bring with it the connotation that the agent is *to blame*? My response to this suggestion starts by looking at moral criticism and blame as different modes of evaluation of agents.[26] Both moral criticism and blame focus on the quality of a person's responses to moral demands. However, moral criticism and blame differ in the way that they understand the object to be evaluated. In non-retributive moral criticism the appraisal is of an authorised agent: one who is capable of grasping and responding appropriately to moral demands. Blame appraises a sub-category of such agents – those who are *qualified* and who can grasp and respond to moral demands by themselves. Qualified agents are blameworthy for their failures to meet even the minimal reasonable conception of their responsibilities in a situation. Non-retributive moral criticism is inadequate as a response to wrongdoers because it does not mark the distinction between those who are qualified and those who are not: it does not treat the status of being qualified as one that should make a difference to how we should treat an agent.

Blame is therefore the mode of moral appraisal that concentrates on an agent's identity as a qualified practitioner: blame assesses her responses to moral demands as a qualified practitioner. I have argued that we need this mode of evaluation specific to the qualified in order to respect the importance of this aspect of our identity. However, the question is why blame has to be retributive. Why does it have to involve, as Strawson claims, a withdrawal of goodwill? Blame expresses a recognition of the fact that, in the wake of the wrongdoing, relations with the wrongdoer cannot remain unchanged. We cannot treat the guilty as we do the innocent if we are to regard them as having done some wrong for which they are responsible. The source of this breakdown in relations is the wrongdoer's failure to take sufficiently seriously the demands underpinning the relationship. The most adequate way to treat the wrongdoer is therefore through the partial withdrawal of the respect normally due to her as a member of that relationship.

---

[26] Let me point out again that the distinction here is an artificial one, since we are used to thinking of blame as a *form* of moral criticism, and moral criticism as in many circumstances *implying* blame. I use these terms as terms of art to distinguish two ways of relating to wrongdoers. The way in which my argument has developed has been to try to show the necessity of a mode of interaction with the wrongdoer that involves characteristically retributive reactions. This is what blame stands for. So what I want to distinguish here is a form of moral criticism in which there is *no* implication of retributive attitudes or reactions as I used the term in chapter 4. It should not, therefore, be confused with our everyday notion of moral criticism.

The withdrawal of respect is partial and temporary. The onus is on the wrongdoer to repair the relationship. The way to repair the relationship is to re-establish commitment. This is done by the wrongdoer coming to a full understanding of what was wrong with her action. Atonement is behaviour that adequately expresses a full understanding of what was wrong with one's action. It involves repudiation of one's action, apology, repair as far as possible of what was harmed, and penance. This latter necessarily involves hard treatment because full understanding of what one has done involves self-blame (or guilt): withdrawal of recognition from oneself. Therefore we can conclude that, if it is reasonable to expect a qualified practitioner to come to a full understanding of the significance of what she has done, we can also and thereby expect her to see the need to do those things in which atonement consists. She will indeed, as Duff says, see these things as a symbolically appropriate vehicle for the expression of her remorse. The appropriateness of these reactions of blame, guilt, apology and penance is unaffected by the sceptical argument from luck.

In terms of the wider argument of the book, we now have in place an important aspect of our defence of a retributive theory of punishment. In chapter 2 we looked at theories of punishment as condemnation. The major problem for such theories was Feinberg's question of why the expression of moral disapproval needs to involve hard treatment. Why can it not be something more symbolic? This account provides us with a response to that question. I agree that the expression of disapproval *is* symbolic, but that the symbols have to be the right ones in order to express condemnation. We have to treat wrongdoers in ways that are adequate to their status. Blame and guilt and the behaviour by which they are expressed are particularly fitting because they recognise that certain actions affect one's status in a relationship: they have to affect it when that status is derived from one's assumed place as a qualified agent in a cooperative endeavour. But these emotional responses that are appropriate in cases of wrongdoing are inextricably and appropriately bound up with certain specific types of suffering. This is why hard treatment is essential to the expression of condemnation. In the next chapter I will argue that the state has a duty to condemn certain types of wrongdoing. And I will argue that in order to express such condemnation in a symbolically adequate way we have to draw on the cycle of blame and apology. We begin the chapter, however, by looking at a different way of using the cycle of blame and apology as a response to crime: informal restorative justice.

PART III

The Apology Ritual

CHAPTER 6

Restorative justice and state condemnation of crime

In part II of this book I developed a 'right to be punished' defence of retributivism. My 'right to be punished' argument takes it that the central cases of wrongdoing involve qualified members of some intrinsically valuable relationship whose actions demonstrate a fundamental failure to respect the demands of that relationship. I argued that where the relationship is a genuinely valuable one, we have a duty to respect the wrongdoer's status as a member of that relationship (to give them the appropriate *recognition*). But if we are to treat such wrongdoers in line with their status as qualified members of these relationships they should be subject to what I called the cycle of blame and apology. Their action – and the lack of concern that it expresses – is something that cannot leave their relations with other participants in the relationship unaffected: the way to express this is through blame (the withdrawal of recognition); the way for the wrongdoer to undo it is through apology and reparation.

In part III I want to look at whether the cycle of blame and apology – which I take to be a familiar feature of our interpersonal relations – can shed any light on how a modern society ought to deal with those who commit those wrongs normally thought of as crimes. What I have argued for in part II is a conception of what the *wrongdoer* has a responsibility to do in response to wrongdoing. However, there are also contexts in which the wrongdoing takes place under the eye of an authority that has an interest in ensuring that people keep to certain rules or standards. An example of this might be the case of Jane that we introduced in chapter 4: the university or school might have disciplinary procedures. Another example is the case of the state, which might have a criminal justice apparatus. Our question about these contexts would be whether these authorities have a responsibility to respond to such wrongdoing, and if so, what they have a responsibility to do. This will inform our understanding of what the criminal justice apparatus in our societies is there for. Thus our subject in this part of the book is: how, as a society, should we organise our response to such wrongs? Note that at this stage I do not want to ask: 'How can the cycle of blame and apology account inform our understanding of state punishment?' For it might be argued that the cycle of blame and apology as it operates in interpersonal relations is a perfectly good type of social sanction by itself, and that it is a mistake to think that we need state punishment as well. According to some of the restorative justice theorists that we looked at at the start of the book, we should stop allowing the state to intervene in those actions it designates as 'crimes', and should instead return the responsibility for dealing with interpersonal conflicts to citizens themselves. Citizens, the argument might go, have an intuitive understanding of the demands of inter-personal relationships and the mechanisms of blame and apology that is far more sophisticated and effective than anything that could be achieved through the unwieldy instruments of law, trial and punishment. I begin this chapter by sketching this 'laissez-faire' alternative and looking at its advantages, before confronting it with a series of objections. Addressing these objections will lead us towards a theory of punishment.

THE LAISSEZ-FAIRE CONCEPTION OF RESTORATIVE JUSTICE

One way in which we could draw on the cycle of blame and apology in framing a societal response to wrongs is to look again at the restorative justice alternative we introduced in chapter 1. Say an advocate of res-torative justice were convinced by my arguments in part II and came to accept (1) the importance of individual responsibility (understood in the context of the relationships we discussed in the last couple of chapters) and (2) an essential role for penance and hard treatment in 'making amends'.[1] Nevertheless, this theorist may still insist that accepting the cycle of blame and apology leads us to something quite distinct from criminal justice as it is usually understood. The position might be as follows:

Society as a whole ought not to try to make any collective response to 'crimes'. Although in some extreme cases it might be necessary to isolate dangerous individuals for the sake of communal safety, as far as possible society as a whole ought to refrain from any heavy-handed intervention. This is not to say that we

---

[1] Cf. the 'making amends' model of restorative justice discussed in von Hirsch *et al.*, 'Restorative Justice: A "Making Amends" Model?' in von Hirsch and Ashworth, *Proportionate Sentencing*, pp. 110–30.

ought not to care about victims or leave people to their own devices. Rather our responses to perpetrators and victims of wrongs are done better when they are left to conscientious spontaneous individual action. What the cycle of blame and apology account uncovers is the presence of a mechanism for regenerating social relations after wrongdoing: a way in which grievances of victims can be given weight and recognised, and through which wrongdoers can be reaccepted into normal relations. This is an important mechanism in itself, on the grounds that, as we have seen, it involves treating offenders as fellow cooperators rather than deviants or 'problem cases'. Furthermore, the felt need for such responses contributes to the sense that victims and offenders have that the event is 'theirs' to sort out: it is not in the first place the business of the state. When the state intervenes it 'disempowers' all parties by taking this responsibility away.

What is recommended by the proponent of this view is what I am calling the 'laissez-faire conception' of restorative justice. According to this conception the state should leave individuals as far as possible to do justice for themselves. It may be compatible with this approach that the state has a role in setting up institutions that will facilitate such citizen action (and perhaps in enforcing ground rules for interaction). But the state and its agents are only mediators: the initiative rests firmly with the main 'stakeholders', that is, the people directly and indirectly affected by whatever has occurred. We can give an example using the case of Bryson (described in the introduction). Immediately upon having caused the accident, Bryson is moved to apologise. As I describe it, his apology is cut off by the arrival of the police who need to take statements and detain him on suspicion of criminal behaviour. From then on the system takes over and anything Bryson might do in the way of apologetic action is hampered or perhaps, in his mind, rendered superfluous by the much larger-scale actions of the criminal justice bureaucracy. However, if we rewind the tape and let it play on without state intervention, what would happen?

On the view that I am presently explaining, it is sometimes held that state intervention in such cases can be disempowering in the sense that when people know that the state will effectively do justice for them they lose the important idea that it is their responsibility to do it for themselves.[2] The corollary of this claim is that left to their own devices people (at least those with moral motivations) are more likely to pursue justice themselves and to take responsibility for their actions. So let us make the assumption – which does seem true to his happy-go-lucky but

---

[2] Christie, 'Conflicts as Property'; J. Braithwaite, 'Restorative Justice and a Better Future', in Johnstone, *A Restorative Justice Reader*.

ultimately unselfish character – that Bryson will decide to take
responsibility for the situation. As soon as he sees what he has done
Bryson understands what an unjustified risk he was taking with other
people's safety. He is immediately filled with an overwhelming wish that
he had never driven so fast and so carelessly. And this remorseful state of
mind is what is expressed when he begins to apologise. Recognising that
the responsibility is his, to try to make up for what he has done he
accompanies his victim to hospital and does what he can to make her
comfortable, phones to inform her relations, and makes the necessary
inquiries with medical staff to ensure that she is getting proper treatment.
Neither does this effort on his part only happen on the day of the crash.
In the following days, weeks and months he continues to attend to his
victim, again making sure that she has what she needs, and generally
going out of his way to make sure that she is as well off as she can be
in the circumstances. The victim is of course devastated by what has
happened to her, and is angry with Bryson. But she finds that this anger
cannot be sustained in the face of his obvious remorse: she accepts his
attempts to help her. She finds what he does for her helpful in practical
terms, but it also gives her some solace. Although of course she would far
rather the event had never happened, and she may be far from forgiving
Bryson for what he did to her, she does at least derive a certain amount of
solace from the fact that Bryson seems to recognise its significance and is
genuinely sorry about it. With her encouragement Bryson joins up to a
schools project that publicises the dangers of drunk and reckless driving.
His audience identifies with his story, and his evident remorse strikes a
chord with them. There is some evidence that his interventions do some
real good in preventing further such incidents in the area. The whole
process also gives Bryson an education, enlarging his perspective and his
sensibilities, and makes him more socially responsible in various areas of
his life.

   This story presents an ideal and optimistic scenario, though not, I hope,
one that can too easily be dismissed as mere fantasy.[3] We can see that
certain goods come from the restorative justice process in this case – goods
that almost certainly would not have been realised if the case had been
dealt with on the conventional court-and-formal-sanction model. Perhaps
the advantages of informal restorative justice could be summarised thus:
it allows victims, offenders and other legitimately interested parties to

---

[3] Cf. Braithwaite's story of Sam: J. Braithwaite, 'Restorative Justice', in M. Tonry (ed.), *The Handbook of Crime and Punishment* (New York: Oxford University Press, 1998), pp. 323–44.

participate meaningfully in justice procedures in a way that conventional Western criminal justice often frustrates.[4]

I use the term 'meaningfully' here with three aspects in mind. The first is about *control*.[5] Informal procedures give parties more opportunity actually to affect outcomes, to have their voice heard and to have it affect what is decided upon. Given that the outcome is simply dictated by the result of the discussion, the parties each have the opportunity to exert influence, though perhaps part of the role of the facilitator might be to ensure that the parties with the greatest stake in the offence are the ones who have the greatest say in what is to be done (for instance, to prevent the proceedings being hijacked by a voluble third party). However, while no doubt the exercise of control over the proceedings is an important one, we should not overemphasise its importance, or concentrate on this aspect to the exclusion of all others. The thing is that a restorative justice meeting ought not to be a meeting in which all parties are simply motivated to exercise the maximal amount of control over the outcome, and to get their way as far as possible in negotiating a compromise. One of the crucial aspects of participation in restorative justice is an ability to see the other parties' points of view: the ideal of restorative justice is therefore an enlarging of experience rather than an exercising of control.[6] This suggests that, to invoke the terms of chapter 4, the model of restorative justice ought to be dialogue as shared inquiry rather than dialogue as negotiation. What proponents of restorative justice aspire to is not so much parties bargaining as parties seeking to understand one another and coming to a decision that reflects the seriousness of the offence. Hence, while exercising control over the outcomes no doubt has some importance, the ideal of restorative justice suggests that this is certainly not the only important thing, and perhaps not the most important.

The second aspect of meaningful participation is about *recognition*. Independently of the outcome the very experience of being listened to and taken seriously can be rewarding and vindicating for all parties.[7] Again informal procedures allow parties to put their own experience across

---

[4] This sort of thought is sometimes expressed by saying that participants can feel as though they 'own' the process. I do not use this language since it seems to me that this makes it sound as though control over the outcomes is the fundamental part of 'owning' the process, whereas I want to emphasise instead the primacy of meaningfulness.

[5] Cf. the reference to the 'personal involvement of those mainly concerned' in Marshall, 'Restorative Justice: An Overview', p. 28.

[6] We touched on this issue in distinguishing dialogue as negotiation from dialogue as shared inquiry in chapter 4.

[7] Zehr, *Changing Lenses*, pp. 26–9; Johnstone, *Restorative Justice: Ideas, Values, Debates*, pp. 64–7.

and – ideally – to have it given due weight in the overall discussion. If the restorative conversation proceeds in a spirit of shared inquiry, in which each person contributes their own perspective, not with the purpose of manipulating an outcome but rather in order to enlarge the common awareness of those participating in the conversation, then each person has a motive to take seriously what others are saying, to find what is of value within it and what they can learn from. Each person's contribution can be treated, in such circumstances, as bringing new evidence to bear on two questions. The first question is: what was the character of the offender's wrong? That is, what was she responsible for? Here the discussion aims to find out the various consequences of the wrong for which the offender can be held to account and can legitimately be asked to make amends. It will sort out rough questions of culpability and the seriousness of the wrong, both in terms of the offender's intention or motive, and the consequences of the action. The second question that the discussion will look at is what should be done to make amends. Here the question will be what amount of amends would be a proportionate response to the wrong.[8] In being treated as a participant worth listening to in such a discussion, the parties have their experiences validated or recognised. To use the terminology of the shared inquiry model from chapter 4, each party is 'authorised' as an interlocutor: they are treated as being able to follow the conversation and as being worth listening to when they contribute. However, let me stress again that this authorisation or validation does not mean that everyone in the room has to agree with the content of what every other party says. The discussion, if it is to be a genuine shared inquiry that aims to reach an adequate answer to these two questions, has to make judgements about the plausibility of the various contributions (the group as a whole has to make judgements, for instance, about how reasonable it would be to hold the offender to account for aspects of an offence, etc.). Therefore it might be that the group decides against a contributor's view that the offender should be held responsible for certain consequences of what she did. But even when this is the case there is an important value in being listened to, taken seriously, and having one's perspective given due weight in common deliberation.

The third aspect of meaningful participation is about *understanding*. If the first two elements that we have looked at emphasise the importance

---

[8] These questions are the relevant ones because, although I take it that the shared inquiry model remains a good model for restorative justice, it is not the purely non-retributive model of chapter 4. Assuming the defence of retribution in chapter 5, we now take it that the restorative conversation is aimed at resolving questions of guilt and amends. See von Hirsch *et al.*, 'Restorative Justice: A "Making Amends" Model?'.

of participation, this third element emphasises the importance of the proceedings being meaningful to their participants. I understand 'meaningful' in this sense to require that the proceedings reflect participants' own understanding of what should go on. However, the idea is more than simply the claim that the participants should be able to become familiar with the procedures, rules and regulations governing the meeting and the way its decisions are made (though of course even this is often lacking in criminal trials). This would be compatible with the rules and regulations themselves being quite unintuitive. Rather it is the idea that each participant should be able to recognise in the substance of what is going on something that corresponds to their deep normative expectations about such situations: they *identify* with the basic structure of the process. This might be thought to be related to the fact that participants have control over the proceedings: because they are in control, the proceedings can reflect participants' own intuitive views of what responsibilities victims and offenders have to one another in the wake of some serious wrongdoing. However, control might not be necessary: what makes the proceedings intuitive is that they reflect the basic cycle of blame and apology. It is when this link is broken that justice procedures become alienating and merely administrative. Of course, it is not possible to accommodate the expectations of all participants, since participants may have vindictive or amoral motivations. Rather, what the meeting has to try to do is to come to a view about which expectations are *legitimate*, and what the offender can *reasonably* be held responsible for and asked to do by way of making amends.[9] Nevertheless, while this means that actual proceedings will perhaps only rarely mirror participants' expectations precisely, the form that restorative justice takes – in that it takes it to be fundamental that wrongdoing creates obligations to take reparative action – is deeply intuitive. So even in cases in which the amount or nature of amends eventually agreed on is different from what a particular participant would judge necessary, there are nevertheless amends being carried out. This has to be an improvement, in terms of meaningfulness, on justice procedures in which no such responsibility of victim to offender features.

The fact that restorative justice enables and encourages meaningful participation helps to explain why it can also bring about further goods for victims, offenders and communities (as noted in chapter 1).[10] For instance, restorative justice might promote an attractive form of reform

---

[9] For some more on this, see Bennett, 'Satisfying the Needs and Interests of Victims.'

[10] On these points see further Braithwaite, 'Does Restorative Justice Work?', in Johnstone, *A Restorative Justice Reader*, pp. 320–52.

or rehabilitation of the offender as an agent with new moral sensibilities. This is something that is quite likely to be good for the offender himself but can also be good for the community in which he lives. We can also see how meaningful participation in a restorative conversation can satisfy some of the needs of victims of crime. For instance, Zehr claims that amongst other things victims have needs to be listened to and taken seriously, and to be *vindicated*.[11] Participation in a restorative justice meeting that culminates in a sincere apology and an offer to make proportionate amends – where these show that the offender now under-stands the moral significance of what he has done – can, so some research suggests, be deeply helpful for victims.[12] Because restorative justice is not openly adversarial but rather presents itself as an attempt to find a rea-soned and morally adequate reconciliation between the parties, it offers – in an ideal case – an environment in which the offender is not confronted with – and hence does not need defensively to reject – accusations and denunciations. He can therefore feel safe to admit that what he did was wrong. He is also confronted – hopefully in a sympathetic way – with the true consequences of what he did, and he is treated as someone to whom those consequences ought to matter, rather than as someone who is always looking to get away with whatever he can. In a restorative justice meeting victims and offenders ought (again, ideally) to be able to find an environment in which they can overcome mutual suspicion and engage in an honest, adult, humanising conversation about what has happened between them. When communities are given the responsibility of staging such meetings then perhaps it might make them more active, stronger and safer.[13]

So an argument can be put forward that some type of informal restorative justice can bring benefits for the victim, the offender and the wider community. Granted that such results will not come about in all cases, but even if something like this happens in some significant pro-portion of cases that should give the defender of punitive and formal sanctions pause for thought. Why should we choose formal sanctions over the informal approach? What is it that makes formal sanctions so valuable that they outweigh the benefits of the informal approach? What valid

---

[11] Zehr, *Changing Lenses*, p. 194.

[12] H. Strang, *Repair or Revenge: Victims and Restorative Justice* (Oxford: Clarendon Press, 2001); Shapland *et al.*, 'Situating Restorative Justice in Criminal Justice'; L. Sherman and H. Strang, *Restorative Justice: The Evidence* (London: The Smith Institute 2007).

[13] Cf. the statement of the primary objectives of restorative justice in Marshall, 'Restorative Justice: An Overview'. For an attempt to imagine in detail how this conception might be put into practice as far as possible, see Daniel Van Ness's 'RJ City': www.rjcity.org.

state purpose is served by formal sanctions, and is it really more important than what the laissez-faire approach can give us? Of course, it might turn out that there is no normatively adequate answer to these questions, in which case it will appear, as many who wish to abolish formal sanctions believe, that less salutary or defensible motives are the real explanation for the persistence of the criminal sanction.[14] Overturning the imposition of formal sanctions would therefore look like an important liberation, a chance to reconnect with the more important goals from which the criminalising mentality has distracted us. But first of all we need to see whether there is some genuine need for formal sanctions. We will do this through an examination of the adequacy of the laissez-faire approach.

QUESTIONING THE LAISSEZ-FAIRE APPROACH

Before we go on to see how far this informalist or abolitionist approach to crime could be taken, let us distinguish two different ways in which the restorative justice theorist might see the importance of informalism. I have characterised this approach as a laissez-faire one, in that it involves thinking that citizens ought to be left to their own devices as far as possible in this matter. However, we can distinguish two quite different motivations for this view. One is the *principled* defence: on this view justice ought to be left to the citizen because it is none of the state's business in the first place. If the state is involved then it steals the responsibility for dealing with these issues from those who really own it: that is, citizens themselves. The other is the *instrumental* defence: on this view, while the state does legitimately have certain criminal justice goals, the best way in which to pursue these goals is through informal social control mechanisms rather than the court-and-sanction approach. In other words, for the latter informalism is the most effective way of furthering or realising a valid state purpose, while the former is more genuinely anti-statist and defends the right of citizens to be left to their own devices on principle. We will begin by considering the principled view on which 'crimes' are really just individual conflicts that are not any of the state's business.

There is a wide range of interpersonal conflict within any society, only a small subset of which is defined by the state as 'crime'. The principled

[14] Cf. P. Hillyard and S. Tombs, 'Beyond Criminology', in P. Hillyard *et al.*, *Criminal Obsessions: Why Harm Matters More than Crime* (London: Crime and Society Foundation, 2005), pp. 5–20, at pp. 11–13.

laissez-faire position holds that the categorisation of an action as crime is morally arbitrary and reflects an illegitimate interest of the state: there is no relevant moral difference between acts that are crimes and those that are not, apart from the fact that they are classified differently, and one type is marked by drastic state intervention.[15] Though prior to their classification as crime such conflicts are taken to be a matter primarily for the parties involved to sort out, once the state is involved it defines the parties as 'victim' and 'offender' (or at least 'plaintiff' and 'defendant') and takes it as a matter of public interest to deal with the issue. However, the effect of this intervention is that the conflict is appropriated from the original participants – to whom the conflict actually 'belongs' – who are not allowed to deal with it in their own way. While this has certain negative consequences in terms of the loss of valuable opportunities for clarification and dissemination of social norms, the fundamental concern for the laissez-faire approach is one of *ownership*: the state claims something as its own business which is really the business of individuals or local communities.[16] It is really up to Bryson, Judith and members of the local community to decide what to do in response to his action: the decision belongs to them in the sense in which they are sovereign with regard to this area of their lives (though this sovereignty may be something they hold collectively as stakeholders rather than individually). Their sovereignty should not simply be violated by the state in the name of the supposed overriding interest of an aggregate (which the anti-statist may take to be a mere fiction) called 'the public'.

This principled laissez-faire view is clearly right in some respects. There is a sense in which the wrong 'belongs' to the immediate participants: this is the sense in which the offender, as a result of what he has done, has responsibilities to make amends to the victim and others who may be indirectly affected. Any account of potential state intervention ought to be sensitive to the existence of these responsibilities and ought not to ride roughshod over them if possible. However, what characterises the principled anti-statist version of the laissez-faire account is the claim that it is only these parties who have any responsibilities or claims arising from the crime: in particular it denies that there are any further responsibilities

---

[15] Christie, 'Conflicts as Property'. See also L. Hulsman, 'Critical Criminology and the Concept of Crime', *Contemporary Crises* 10 (1986), pp. 63–80; Hillyard and Tombs, 'Beyond Criminology'.

[16] Cf. McCold and Wachtel: 'A fundamental principle of restorative justice is that society is not the victim, government is not the victim, the victim is the victim.' See P. McCold and B. Wachtel, 'Community Is not a Place: A New Look at Community Justice Initiatives', in Johnstone, *A Restorative Justice Reader*, pp. 294–302, at p. 297.

on the state's part. On this view the event only belongs to those most immediately involved. In particular there is scepticism about the reification of 'the public' or 'public interest'. At most, on this view, the state's role should be to facilitate restorative justice meetings. But is this denial of public interest and public responsibility really plausible? Say Baxter has committed the same crime as Bryson, but his case is a hit-and-run. He panics after hitting the cyclist and accelerates away as he sees her in his rear-view mirror sprawling on the ground. His concern is only with avoiding the humiliation and disruption of being caught. Baxter would never comply voluntarily with a restorative justice process. Can such people be required (presumably by the state) to make amends if they will not do so willingly? Or if the matter is really not the state's business to interfere in is the correct response for the state simply to leave events to run their course?

We can distinguish three broad lines of possible response from restorative justice theorists to the Baxter case. One (which we might dub the pure informalist or laissez-faire approach) claims that the state has no responsibility to do anything to the offender as a result of the crime (or 'crime') and hence would reject the idea that Baxter should be held to account against his will. This position can acknowledge that Baxter has real responsibilities to his victim as a result of what he has done. It simply claims that no one (at any rate not the state or a public authority) has the right to compel him to meet those responsibilities. The problem with this approach, though, is that refusing to take action against Baxter on the grounds that it is only the victim's business seems to be a false delimitation of responsibility. If all were to stand by and let Baxter drive off and do nothing for those he has harmed, this would fail to recognise the significance of the offender's responsibility for the action and hence leave the victim's plight as the victim not of an accident but of responsible wrongdoing insufficiently acknowledged. In a case in which the offender absconds and leaves the victim to their fate, and where the state has the power to track that offender down, surely it should do so. Not to do so would represent a failure properly to care about what he has done to the victim. It is not only retributivists who need be concerned about offenders 'getting away with it': restorative justice theorists can share the retributive concern that offenders should be made accountable.

In response to the problems with the pure laissez-faire line, a second, 'semi-formalist' response could argue that the state should be seen as having a responsibility to make sure that the offender meets his responsibilities to the victim, coercively if necessary. This position would accept some role for state coercion, and hence would accept that the state has genuine responsibilities to take action against offenders in the case of certain actions. However, these state responsibilities would on this view be derivative from the offender's responsibilities to the victim: the state would simply have the responsibility to ensure that the offender meets these responsibilities. It would be like a civil rather than a criminal law model of dealing with such actions.[17] (Perhaps there are simply harms that individuals can cause one another that create obligations for redress and are serious enough to warrant state intervention to ensure that redress is given.) Hence this view would argue that there is no genuine *public* interest in crime. On this view the state might compel Baxter to do something for his victim. Given that – as we will stipulate – Baxter has no intention of saying sorry or admitting responsibility (he is a thoroughly uncooperative offender) it would be inappropriate to stage any face-to-face meeting between victim and offender, but perhaps some form of indirect mediation might be a suitable way to arrange a level of amends.

However, this second line of response still denies that there are any collective goals that a political society – through the agency of the state – properly pursues through the justice system, and hence denies that there is any genuine public interest in those acts we designate as crimes. This assumes that, when we think that we ought to take action against Baxter rather than letting him get away with it we are really just acting on behalf of the victim. But now consider a case in which the victim does not want to take action against the offender for what was clearly a criminal act. Is the victim's wish a conclusive reason for the state to let the matter rest? After all, the offence is an act that takes place in the context of a society, and that society belongs to others as well as the victim. Perhaps the victim is not the only one who has legitimate interests in the offence. Thus many would say that the state – acting on behalf of the public – has independent reason for taking action against Baxter.[18] The public has collective criminal justice goals that have weight independently of the interests of the victim.[19] For instance, it might be argued that we have a legitimate collective goal of keeping crime rates low. Or it might be argued that we have a legitimate collective goal of making appropriate

---

[17] Barnett, 'Restitution.' For some discussion of this approach, see Zehr, *Changing Lenses*, pp. 215–22; G. Johnstone, 'Introduction: Restorative Approaches to Criminal Justice', in Johnstone, *A Restorative Justice Reader*, pp. 1–18, at pp. 8–14.

[18] This is a version of the common criticism that restorative justice 'privatises' wrongdoing when it denies a public interest. See e.g. von Hirsch *et al.*, 'Restorative Justice: A "Making Amends" Model?', pp. 123–4.

[19] Cf. N. Lacey, *State Punishment* (London: Routledge, 1988), pp. 182–3.

condemnation of the offence. Which understanding of these goals is correct will depend on the success of a philosophical justification of punishment. But if an argument to this effect can be made out then it will show the inadequacy of the civil law model. It would show that, even though a crime is usually an act committed against particular individuals, it is not only those particular individuals who are responsible for deciding how to deal with it. Perhaps we should concede that the crime clearly *is* the victim's business, and that this fact has often been overlooked in criminal justice, but deny that it is ever *only* the victim's business: it is not *just* up to the victim to decide how we should respond to crime.

This takes us to a third line of response to the Baxter example, which is what I earlier called the instrumental defence of the laissez-faire model. This view holds that, while there are collective goals that we appropriately pursue through the criminal justice apparatus, they need not be incompatible with restorative justice, since as a matter of fact these collective goals are best pursued through the laissez-faire model. In fact, this view could accept that there are many interests to be served by a conception of justice – interests of victims and offenders, but also interests of the wider community which may itself have been harmed by the crime – and that the restorative justice model of a process involving victim and offender is the most effective way of furthering these interests.[20] An example of this instrumentalist view is that put forward by Braithwaite and Pettit.[21] They take it that we do indeed have certain collective criminal justice goals, goals that stem from the overall goal endorsed by their republican political philosophy: the promotion of dominion (where dominion is a person's freedom to do what they want – negative liberty – in a social context: in other words, their freedom from domination or undue influence by others).[22] They think that from this overall goal we can identify aims – including reducing the level of crime, restoring the confidence and empowerment of victims, reintegrating offenders into productive society, building strong and active communities[23] – that the laissez-faire conception of restorative justice is likely to be more successful at promoting than conventional approaches such as the court-and-sanction model.[24]

---

[20] See, for instance, L. Walgrave, 'Restorative Justice for Juveniles: Just a Technique or a Fully-Fledged Alternative?' in Johnstone, *A Restorative Justice Reader*, p. 255–69.

[21] Braithwaite and Pettit, *Not Just Deserts*.

[22] Braithwaite and Pettit, *Not Just Deserts*, pp. 56–7, 63.

[23] Braithwaite and Pettit, *Not Just Deserts*, e.g. pp. 69–71, 91–2.

[24] See for instance Braithwaite's 'Does Restorative Justice Work?', which takes the form of defending the hypothesis that restorative justice restores and satisfies (1) victims, (2) offenders and

Whether this instrumental defence of the laissez-faire conception is plausible depends in part on the extent to which restorative justice works as we imagined it might in the example of Bryson, above.[25] Coming to a conclusion about this would require analysis of empirical data that I will not go into here. However, I want to raise a set of independent problems with this approach, problems that again centre on cases of non-compliant offenders like Baxter. The issue concerns the basic claim that criminal justice procedures are simply the most effective means to the promotion of dominion. A state that takes itself to have a responsibility to promote dominion by lowering crime, aiding victims and increasing public confidence will not leave Baxter alone because he has refused to comply with restorative justice. If the state's criminal justice goals ultimately boil down to that of promoting dominion then whether restorative justice is appropriate in any particular case will depend on the probability of getting a good outcome. But minimally the state's response will simply involve deterrence and the protection of the public. Baxter's is a case, let us imagine, in which it is judged (in whatever way such decisions might be made) that there is no point in pursuing the more ambitious aims. Therefore the logic of the aim of promoting dominion is that we should deal with Baxter by attempting to deter or incapacitate him as necessary. This means that non-compliers are treated quite differently from those who comply, and Braithwaite makes this point quite explicit.[26] Offenders who cooperate and go to restorative justice willingly are treated as moral agents, capable of understanding and acting on moral reasons. But those who do not are treated as merely rationally self-interested agents; the restorative paradigm is abandoned for such agents and they are subjected to either deterrent or incapacitative measures.

There are a number of problems with this. The first is a concern that, because it confronts offenders with a choice between restorative justice or a deterrent sanction, Braithwaite's proposal amounts to coercing offenders into restorative justice. And this, the objection goes, is unacceptable because restorative justice is an emotionally demanding process in which offenders will be put under a certain amount of situational pressure to

---

(3) communities better than existing criminal justice practices. One can agree with many of these aims independently of one's support for their wider republican project. For instance, compare the list in Sherman and Strang, *Restorative Justice: The Evidence*.

[25] Thus Braithwaite acknowledges that there are 'optimistic' and 'pessimistic' scenarios for restorative justice. See e.g. his 'Restorative Justice: Assessing Optimistic and Pessimistic Accounts', *Crime and Justice: A Review of Research* 25 (1999), pp. 1–127.

[26] See, for instance, Braithwaite, 'In Search of Restorative Jurisprudence', in Walgrave (ed.), *Restorative Justice and the Law* (Cullompton: Willan, 2002).

accept responsibility, apologise and display the relevant emotions. In one way the Braithwaite proposal looks innocent enough: we reward those who comply and deal more harshly with those who do not; we do so in order to encourage compliance. But compliance in this case involves something morally intimate, an acknowledgement of wrongdoing and hence of deep personal failure. While one person might require such emotional honesty of another in the context of a close personal relationship, this is not the sort of avowal that the state should coerce a person into making: indeed perhaps the state should always stop short of requiring people to mouth 'appropriate' sentiments as though they really mean them. Braithwaite may of course deny that there is any coercion going on here and argue that it is all to the good to give people a prod in the direction of appropriate and beneficial responses, attempting to break down the emotional defences of offenders if need be. But many will say that the offender can legitimately have his own reasons for declining to be involved in the restorative justice process, reasons which might be good as well as bad (e.g. he has been wrongfully convicted; the offence is an unjust one; he is not good at showing emotion, at least under pressure; he has the wrong values; he is simply wilful).[27] The state can, and sometimes should, disagree with such reasons but it is not always legitimate to pressure the offender to disavow them.[28]

The second problem with Braithwaite's approach is that it involves treating non-compliant offenders as though the only considerations that can move them are ones that appeal to their own self-interest. This is hard to reconcile with the claim – defended in this book – that we should respect a person's status as a qualified member of those relationships the terms of which he has violated. Someone like Baxter, insofar as we hold him responsible for such violations, has to be seen as being capable, by himself and without external intervention, of complying with the obligations of the relationship. But if he is such a qualified agent then this is an important thing about him, something that we should recognise as giving him a certain status, and affecting the way we treat him. Thus we owe it to the Baxters of this world to treat them as more than merely self-interested agents. Braithwaite's argument is presumably that the most efficient way to deal with cases like Baxter is to treat them as merely self-interested: it is not cost-effective to try to engage with them. But this is to

[27] Cf. the discussion in Hampton, 'Moral Education Theory of Punishment', pp. 232–4.
[28] See e.g. von Hirsch, *Censure and Sanctions*, pp. 83–4; Ashworth, 'Rights, Responsibilities and Restorative Justice', *British Journal of Criminology* 42 (2002), pp. 578–95; von Hirsch *et al.*, 'Restorative Justice: A "Making Amends" Model?', pp. 122–3.

assume that there is no more to morality than the cost-effective pursuit of valuable ends. I have been arguing that in addition we have responsibilities to treat one another in line with morally valuable forms of status. Just because Baxter, as we have been imagining him, is not likely to comply with his obligations does not mean that his status as a qualified member of these relationships is not an important aspect of his identity and one that we ought to respect.

A FINAL OBJECTION: THE NEED FOR STATE CONDEMNATION OF CRIME

Up till now I have sketched some variants of the laissez-faire approach and have looked at some problems with these proposals. I have tried to make the alternatives and the sorts of problems that they face reasonably comprehensive, but readers may be left unconvinced that their preferred version of the laissez-faire approach is vulnerable to the charges I have made.[29] It is of course a weakness of the rather broad way in which I have characterised the positions here that I cannot do justice to the subtleties of particular positions, and there are many variants that I have not addressed. Therefore we should not regard the criticisms I have made so far as conclusive.

Nevertheless there *is* a conclusive objection to the proposal that something like laissez-faire restorative justice should be the main response to crime and interpersonal conflict in the good society. This is an objection to which laissez-faire conceptions are vulnerable no matter what their particular variant, for the objection focuses on what the laissez-faire approach, by its very nature, excludes. The argument goes like this. The laissez-faire approach involves citizens resolving disputes for themselves and making their own decisions about how seriously to treat what someone has done and what must be done to address it. This procedure might serve collective goals of reducing crime (*à la* Braithwaite and Pettit). But it cannot serve the collective responsibility we have to

---

[29] See, for instance, the sophisticated responses to these and other issues for restorative justice in e.g. M. Cavadino and J. Dignan, 'Reparation, Retribution and Rights', in von Hirsch and Ashworth, *Principled Sentencing*, pp. 348–58; J. Dignan, 'Towards a Systemic Model of Restorative Justice: Reflections on the Concept, its Context and the Need for Clear Constraints', in von Hirsch *et al.* (eds.), *Restorative Justice and Criminal Justice: Competing or Reconcilable Paradigms?* (Oxford: Hart, 2003), pp. 135–156; D. Van Ness, 'Creating Restorative Systems', in L. Walgrave (ed.), *Restorative Justice and the Law* (Cullompton: Willan, 2001); D. Van Ness, 'Proposed Basic Principles on the Use of Restorative Justice: Recognising the Aims and Limits of Restorative Justice', in von Hirsch *et al.*, *Restorative Justice and Criminal Justice*, pp. 157–76.

condemn or censure particularly serious moral wrongs that people can commit against one another or against the polity as a whole. Some wrongs, in other words, give the members of political society as a whole a duty to express their disapproval, and they do this through punishment.[30] The essence of the laissez-faire approach, however, is to treat these disputes as a private matter for the parties involved to sort out and not for the state to get involved with. Therefore if there is a collective responsibility to condemn certain categories of crimes then the laissez-faire approach, which fails to recognise such a responsibility, will be to that extent inadequate.

The argument here involves a number of ideas. First of all there is the idea that some things that people do *call for* condemnation from others, to the extent that a failure to express condemnation would be a moral fault. There are some things that people can do to one another about which we can say that, if we let them pass and said nothing about them, if we did not make clear our disapproval or condemnation or outrage, we would be condoning or acquiescing in the wrong. In our silence we would be acquiescing because we have a responsibility to say something. I take it that this is a familiar idea. Imagine that one of your friends engages in some low-level racist joking. Should you say something to him about it? There is a dilemma here because, while on the one hand you do not want to step on your friend's toes, on the other hand you would feel implicated by saying nothing. You would be failing to be honest to your friend, and failing to stand up for those who are in the end the victims of such abuse. This example shows that we take ourselves to have a responsibility to protest against certain actions and not treat those who perform them as though nothing were wrong.

Now an objection to this claim might be that we would turn into a nation of prying busybodies if we were forever to be condemning one another for what we do. Say I lie to my close friends about my past, or commit adultery though I tell my partner our relationship is monogamous: do we really think that publicly condemning one another for such things would be a positive advance in our morality? In response to this objection we should acknowledge that there are many wrongs for which, though they may give us grounds for disapproving of a person, or thinking (morally) badly of them, it would be intrusive publicly or overtly to condemn them (either to others or to the person themselves). (Thus imagine that someone I had never met and had no connection with, but who had heard about my infidelity, came

---

[30] As on the censure theories we discussed in chapter 2.

up to me one day and started haranguing me about it. Maybe I should still feel bad about my infidelity, but would not this person be talking out of turn?) This suggests that the mere fact of wrongdoing does not give us grounds for collective condemnation.

So the second idea involved in this argument is that, while there is no duty overtly or publicly to condemn wrongdoing as such, there are some wrongs – say, those that are particularly serious or particularly related to the business of political society – that we do have a collective responsibility to condemn. A clear example of such a case is domestic violence.[31] What is now widely accepted is that violence in the home is not just a private matter for the disputants to sort out, but rather an intolerable act the perpetrators of which we have a collective responsibility to condemn. A society in which the state took no action against people who committed such wrongs would be a state whose citizens collectively acquiesced in what was done to the vulnerable. Therefore in this case the argument is that the state has a duty to take action against this public wrong.

Nevertheless we might wonder why the need for an institution of the state that expresses collective condemnation of offences rules out the possibility that laissez-faire restorative justice could be the main societal response to crime. Thus one might suggest that restorative justice procedures should distinguish between criminal and non-criminal cases, where the former only come into play once a conviction has been made. The conviction does the job of expressing collective disapproval of the crime. But the job of sentencing is left up to the restorative justice process to sort out.[32] The reason that this proposal is inadequate is that the process of sentencing is essential to the task of state condemnation of crime. And this leads us on to the third idea contained in our objection to the laissez-faire approach: that collective condemnation is expressed through the imposition of sanction.

When the state expresses collective condemnation of an offence it has to be able to express how one crime is more serious than another, or one person more deeply implicated in the crime than another (and hence more responsible for it). The way it does this is through the severity of the sentence: a more onerous sentence for more serious crimes and higher degrees of responsibility. If it is the state's job to express condemnation of crime and to express not just blanket condemnation of all crime but to

---

[31] Duff, *Punishment, Communication and Community*, p. 62.
[32] Cf. Johnstone, *Restorative Justice: Ideas, Values, Debates*, pp. 138–9.

differentiate between more and less serious offences and acts then it is also the state's job to fix sentences. The state cannot therefore delegate this responsibility to private individuals. Again, it might be argued against this that the judge in convicting the offender could verbally express an 'official' collective view about how serious the crime was. However, the problem with this goes back to an issue we considered first in chapter 2. There we considered the retributivist argument that for condemnation to function as such it has to be expressed in symbolically adequate terms. When a person condemns he does not merely *say* that the act was wrong: he shows how the offence *matters* in the way that he then treats the offender. Similarly, in the institutional case, it cannot be enough that the offender is simply informed of the seriousness of the crime. The state has to *act* as though it condemns. It has to treat those who commit serious crimes in a way that is markedly different from the way it treats those who commit minor crimes. Otherwise we would not really understand or identify with the claim that there was a different degree of condemnation. Hence the state must keep control over sentencing; this is incompatible with the laissez-faire approach.

The conclusion of this argument against the laissez-faire approach is that the state has a job to do in condemning crime through the imposition of punishment, and therefore that decisions about how to respond to offenders cannot just be left to individuals. But note that the crucial objection to the laissez-faire approach is not that citizens when left to their own devices are not *capable* of coming up with good decisions, and that restorative justice could end up being too lenient or mere vigilantism. This may or may not be true. But my point is separate from this. It is not about whether the state is more capable than individual citizens of coming up with justifiable results, but rather whose *business* it is to make the decisions. I am arguing that for certain wrongs, it is the business of the public as a whole. These are the acts that should be classified as crimes. Crimes are, as Duff has written, 'public wrongs',[33] where public wrong is not to be understood as a crime against the abstract body of the public, but rather a wrong (usually committed against identifiable individuals, though not always) that it is the business of the public to condemn. This in effect makes it the business of the state, since the state is the only agent capable of representing the collective and common interests and responsibilities of all citizens.

[33] Duff, *Punishment, Communication and Community*, pp. 60–4.

SYMBOLICALLY ADEQUATE CONDEMNATION OF CRIME:
THE APOLOGY RITUAL

Now the reader might think at this point that if we are to accept the importance of collective condemnation as I have urged, and hence accept the need for a state institution that expresses such condemnation, then we will have to abandon any attempt to integrate the account of apology and atonement from the last chapter into a theory about criminal justice. We have pointed to some important benefits that restorative justice can have. But we now have an answer to the question we asked at the very start of the book when considering the case of Bryson. Our question was: what purpose of the state is so important that it gives us reason to interrupt the natural process of apology and reparation that Bryson feels compelled to go through, diverting him instead into the bureaucratic and artificial official system of criminal justice? We asked it again in this chapter: what state purpose is so important that it overrides those benefits for victims and offenders that could come from engaging in a restorative justice process that sticks closely to our intuitive expectations about the need for apology and reparation? The answer is that the fundamental state purpose is the expression, through the institution of state punishment, of collective condemnation of public wrongs. The reason that this has to be an official, centralised and hence to some extent procedure-driven and bureaucratic process is that the state has to be involved in assessing guilt and fixing a sentence, since only the state can claim to act on behalf of the members of political society as a collective. If the state had no such institution, then the fact that a person had acted in a criminal way would have no effect on her civic status. But this would be morally questionable as it means that the state would not be acting as though the criminal act *matters*. The argument is therefore that it is more important that we meet our responsibility to condemn appropriate acts as intolerable – and hence express solidarity with their victims – even if that means sacrificing the benefits discussed earlier in the chapter.

Of course, this does not mean that restorative justice procedures could not take place. There could be citizen initiatives in the non-state sector. Perhaps the state should also fund and facilitate such initiatives, since society would no doubt be better off for them. But restorative justice would not be the major or fundamental criminal justice response. The fundamental response is carried out by that institution that expresses collective condemnation. At best restorative justice could have a merely supplementary role.

However, while I think that to some extent this verdict on the proper place of laissez-faire restorative justice is correct (though I have more to say about it at the end of the chapter and in chapter 8), it is too pessimistic to say that we must now abandon the account of apology and reparation that we developed in the last chapter. We can see what role this account can play in criminal justice if we think in more detail about *how* the state could express collective condemnation through the institution of punishment. Those who talk about the expressive or communicative or censuring function of the state generally talk about this function being carried out through punishment. But, as we saw earlier, all such theorists need an answer to Feinberg's question of why punishment is necessary to the expression of condemnation.[34] We saw that a common retributive response to this question is, first, that the expression of condemnation has to be symbolically adequate – the 'condemnation' must really express condemnation – and, second, that it is only through the use of punishment that condemnation will really be symbolically adequate. While something in this latter claim will strike many people as correct, we have not yet seen a compelling explanation of why this should be. However, the account that we developed in the last chapter puts us in a position to do so.

In chapter 2 I suggested that where we might expect to find adequate symbols for expressing condemnation is by looking at the way in which the emotions relevant to cases of wrongdoing tend to be expressed. (Or to put it more exactly and in a way that allows for normative debate about such emotions and their expressions: we should look at the emotions *appropriate* to cases of wrongdoing and how those emotions are *appropriately* expressed.) In general people who have thought about this issue have tended to think only about the emotions of those who condemn.[35] They have thought about the expression of outrage or indignation, even disgust. But I would suggest that if we want to express condemnation in a symbolically adequate way it is more fruitful to think about the crime from the offender's point of view. What we looked at in the last chapter was in part a story about the emotions that it is appropriate to experience *having done wrong*, and how it is appropriate to express those emotions. I suggested that when one has (culpably) done wrong it is always appropriate to feel guilt or self-blame, and that the appropriate expression of this is through apology, restitution and penance. What I want to suggest

---

[34] Chapter 2, section 3.
[35] See notoriously Devlin, 'Morals and the Criminal Law', p. 17: 'No society can do without intolerance, indignation and disgust; they are the forces behind the moral law'.

now is that this points to a rich source of symbolism for expressing condemnation. We can communicate our condemnation by putting into symbols, not how indignant or outraged we are, but how *sorry* we think the offender ought to be for what she has done. And we can do this by imposing on the offender an amount of amends that reflects – and thus is proportional to – the seriousness of their crime. Since how sorry someone feels will be expressed – according to our story from the last chapter – in the amends that she feels the need to make, we can communicate how sorry someone *ought to be* for a crime – that is, how serious we think it is, the degree of our condemnation – by setting a certain level of amends to be made for a crime (given a level of responsibility): a level of amends that represents a view of what the offender ought to be motivated to undertake if she were appropriately sorry.[36]

Thus a good way to express how wrong we think an act is would be by making the offender do what we think someone who was sorry enough for their offence would feel it necessary to undertake by way of making amends. This suggests a way of making use of the account of the cycle of blame and apology from the last chapter that is an alternative to restorative justice. Rather than staging an event in which real apologies might be forthcoming, this account suggests that we instead draw on the symbolism of apology in order to express condemnation. Because it recommends making the offender act as she would were she genuinely sorry for her offence, we can call this theory of punishment the Apology Ritual.[37]

I claim that this way of expressing condemnation is more symbolically adequate than accounts that look primarily to the emotions of those who condemn. After all, many people are turned off the idea that the state should condemn crime precisely because they think of it in terms of the expression of outrage and disgust. We rightly find the idea of such expressions problematic for at least two sorts of reasons. Firstly, if we express our condemnation through symbols of outrage and indignation then we will be led to think about doing things to the offender that are angry and aggressive, even violent. But these are not things that the decent state should consider doing to its citizens, and hence concentrating on this

---

[36] See C. Bennett, 'Taking the Sincerity Out of Saying Sorry: Restorative Justice as Ritual', *Journal of Applied Philosophy* 23 (2006), pp. 127–43.

[37] R. A. Duff appeals to the idea of ritualistic apology in *Punishment, Communication and Community*, pp. 94–5. For further discussion of the difference between Duff's account and my own, see Bennett, 'Taking the Sincerity Out of Saying Sorry'; and this book, ch. 8.

sort of case undermines the claim that there is a useful analogy between punishment and condemnation. Secondly, thinking about expressions of outrage and so on seems to say the wrong sort of thing to and about the offender. Expressions of outrage emphasise the distance between the offender and the community of decent persons. But although this does have to be part of the message, the fact is that after the offender has been subjected to the expression of condemnation she will then resume her life and be returned any civic rights and liberties that were suspended during her punishment. In one fell swoop at the end of the sentence the state's attitude will go from outright condemnation back to normality. It might be more adequate from a symbolic point of view if the language of punishment communicated rather what the offender will have to do in order to resume her place in the polity. Rather than emphasising distance, it emphasises a process of reconciliation. And because of this we express better what we want to say in the condemnation of an enduring though errant member of some relationship when we take our symbols rather from the process of apology and amends that the offender ought to feel it necessary to undergo before she could feel that she had redeemed herself in that relationship.

Of course, emphasising distance (which is a metaphorical way of saying that the offender cannot be treated as if the action were not a criminal one) *is* part of what punishment has to do, and on my story we express this by partially suspending the offender's rights and liberties. According to the story of the last chapter, an offender only needs to apologise for something (in the way that expresses guilt and repudiation) because she has done something that merits *blame*. An action merits blame when it changes the terms of our relationship with the agent, making it wrong to treat them as though their place in the relationship were unaffected by what they had done. And it is important that the way the offender is treated does express such blame, since public wrongs are precisely those acts by which offenders can be understood to change their relationship with their fellow citizens as a whole: more on this in the next chapter. But blame is a different emotion from the hot-headedness of outrage: blame is disposed rather to cut a perceived offender off, give the cold shoulder, sever relations (at least partially and temporarily). This is appropriate as the most basic response to wrongdoing because severing relations (at least partially) is constitutive of treating the offender differently because of her offence. If one were not prepared to sever relations to some extent, and to withhold the standard of treatment that the offender would normally expect, then it is not clear that one is condemning or disapproving of the offence at all. Therefore blame, understood as the proportionate withdrawal of respect or recognition, is the minimal response to crime. The way that this severing of relations is expressed in institutional terms is through the proportionate suspension of the offender's rights and liberties. The offender loses something of her civic status as a result of her crime and hence it becomes legitimate to impose amends on her. But the suspension of rights is not symbolically adequate by itself. It merely emphasises distance: it does not say anything about how sorry the offender ought to feel or what would have to be done before she could be redeemed. Therefore this account of punishment recommends an Apology Ritual and not just a blaming ritual.

We look in more detail at the Apology Ritual in the next two chapters. Before I conclude this chapter, though, let me make two points briefly in order to clear up possible misunderstandings. First of all, it might be argued that my account has precisely – and more brazenly – the flaw that I claimed lay in Braithwaite's view. Does my view not recommend actively coercing people into saying sorry? And yet did I not criticise Braithwaite for doing just this? The answer to this objection is that my view does not require people to say sorry: it simply requires them to make the level of amends that it would be appropriate to make for their offence (the level of amends that they would feel it necessary to make were they appropriately sorry for it). My view does not involve offenders having to confront their victims (though this could be made an option: see chapter 8). Furthermore, it does not require offenders to undertake these amends in a spirit of sincere remorse or even to put on signs of such remorse. A person should be judged to have completed their sentence perfectly well simply by carrying out the level of amends, regardless of the spirit in which they do it.[38] It is not necessary for an offender to perform in front of a parole board in order to secure their release.[39] The reason for this is partly that requiring offenders to put on a show of remorse would be incompatible with their integrity. But it is also because the fundamental job of the criminal sanction is not to induce repentance or to achieve moral reconciliation between offender and community: its job is simply to express proportionate condemnation, and this is done perfectly well regardless of how the offender receives that condemnation.

---

[38] See Bennett, 'Taking the Sincerity Out of Saying Sorry'.
[39] See J. Hampton, 'The Moral Education Theory of Punishment', p. 234.

The other issue that I want to address is the extent to which the benefits of restorative justice are really being abandoned. I discuss this issue in detail in chapter 8. But just to anticipate that discussion and round off this one, let me make the following quick points. I argued that we could see restorative justice as bringing about benefits to victims, offenders and communities because it encourages meaningful participation by all of these parties in the justice process. I have now argued that there is a more important public interest in condemning crime. But although the institution of state condemnation would rule out certain types of citizen participation in the justice process, I am hopeful that the Apology Ritual nevertheless represents a more meaningful way to think about how we do justice than alternative theories of punishment. The Apology Ritual is an artificial and symbolic procedure. It can insist on the importance of due process, proportionality and so on, and therefore insulates the fate of offenders to some degree from the vagaries of public opinion. Offenders are not simply subject to public outrage. But it draws its symbols from emotions and expectations that are deeply intuitive. Offenders end up having to do something that would constitute meaningful amends for their crime: that is something that victims, offenders and communities can identify with. They can feel that justice has been done. My account of what the state has a responsibility to do to offenders is based on an intuitive understanding of what responsibilities offenders have.

CONCLUSION

In this chapter we have looked at two ways in which the account of the cycle of blame and apology from chapter 5 might be deployed in our thinking about societal responses to crime or wrongdoing. The account of the cycle of blame and apology gives us a certain picture of what responsibilities offenders have as a result of wrongdoing. The two accounts we have looked at disagree over whether the fact of wrongdoing also gives an authoritative body such as the state a responsibility to react. The laissez-faire conception of restorative justice claims that it does not, and that crimes remain essentially the business of those most intimately affected. On my favoured account, however, bodies such as the state do have a responsibility arising from crime, which is to express proportionate condemnation of wrongdoing (or whichever wrongs turn out to be 'public wrongs'). I have claimed that such condemnation has to be expressed in symbolically adequate terms, and that this can be done by imposing a certain amount of amends on the offender. The amount of amends symbolises how sorry the offender ought to be, where this indicates an understanding of how serious the crime is and the degree of the agent's responsibility for it.

The plausibility of this account of sanction can be illustrated by looking at a non-criminal but institutional instance of wrongdoing. Let us look again at the case of Jane that we introduced in chapter 4. Jane's neglect of her students is not criminal, but there does exist an authoritative body – such as a university – that has overall responsibility for ensuring that educational standards are upheld. The university might – and perhaps ought to – promulgate certain rules that its teaching staff are expected to uphold. At least a subset of these rules will be concerned with what at the very minimum is expected of staff. Violation of these minimal expectations – as in the case of crime – has to bring some sort of response from the authority if the members of the university as a whole are to be able to claim to be concerned that these standards are upheld. An entirely laissez-faire response would imply that the members of the university are not really responsible to one another for what they do, and hence that they are not really engaged in a common educational project at all.

Consider now whether my claim about the nature of the sanction to be imposed on Jane is a plausible one. In the first place, Jane's failure would, according to my argument, have to be condemned by the university. Her actions are such as cannot go unremarked. They need to be taken to change her status within the university in order to reflect the gravity of her failure to meet the minimal promulgated standards. The way in which to do this, according to the Apology Ritual account, is for a disciplinary committee temporarily and partially to suspend her official status within the university (thus expressing blame) and to ask her to make some sort of amends for what she has done. Of course, if we are thinking about amends or penance then there are limits to what the university could require Jane to do in terms of extra unpaid work. But as far as possible the sanction should be modelled on what she might choose to do for herself if she were genuinely sorry.[40] She will not be asked to perform a sincere apology in front of a disciplinary committee. Neither is the imposition of amends done in order to make her feel repentant. It seems plausible that the university has no *duty* to attempt to try to make Jane repent. Indeed it might be claimed that the university is not in the sort of relationship with its staff that would make it appropriate for it to

---

[40] This is discussed at the end of chapter 5.

seek to make them morally better through imposing penances.[41] Jane's actual feelings of repentance or otherwise, it might be said, are her own business, in the sense that it is not the place of the university disciplinary committee to try to make her repentant. But it *is* the place of the committee to issue condemnation. Members of staff are responsible to one another for their conduct as it regards the common project in which they are engaged. Hence she will be asked to do something that, if she were sorry, would express how she felt. Thus the university treats Jane as one who has committed a wrong of a particular gravity. And hence it discharges its duties. It issues symbolically adequate condemnation of her wrong and imposes a sanction on Jane after the performance of which she can resume her duties with her official status fully restored.

This, I submit, is an attractive way of understanding how an institution like a university ought to respond to misdemeanours amongst its staff. Hence, if the state is in relevant respects an institution like a university then this should lend strength to the argument that the Apology Ritual is a promising account of state punishment. However, this might legitimately be viewed as a big 'if'. Thus it is to the question of how we ought to think about the state, and whether it can be viewed as a cooperative endeavour, that we turn at the start of the next chapter.

---

[41] This point means that my account avoids some of the criticisms levelled at Duff's theory of punishment. Like mine, Duff's account centres on the importance of repentance. However, my account is able to give a satisfactory justification of hard treatment and is not tied to an implausibly interventionist account of the state. It therefore aspires to be able to answer the criticisms of Duff made e.g. by M. Matravers in *Justice and Punishment*, p. 92. Similar criticisms are made against Duff by von Hirsch and Ashworth: see e.g. *Proportionate Sentencing*, p. 95.

CHAPTER 7

Institutional blame and apology

In the last chapter I put forward a theory of punishment that I call the Apology Ritual. According to this theory the main purpose of punishment is condemnation of the offender for a 'public wrong'. And I have argued that the most symbolically adequate way for such condemnation to be expressed is through requiring the offender to undertake proportional amends for her crime – that is, to do the sort of thing that she would be motivated to do spontaneously were she appropriately sorry for her offence. In this chapter I explore and try to defend some of the ramifications of this claim.

APPLYING THE ACCOUNT OF THE CYCLE
OF BLAME AND APOLOGY

The task of this chapter begins with a simple question. While I take my claim about the symbolism of punishment to have some intuitive plausibility, the reader might ask for a better explanation of *why* the performance of amends is the right sort of symbol. Why is a crime something for which it would be appropriate for the offender to say sorry in this public way? The answer to this question ties the Apology Ritual account more tightly and more explicitly to the argument of previous chapters of the book. The claim is that the reactions of blame and penitent making of amends are appropriate reactions to crimes. Let me explain the significance of this claim in more detail. The Apology Ritual account sees punishment as an institutional version of the cycle of blame and apology, where the offender through doing wrong alienates herself from (those engaged in) a cooperative enterprise or common project, and is then restored to it by making amends and repudiating the wrong. In the Apology Ritual the offender is subjected to condemnation or blame for what she has done, and I have argued that the way in which the condemnation is most adequately expressed is through the imposition of amends. The reason that this symbolism is fitting is that the offender is rightly regarded as having damaged her status within political society through having committed the crime, and as restoring her status by undergoing punishment. As I understand it, therefore, for the Apology Ritual account to be successful it would have to be the case that those acts legally defined as crimes are acts for which it is appropriate to apologise, make amends, and seek restoration to the moral (legal, political) community.

The cycle of blame and apology account from chapter 5 started with the view that our actions take place in a social context where we have responsibilities by virtue of our membership of a variety of relationships. Where these relationships are valuable in their own right and not merely instrumentally, people gain an important status by virtue of membership: participants treat one another with particular signs of respect or recognition; these are signs that they are engaged in doing something important together. When there is some serious violation of responsibilities, that violation alters – or ought to alter – the offender's relationship with the rest of the group (those who are committed to the appropriate standards). The respect or recognition ought to be partially withdrawn as a response to the fact that the offender has acted in such a way as no member of that relationship (that is, someone with the appropriate understanding of, and commitment to, those values) ought to act. Violating the basic, minimal responsibilities of one's role gives a member of such a relationship responsibilities to put things right. By meeting these responsibilities she thereby redeems herself as a member of that relationship: these responsibilities include apologising and undertaking a penance. The responsibilities constitutive of atonement (that is, at-one-ment) are what someone who understood and fully repudiated his wrong would be motivated to do spontaneously.

The Apology Ritual view takes this model and applies it as far as possible to the case of political community. In order for such an application to be successful a number of things would have to be established. First of all, that political community is a valuable type of relationship structured by important values and standards of behaviour. Secondly, that citizens have responsibilities to one another that follow from the nature of that common enterprise – responsibilities to treat one another *as fellow citizens* in some important way – with respect to which we can identify 'qualified' citizens who can be expected to grasp and comply with their responsibilities independently of external guidance. Thirdly, that a person who fails to do what is required of her with respect to these responsibilities (for instance, fails in her actions to show even minimal respect for her fellow citizens) ought not any longer to be treated with the same respect as she would get were she in good standing. Fourthly, that crimes are therefore those acts the performance of which ought not to be taken to leave one's relationship with the political community unchanged: crimes are those actions that would merit *blame* in the context of the particular relationship of political community (and hence that criminal culpability is a specific type of blameworthiness). Fifthly, that the way in which the political community collectively treats an offender differently as a result of her offence is through the agency of the state and in particular through the criminal sanction. Sixthly, that in treating the offender differently in this way the state expresses collective condemnation of the offence. Seventhly, that in order properly to express such collective condemnation the state must use the appropriate symbols, and that such symbols can be found in the cycle of blame and apology (suspension of some civic rights and imposition of amends). Eighthly, that an offender who undertakes such apologetic action ought to be considered as restored to the political community, her civil rights fully returned, and that this should be the case regardless of whether the attitude with which she made her amends was genuinely apologetic.

If the Apology Ritual can be defended it would meet the desiderata for a theory of punishment that we have articulated as the argument of the book has progressed. Thus, because it sees the criminal sanction as essentially an expression of proportionate condemnation, it takes the offence seriously. It also takes the offender seriously as a qualified participant who is responsible for meeting the obligations of political community. This view, therefore, sees the state as having certain responsibilities in the case of crime to deal with the offender in a way that reflects the gravity of what she has done, and through doing so to express appropriate collective condemnation of the offence. But it is also restorative in that it sees the shape of the criminal sanction as based on the obligations that the offender has to put things right and restore her relationship with the political community. Finally, this account is compatible with freedom of conscience in that, although it focuses on making offenders undertake apologetic action, the action has to be such that it is possible successfully to complete it regardless of whether or not it is sincere. It is for this latter reason that the view is called the Apology Ritual: rituals are often castigated as empty and formal because they need not engage 'inner' attitudes, but it is precisely this vice that is a virtue in this context, since – it might be argued – the state (like the university disciplinary committee) has no business giving out sentences the explicit aim of which is to make offenders genuinely penitent.

In this chapter I cannot address all the objections that might be made to this theory of punishment, but I explore some critical questions about the analogy that I draw between the cycle of blame and apology and the institution of state punishment. We will look at how good an analogy there is between political society and the sorts of cooperative enterprises and relationships we have looked at up to now. We will look at the extent to which legal culpability should be modelled on moral blameworthiness. And we will look at the extent to which an offender can really be regarded as restored to political society if, as I insisted in the last chapter that she might, she undertakes her punishment in an entirely unrepentant spirit.

POLITICAL COMMUNITY AS AN INTRINSICALLY VALUABLE RELATIONSHIP

The account of the cycle of blame and apology begins with the idea of community as an intrinsically valuable shared cooperative enterprise or relationship. Can the modern state be considered as a community in this sense? Some readers will be concerned that this appeal to community rests on a form of nostalgia for a premodern *Gemeinschaft* that is inapplicable to modern, liberal, pluralistic states.[1] We can interpret this criticism that the model of community I am working with is 'inapplicable' to modern states in two ways. On one interpretation the criticism is that the model is infeasible. Thus it might be claimed that if we want to understand modern societies the idea of a community I am using will not help us very much. Modern states as they exist are not communities in this sense, and so any theory of punishment that will only be true in ideal social conditions will not be applied to our actual situation: it cannot inform our actual criminal justice system. However, while this is an important point when we are concerned to draw practical lessons from our theory, I am not sure that this criticism need necessarily derail the whole attempt to specify social conditions in which the theory would be applicable. For while it may well be true that our current society falls well below the ideal, that need not in itself affect the validity or

---

[1] For instance, this has been a major criticism of Duff's theory, particularly in its original formulation in *Trials and Punishments*. See e.g. J. E. Bickenbach, 'Critical Notice of R. A. Duff, Trials and Punishments', *Canadian Journal of Philosophy* 18 (1988), pp. 765–86; R. J. Lipkin, 'Punishment, Penance and Respect for Autonomy', *Social Theory and Practice* 14 (1988), pp. 87–104; B. Baker, 'Penance as a Model for Punishment', *Social Theory and Practice* 18 (1992), pp. 311–31.

critical power of the theory of punishment. Thus it is open to someone putting forward a normative theory of punishment to argue that, although their theory of punishment requires genuine community in order to be applicable, and such genuine community is lacking, this simply shows that (a) we need to recover such community, and (b) only when we do so will punishment be fully justifiable. Thus it might be naïve to think that we can apply the normative theory in which we are engaged here straightforwardly to our current justice institutions. But this does not make the theory redundant, since it can act as a critical model, which provides a standard to which actual practice can aspire, and informs our decisions about how to act in non-ideal circumstances.

Nevertheless in order to have critical leverage a normative theory has to present an ideal that is attractive and in principle achievable. And the other way of interpreting the claim that the model of community is inapplicable to modern conditions is as a complaint that it fails as an attractive normative standard. On this criticism, the concern is that anything that qualifies as a community in my sense will fail to respect important liberal values of *individualism* and *neutrality*. For instance, when one talks of community one inevitably raises the question of the individual's right to disagree with and depart from community values. Thus it might be suggested that my model for the political community suggests the need for a strong common project. This strong common project must issue in standards of behaviour which the members are responsible to one another for meeting. Furthermore, these standards of behaviour are, like the standards embodied in our conceptions of friendship, not merely instrumentally valuable: they are not just the rules that are necessary for peaceful coexistence. Rather they are meant to constitute an intrinsically valuable form of relationship. A paradigm case of such a community, the critic might suggest, is a religious community.[2] In that community there is a strong common conception of the good that structures relations between members. The community is founded on a particular idea of how members ought to live, what the good of its members is, and through the apparatus of the central authority (for instance, the dictates of the abbot)[3] it organises the community in order to promote and protect their development of this good.

The problem with taking such a community as a model for political society, it might be said, is that people disagree deeply and fervently about what is the right way to live. However, it is not merely the fact of

[2] Duff, *Trials and Punishments*, pp. 247–54.   [3] Von Hirsch, *Censure and Sanctions*, ch. 8.

disagreement that is important here: we need to know why the disagreement has moral significance, why people should be taken to have a right to disagree. We want to know what the moral basis of liberal neutrality is. The argument that I want to explore has been put forward by those who defend 'political liberalism', which I take to be a form of liberalism that is meant to be free from commitments to any particular substantive (or 'comprehensive') conception of the good.[4] For political liberals the real significance of the fact of disagreement has to do with the justification of political coercion. What Rawls has called the liberal principle of legitimacy holds that coercive political power can only properly be exercised on the basis of principles that all citizens can reasonably be expected to accept.[5] The problem with the political society modelled on the religious community, on this view, is that it attempts to enforce a vision of the human good that, in conditions of disagreement, it cannot expect all citizens, by their own lights, to accept as the right way to live. The fact of disagreement therefore militates in favour of liberalism, with its characteristic range of individual freedoms, because if one accepts the liberal principle of legitimacy one thereby rules out enforcing matters on which individuals cannot reasonably be expected to be brought to agreement.[6]

If one accepts the liberal principle of legitimacy must one reject the conception of political community as an intrinsically valuable form of cooperative relationship? The parallel with the religious community suggests a deep lack of fit. The question is whether the religious community is a good example of the sort of community we have been discussing. Luckily the answer to this question is no. There is a good example of political community that fits just the model we have invoked in the argument of the book. And it is a model that is used by political

---

[4] See e.g. J. Rawls, 'Justice as Fairness: Political Not Metaphysical', *Philosophy and Public Affairs* 14 (1985), pp. 223–51; C. Larmore, *Patterns of Moral Complexity* (Cambridge: Cambridge University Press, 1987), ch. 3.

[5] See e.g. Rawls, *Political Liberalism* (New York: University of Columbia Press, 1996), p. 137: 'our exercise of political power is fully proper only when it is exercised in accordance with a constitution the essentials of which all citizens as free and equal may reasonably be expected to endorse in the light of principles and ideals acceptable to their common human reason'. For the centrality of the principle of legitimacy to Rawls's work, see also S. Mulhall and A. Swift, *Liberals and Communitarians* (Oxford: Blackwell, 1992), pp. 190–1; L. Wenar, 'The Unity of Rawls's Work', *Journal of Moral Philosophy* 1 (2004), pp. 265–75.

[6] There is plenty of room for discussion about what is meant by 'reasonable' here. See L. Wenar, 'Political Liberalism: An Internal Critique', *Ethics* 106 (1995), pp. 32–62; and the two different options discussed in C. Bennett, 'A Problem Case for Public Reason', *Critical Review of International Social and Political Philosophy* 6 (2003), pp. 50–69.

liberals themselves.[7] In rejecting the 'perfectionist' conception of a political community founded on a substantive conception of the human good, the political liberal does not reject the idea of political community altogether: rather she invokes a rival conception. Thus the crucial point in the political liberal's argument – the liberal principle of legitimacy – rests on an idea of the moral relation between, on the one hand, the state and its exercise of coercive power, and on the other hand, the body of citizens. In order to make the Rousseauian heritage of this idea clear we can call it the *self-government* conception of political community.[8] On the self-government conception, the key idea is that the body of citizens should, collectively, govern themselves. The true sovereign, in other words, is the body of citizens considered as a whole. The moral force of this ideal lies in the fact that each citizen is treated as a free and equal member of the political community, both the author and the subject of the law. We are free and equal in such a community because we obey a law that we give to ourselves, the law of our own will. We – the body of citizens considered as a whole – obey a law that we – again, the body of citizens as a whole – give to ourselves. Cases in which one faction of the community – the one with most political clout, say – takes power and is able to impose its will on the others are inconsistent with collective self-government and with each citizen being an equal author of the law. In such cases those in the minority are subjugated to the will of another.

Now the self-government conception is often thought to be inapplicable to modern societies (in both the senses discussed earlier). For in order for there to be genuinely collective self-government there notoriously has to be a General Will, something that is not merely the aggregate of individual desires but somehow a common purpose in which all citizens participate. But this is where the political liberal steps in and suggests that, although for collective self-government there does have to be such a common purpose, it might be more minimal than the critics of Rousseau have generally thought. The common purpose might just be

---

[7] I should make it clear that in what follows I provide what I take to be an attractive interpretation of the political liberal position and will not be concerned to show that it is also a good exegesis of its main theorists.

[8] See Rawls, *Political Liberalism*, pp. 139–40 on the 'liberal political ideal': '[S]ince political power is the coercive power of free and equal citizens as a corporate body, this power should be exercised, when constitutional essentials and basic questions of justice are at stake, only in ways that all citizens can reasonably be expected to endorse in the light of their common, human reason.' To the liberal principle of legitimacy quoted in n. 5 this statement adds the explanation that the reason for this principle is that political power is 'the coercive power of free and equal citizens as a corporate body': this is what I interpret as a Rousseauian General Will.

that of finding grounds for the actions of the state that we can justify to one another and that can therefore be regarded as common to all. The common purpose simply is self-government. And this is how we reach the liberal principle of legitimacy. Thus in order for a political society to be self-governing the coercive power of the state – the power that would otherwise be merely imposed on citizens – has to be deployed on the basis of principles that all citizens can reasonably be expected to accept. Only political power that is exercised on the basis of such principles can be seen as the action of the body of citizens as a whole governing itself – and only thus can the exercise of political power be legitimate. The political liberal makes equal participation in the sovereign the central political value. Societies in which the reasonable disagreement of some citizens is regarded as irrelevant to the deployment of the coercive power of the state are societies that cannot regard all citizens as politically equal. Thus political power is, for such liberals, only used legitimately when it is in accordance with principles that all can accept.

This explains what the political liberal thinks is wrong with the perfectionist political community. Given the fact of widespread and deep moral disagreement, there is unlikely to be agreement on any one substantive or comprehensive conception of how to live. In that case the perfectionist who decides to enforce one particular view despite the disagreement must be rejecting the self-government conception and its associated privileging of political equality. But the self-government conception is not antithetical to the idea of political community, or the idea of citizenship as an intrinsically valuable relationship. The liberal who criticises the perfectionist conception of political community as violating a principle of legitimacy has her own preferred conception of political community. Thus one way of understanding the liberal rejection of perfectionism is to see that for liberals perfectionism violates a particularly valuable way of relating to one's fellow citizens. Perfectionism is incompatible with regarding one's fellow citizens – all one's fellow citizens – as agents with whom one participates as an equal in legislating for the political community. It is incompatible with regarding one's fellow citizens as agents with whom one is engaged in the project of collective self-government. The thing with perfectionists, the liberal thinks, is that they try to get hold of political power for their own perfectionist ends, regardless of whether those ends could be accepted by all. The liberal thinks that such behaviour is illegitimate *even if the perfectionist is correct in her view about how we ought to live.* The political liberal holds that citizens should accept a constraint on the proposed exercise of political power, namely that it be exercised only in the name of all citizens.[9] The moral basis for this constraint seems to lie in a conception of collective self-government as an intrinsically valuable relationship.

At this point let me make the limited aims of the above argument clear. I do not claim that the self-government conception is the basis of liberalism: clearly there are perfectionist versions of liberalism that could be based, amongst other things, in the claim that the good human life is an autonomous one.[10] At best the self-government conception underpins what has been called *political* liberalism. Neither do I claim that all political liberals are committed to seeing collective self-government as an intrinsically valuable form of (political) relationship. There may be ways in which the political liberal can explain why the would-be perfectionist should accept the constraint I have discussed without appealing to such a notion. I do not need to make either of these claims because my aims are more limited: simply to show that accepting the view of political community on which my theory of punishment is based does not entail accepting an anti-liberal political theory. So my point in this part of the argument has not been to defend the political liberal viewpoint. Rather my purpose has been to defuse a worry that the modern liberal state ought to be in some way neutral, and that such neutrality is incompatible with my assertion that political community can be regarded as an intrinsically valuable relationship. My response to this problem has been to point out that this neutrality can only go so far. Liberal neutrality is rooted in important values about which the liberal cannot be neutral. These values, I have claimed, have to do with a conception of political community as collective self-government, an intrinsically valuable relationship. Therefore the political liberal position is compatible with my conception of punishment. What this argument has also allowed us to do is to give some examples of the sorts of political communities that might count as intrinsically valuable relationships. Both the collectively self-governing community and the perfectionist community in which people express and promote their good are such examples. For the purposes of our argument here we do not have to choose between them.

Having made this clear let me briefly confront the concern that even this liberal pluralistic self-government conception of political community is inapplicable to modern societies. The self-government conception claims that coercive political power ought only to be exercised in the

---

[9] I call this the public reason constraint.

[10] For an example see J. Skorupski, *Why Read Mill Today?* (London: Routledge, 2006).

name of all and hence on the basis of principles that can reasonably be accepted by all. But in order for this ideal to be realisable we must be able to find such principles as can be reasonably accepted by all. Is this likely in modern societies? Or are the disagreements in such societies really too deep? Political liberals respond to this sort of criticism by pointing to two sources of consensus. One is the overlap between the different moral conceptions to which people hold. Thus there may be some values that people share even though they have quite different views otherwise. Furthermore, since the values on which we seek consensus are political values, they can be values to which people hold for quite different moral reasons.[11] The other source is the values implicit in the political culture of the society itself. Thus public political discourse and argument in a society will be carried out in certain terms: the major political institutions in a society may have a certain self-conscious justifying narrative expressed in terms of particular ideas, and these terms and ideas can enter the general public consciousness to the extent that, in a reasonably well-functioning society, all citizens can be expected to share them or see their attractiveness. Participation in these institutions, in other words, presupposes an understanding and to some extent acceptance of certain ideas and values.[12]

The political liberal view is that public and political discourse about the justification for deploying coercive political power ought to be carried out in these terms. The idea is roughly that if these terms are acceptable to all, then good arguments made using these terms can also be expected to be acceptable to all. Is it plausible to expect sufficient consensus on such values? It is beyond my task here to pass judgement on this complex question. I will limit myself to noting that if such consensus turns out to be impossible then an attractive relationship between citizens and the coercive power of the state becomes impossible. This would doubtless be problematic in many ways. However, it would not be fatal to my argument. For my argument is compatible with more perfectionist accounts of political community. One of the major objections to perfectionism, as we have seen, comes from the political liberal claim that the

---

[11] J. Rawls, 'The idea of an Overlapping Consensus', *Oxford Journal of Legal Studies* 7 (1987), pp. 1–25.

[12] Rawls, 'Justice as Fairness'. This is also a theme in Charles Taylor's work. See the example of voting in 'Social Theory as Practice', in *Philosophy and the Human Sciences: Philosophical Papers*, vol. II (Cambridge: Cambridge University Press, 1985), pp. 91–115, at p. 93. See also Taylor, *Hegel* (Cambridge: Cambridge University Press, 1975), p. 382, on 'the institutions and practices of a society as a kind of language in which its fundamental ideas are expressed'. Note also, though, that it seems quite possible that people participate in social institutions on the basis of understanding though not accepting their foundational ideas and values.

actions of the state should be actions of the body of citizens acting together. However, the force of the political liberal criticism rests on the assumption that its alternative self-government conception is authoritative. But the self-government conception can only be authoritative if it is in principle realisable. If this is not the case, then perfectionism correspondingly will start not to look so bad.

What I have tried to show here is that political community can be understood, on a liberal account, as an intrinsically valuable relationship. Let me just restate the significance of this conclusion. My overall reason for claiming that the symbolism of blame and apology is appropriate for offenders – and hence that punishment is appropriate – is that this symbolism recognises an offender's status as a qualified member of an intrinsically valuable relationship. Now being qualified does not require any formal process of training (as it might in the case of the teacher that we introduced in chapter 4). Rather, being qualified in such a relationship involves having a certain *moral competence*: an ability to understand what one's basic responsibilities are and to comply with them *independently*, without external guidance or supervision. Where the relationship is a valuable one then the status of having this moral competence is a valid source of self-respect, and something that affects how we should treat one another. If political community is an intrinsically valuable relationship then, by the rest of the argument developed in the book, citizens are deserving of a particular kind of respect when they are qualified members of this relationship; their status makes it wrong – at least prima facie – to treat them in ways that make no acknowledgement of this status (such as by manipulating or coercing them, or subjecting them to 're-education'); and more positively their status requires that when they do wrong this is recognised as incurring blame. If it makes sense to talk of liberal political community as an important common project, then it makes sense to talk of citizens as having a 'right to be punished'.

CRIMINAL GUILT AS BLAMEWORTHINESS RELATIVE TO THE POLITICAL RELATIONSHIP

What I have tried to defend so far is the idea that political community should be seen as an intrinsically valuable relationship. In this section I want to suggest – in sketchy and somewhat speculative terms – a way in which we might develop this view into an understanding of law, in particular the criminal law, and the legal culpability that calls for the criminal sanction. Let us start by returning to the notion of relationship that I invoked in earlier chapters. On this notion a relationship carries with it certain sorts of responsibilities: one is only said to be in a relationship in these terms when one has certain responsibilities or a role with some sort of duty. If political community or citizenship is thought of as such a relationship, then we can see how, given a certain conception of what citizenship involves and what its importance is, a picture of the responsibilities involved will emerge. Consider, for instance, the collective self-government conception. On this view the central political value is equality in legislation: the attitude consonant with this central political project is that of regarding one another as equals in the search for political principles that we can hold in common. Within this project each of us has certain responsibilities. For instance, we have a broad responsibility to abide by those principles that we do or can hold in common. For instance, if there are compelling arguments on the basis of principles we hold in common for an institution of property, then we ought to regard certain sorts of appropriation as theft. We will also have certain responsibilities to one another by virtue of our participating in a common project together. We will have duties to respect one another's status as fellow participants. For instance, we may have positive duties to ensure that each citizen has the education and material welfare sufficient to contribute to the project of finding and abiding by grounds for collective self-legislation. We may also have a responsibility to contribute to the search for such principles by following and engaging in public political debate. We may also have negative duties not to violate our fellow citizens' status as our political equals, either in drastic ways by murder or assault, or in more minor ways by proposing public policies that could not reasonably be affirmed by all.[13]

The responsibilities that I have enumerated here are only meant to serve as examples. The point that we can agree on at the moment is that participating in a relationship like citizenship (or like friendship or academic collegiality) carries with it certain responsibilities, even where we may disagree or be uncertain about their precise nature. From this point we can make a speculative link between this view of political community and the nature of law. This is that law ideally has to do with the responsibilities that we have by virtue of the collective project in which we are engaging with one another as citizens. This is the matter *relevant* to law: this is the law's business. Some of the responsibilities that we may have towards one another as members of this common project

---

[13] For the latter responsibilities, see Rawls, *Political Liberalism*, pp. 216–20.

may be unsuitable for being put into law. There might be responsibilities (like positive, imperfect duties) that it is better to leave to citizens themselves to discharge rather than legislating for. But the sorts of things that *should* be put into law are only those things that are aspects of our responsibility to one another as participants in the common project. When the law seeks to legislate on matters that go beyond the common project then it oversteps its bounds: here is where the boundary between the public and the private emerges. For instance, one reason for not legislating against certain sorts of sexual immorality might be that such wrongs (assuming there are such) are no business of the political community: they are none of its business because they have nothing to do with the terms of the political relationship. Of course, where one thinks the line between public and private is to be drawn will depend on what one takes to be the nature and demands of our political relationship. But if what is at the heart of such a view is a conception of the political relationship as an intrinsically valuable one, then the proper content of the law will reflect the project that this relationship involves. This suggests a view on which the overall task of the law is to make determinate and adjudicable the responsibilities (and rights) that we have by virtue of our status as participants in the common project.

This idea of law as articulating the responsibilities of our roles in a certain form of relationship has been articulated, for instance, by Ronald Dworkin.[14] For Dworkin, a polity can properly be seen as a type of community and its law as a set of 'associative obligations' that are constitutive of that form of community. On this view the law articulates the duties of our role as citizens. The reason why we should obey the law is that it corresponds by and large to what we owe to our fellow citizens anyway by virtue of our participating in this valuable project. The law on this sort of view might be an attempt to realise through formal structures a moral conception of how citizens should relate to one another, a conception based in a vision of what the common enterprise of political society really is. If law articulates the associative obligations of citizenship, how are we to understand criminal law in particular? If we took the Dworkinian view we might say that criminal law defines that area of our associative obligations which will merit criminal sanction if we fail to meet them. Now add to this view the claim that the actions that merit the criminal sanction are those that are blameworthy (since the criminal sanction is itself in part an expression of blame) and that blame works as

---

[14] Dworkin, *Law's Empire*, pp. 195–202.

I have suggested in previous chapters. In other words, we merit blame when we do something that it would be wrong for others not to take as reason to withdraw respect: blameworthy acts are those that it would be wrong not to treat as changing the terms of our relationship (because they cast doubt on one party's commitment to the terms of that relationship).

On the view I am now developing, crimes are those acts that ought to be understood as altering the relationship between the perpetrator and the other members of the political community, making it inappropriate to treat the perpetrator with the respect due to a citizen, to the extent that the state must – temporarily and in proportion to the seriousness of the crime – withdraw his civil rights and liberties. Those acts that are really crimes – that ought to be designated as crimes – are those that violate the values of the common enterprise in the sense that they express a lack of even minimal commitment to those values. When members of the political community regard themselves as such, that is, as participants in a particular shared enterprise, an enterprise which is valuable and has a claim to their allegiance, they ought to see that what the perpetrator of a criminal act has done means that he cannot unproblematically retain his place within the community. The perpetrator is a member of that community, and is accountable to its values, but has done something that no qualified member of that enterprise – that is, no person independently capable of appreciating the force and demands of those values, without further external guidance, as a qualified citizen – ought to do. To take the self-government conception again as an example, the view would be that citizens are taken to be able to see for themselves the importance of at least the basic minimal responsibilities imposed by the project of collective self-government.[15] In such a political community, where this common project is held to be authoritative for all, citizens are required to act in a manner consistent with respect for these values. Criminal acts are those that express a failure to respect these values, and hence a failure to meet the responsibilities of one's role in the shared enterprise. Such actions cannot go unremarked. Therefore they are the actions that call for a specifically criminalising response.

---

[15] Although citizens are taken to be able to grasp or understand these values, this is not to say that they are expected to be able to articulate them in the way that philosophers and political theorists do. I take it that there is a perfectly adequate way of grasping a moral value or principle that need not involve being able to state it or articulate it with any clarity. If this were not the case then only philosophers and political theorists would have any real moral understanding: much as I esteem my colleagues, I cannot believe that that is so.

The idea that criminal guilt should be modelled on intuitive blameworthiness is one that many retributivists accept. One objection to such accounts has always been that it is hard to explain why blameworthiness should in itself call for a state response: why there should be a state institution that is concerned with (in Michael Moore's phrase) 'placing blame'.[16] My account seeks to answer that question with a particular conception of blame that sees blameworthiness as having to do with one's standing within the relationship of political community, a relationship in which we are responsible to one another for meeting the demands of a collective project. It argues that the reason the state needs an institution of blaming is that it is in the nature of such a relationship that its participants have certain responsibilities – responsibilities are attached to their role within that relationship – and it is part of appropriately valuing the maintenance of this relationship that one should condemn infractions of those responsibilities. But a second concern with the idea of equating criminal guilt and blameworthiness is that it implies a straightforward type of legal moralism. For instance, on Michael Moore's account, criminal law is a functional kind: it exists to bring about retributive justice.[17] On Moore's view, the demands of retributive justice are independent of the existence of law and legal and political relationships. His view is a moralistic one in that law is taken to have a job of enforcing morality, and the limits on the morality that it can enforce are external limiting principles: were it not for the limiting principles the criminal law would be concerned with all moral wrongdoing. On the account presented here, on the other hand, moral considerations also inform the criminal law, but in the sense that legal relationships are taken to be (one type of) moral relationship. Criminal law sets the limits to the legal relationship, as it were, setting out that basic respect for the norms and values of the relationship in the absence of which a person will (partially) lose their status as citizen and have some action taken against her. However, it is not the case that the criminal law has a writ, even prima facie, to concern itself with the morality of its citizens' behaviour as such. The concern of the criminal law is with the maintenance of a certain relationship between citizens. Unless what citizens do offends the standards internal to this political relationship the criminal law has no business with the morality of its citizens' actions.

---

[16] M. S. Moore, *Placing Blame* (Oxford: Clarendon Press, 1997).
[17] Moore, *Placing Blame*, e.g. p. 71.

DO WE NEED AN INSTITUTION OF COLLECTIVE CONDEMNATION?

At this point we need to consider an objection that threatens my argument for the moral value of an institution of collective condemnation. This objection suggests that my argument in support of the collective condemnation of crime conflates two separate issues and that in fact there is no moral duty to issue a collective condemnation of crime. We can distinguish, the objection begins, the conditions that make a person *blameworthy* from the conditions that make it appropriate *overtly* to blame them, or to *express* our blame.[18] Often it can be the case that a person is blameworthy, and that his blameworthiness is not merely a private matter (as it would be in, say, the case of many sorts of dishonesty): perhaps he has been fiddling his taxes or some other issue of public interest where the action is one that we can agree ought to be a crime. Nevertheless, the objection goes, it would be inappropriate for one of his fellow citizens overtly to blame or condemn him. And this is because his fellow citizens are strangers to him. Unless there is some fairly specific pre-existing relationship it would be inappropriate for anyone actually to express the blame that this person merits. It may be true that a person who does such a thing changes the terms of our relationship with him in the sense that he becomes blameworthy. But it does not follow that it would be wrong not to blame him or to treat him differently as a result. Whether it is wrong not to blame depends not just on the person's blameworthiness but also on whether those who condemn have the standing or the authority to blame.[19] Having such standing or authority depends on the relationship one has to the person, and simply being engaged in a collective project with him is not enough. The argument I have given in support of collective condemnation, it might be said, moves from the fact of someone's blameworthiness when he violates the terms of our political relationship to our having a collective duty to condemn, a duty that it is right for the state to discharge. But this step of the argument does not follow. My argument may establish that those who violate the basic responsibilities of the political relationship are blameworthy. But it does not establish that anyone in particular has

---

[18] See, for instance, H. Jensen, 'Morality and Luck', *Philosophy* 59 (1984), pp. 323–30.
[19] Duff, *Punishment, Communication and Community*, p. 185; von Hirsch and Ashworth, *Proportionate Sentencing*, p. 95.

the standing to blame them, and certainly does not establish that we need a state institution for expressing such condemnation.

In response to this objection let us initially consider an example that seems to strengthen its case. Consider again the case of Jane from chapter 4. Jane has grossly failed in her responsibilities as a member of the common educational project of the university. She has let her colleagues down and they as well as the students who are her direct 'victims' have reason to feel aggrieved at what she has done. However, does this in itself make it all right for any member of staff to blame her, to express condemnation, to withdraw respect from her? The inference here seems wrong. Bad as she ought to feel about what she has done Jane may legitimately feel that, if a member of staff with whom she has no specific further relationship came up to her in passing and told her to her face that she had let everyone down, he would be speaking out of turn. And this might suggest that I am wrong to talk about a collective right or duty to condemn infractions. However, while our intuitions may be with the objection thus far, the conclusion the objection seeks to draw is that it does not follow from a person's blameworthiness that a political community as a whole has reason, through the agency of the state, to issue condemnation: in terms of this example, the objection draws the conclusion that it does not follow from Jane's infraction that the *university* has any responsibility to sanction her. And here our intuitions may be less clearly on the side of the objection. What I have argued before (at the end of chapter 6) is that were the university to fail to take some condemnatory action against Jane then it would be failing to treat her as engaged in an enterprise whose members are responsible to one another for what they do. In that argument I was relying on the thought that surely in an institution like a university, where there is arguably some sort of common project, the members are responsible to one another for playing their part. The objection points out a gap between, on the one hand, our being responsible to one another in the sense of being members of a common project and, on the other, our having the right to condemn one another (as individuals at least) for violations of our responsibilities. But does it follow that my argument provides no support for the university or the state having an institution that does issue condemnation?

What my case would need here is an argument that shows why, although it is true that the members of the enterprise have no right *as individuals* to issue condemnation, nevertheless they have a *collective* duty to condemn – or the institutional authority has a duty to condemn on their behalf. However, I think that there is such an argument, which goes like this.[20] What we are dealing with in the case of infractions of criminal law or university disciplinary code are specific contexts of wrongdoing. These contexts are – I have argued – cases in which participants are members of an intrinsically valuable relationship. But they are also cases in which there is an institutional authority that *presides over* the enterprise in the sense of promulgating standards that participants are meant to regard as authoritative. In other words, there is a central body that has the job of putting forward a view of what members' basic responsibilities are, a view that members are supposed to take into account when they act.[21] My argument is that where we have these two elements to the situation the central body has a duty to mark cases of infraction as such. Not to do so would be to undermine its claim to provide an authoritative account of basic responsibilities. Let us examine this argument in some more detail.

When one participates in a relationship or enterprise of the sort I have described, one's actions take place in a context that compels one to think of what one does in universal terms.[22] What I mean by this is that when one acts one does so not merely as a brute individual but as a member of that norm-governed relationship. In such a relationship, when one acts, one acts not simply as oneself but as an occupier of a role that is hemmed in with rules and responsibilities. When acting in such a context – at least when one can be expected to understand the context – what one does carries with it the implication that it is *permissible* within that relationship for one to act in this way. One implies that the rules permit such action. Implicit in all actions performed in such a context is a claim that what one does is all right for anyone in that situation to do. I do not mean that this claim must be 'in one's mind' when one acts but that we can see the act as expressive of that attitude. The actions that I am suggesting should be understood as criminal are acts that make a false claim to

---

[20] I have put forward a version of this argument under the name 'the Hegelian argument' in C. Bennett, 'State Denunciation of Crime', *Journal of Moral Philosophy* 3 (2006), pp. 288–304. In that paper the focus of the argument and some of its details are different from the way I state it here.

[21] As part of the argument here I do not need to take sides in the debate about whether in order to be authoritative the pronouncements of the central bodies need to make a difference to the reasons for action that participants have or whether the authority can simply derive from the authority of the pre-existing reasons. For the first view, see J. Raz, *The Morality of Freedom* (Oxford: Clarendon Press, 1986), ch. 3. For the second, see Duff, *Punishment, Communication and Community*, pp. 56–8, 64–6.

[22] The relevance of universalisation here is meant to depend on a specific social context in which deliberation takes place. I am not committing myself to the Kantian claim that such universalisation is constitutive of rational agency or rational deliberation. The argument here would be compatible with the Humean or Hegelian claim that the Kantian starts with something correct – the need for universalisation when deliberating in certain social contexts – but generalises it illegitimately to rational deliberation as such.

permissibility: they violate acceptable terms of the relationship. They present a false claim.

Now false claims in themselves are no big deal. Why should falsehood itself need to be confronted?[23] The objection correctly points out that simply by virtue of the claim being false there is no duty to correct the person who makes it, even when it is a false claim about what it is permissible to do. The crucial thing is that in the cases we have been discussing, as well as it being the case that the agent acts in the context of a norm-governed relationship, there is also a central institution that decides and declares what the rules are. This institution has authority over the members of the institution in the sense that its decisions and declarations about the content of the rules are ones that members are *meant to* follow in deciding how to act. This institution claims the authority to say definitively how it is permissible for members to act in a way that in everyday life individuals do not do. In everyday informal cases of wrongdoing there is no duty on persons generally to express condemnation to a wrongdoer since no one claims the authority to make such definitive decisions for all. However, in the case in which there *is* such an authoritative body then it *does* have a duty to reject the false claim, to mark it out as false. This is for the simple reason that if it did not then its claim to be issuing authoritative standards would be empty. The state or the university claims that the standards that it promulgates are ones with which its members have to comply as occupiers of certain roles in a common enterprise. It must regard its members as *bound* by those standards. But if this central body did nothing to mark infractions of its standards then its claim that the standards were binding would be empty. Hence there is good reason for the central body to issue condemnation even where there is no reason for members of the enterprise as individuals to do so.

RESTORING RELATIONSHIPS AND RIGHTING WRONGS

The overall picture of the Apology Ritual as we have developed it so far looks like this. We have claimed that political community can be seen as a relationship with values specific to it, from which associative obligations arise, the failure to meet the most fundamental of which requires that

---

[23] This is a question, for instance, for Jean Hampton's expressive account of retribution, which lacks the answer I go on to provide. See e.g. 'A New Theory of Retribution', in R. G. Frey and C. W. Morris (eds.), *Liability and Responsibility* (Cambridge: Cambridge University Press, 1991), pp. 377–414.

some action be taken against the perpetrator by a central authority that presides over the enterprise. For such an authority not to take action would be for it not to treat the infraction as unacceptable or impermissible. The presiding authority therefore has an obligation – arising from its role – to issue condemnation of the offender for the offence. But the condemnation has to say what it claims to say: it has to be symbolically adequate. And we have claimed that where the context is an intrinsically valuable form of relationship the adequate symbols are to be drawn from the account I have called the cycle of blame and apology: we impose on the offender a duty to make amends of the sort that he would be spontaneously motivated to make were he genuinely sorry for what he has done.

In this section we will consider a series of objections to this claim that symbolic amends is the best way to express appropriate condemnation. The objection begins by proposing an alternative to the imposition of amends. It points out that the 'imposition of amends' on my story is really the conjunction of two elements: firstly the partial and temporary suspension of the normal rights and liberties – deprivation of freedom – which is necessary so that it becomes legitimate to *require* the offender to make amends; and then secondly the imposition of amends itself. On my story the deprivation of freedom symbolises a 'withdrawal of recognition', that is, the withdrawal of the respect normally due to the offender given his status in the common project, while the amends symbolise what he would have to do to redeem himself as a member of the enterprise. However, the objection continues, I have claimed that the fundamental job of the criminal sanction is to express proportionate condemnation. And this raises the question of why the imposition of amends is necessary as well as the deprivation of freedom. Why can the job of proportionate condemnation not be carried out perfectly well by the proportionate deprivation of freedom or status rather than the imposition of amends? Consider again the case of Jane, or a case of a doctor being disciplined by the General Medical Council. Would it not be quite plausible to think that the sanction imposed by such bodies would be more likely to consist in temporary suspension of status rather than temporary suspension plus the imposition of an obligation to make some amends? Would those bodies not be likely to feel that they had satisfactorily issued proportionate condemnation by handing out a suspension of a determinate length, where the length of suspension signals the degree of condemnation?

I considered this possibility in brief in the last chapter, where I discussed what was wrong with drawing the symbols of punishment simply from the structure of blame as opposed to blame *and* apology. The answer that I gave there was that there would be something symbolically inadequate in such condemnation for the reason that once an offender has done his time then he resumes his place in the enterprise. He has full status returned to him. In making this argument I was assuming that this reacceptance of the offender looks a bit as if he has been granted a sort of forgiveness: the offence is not quite forgotten, but put into the past: it no longer conditions the offender's relations with the authority and his official status in the group. In particular the offender's reacceptance looks like the kind of forgiveness that results from a person's having made a sincere and adequate apology.[24] This is why it is the symbolism of apology that is appropriate rather than the symbolism of blame: in order to earn the institutional version of forgiveness the offender has to be made to do something that is an institutional version of apology.

However, this leads us to a further objection to the appropriateness of the symbolism of apology when transferred to the institutional case. The reason for this has to do with the need for sincerity.[25] In standard cases of apology we need at least to assume that the apology is sincere in order for it to earn the offender forgiveness. As we saw in chapter 5, apology and penance work to redeem an offender as a member of a relationship because and insofar as they express the offender's repudiation of the act that caused the rupture in relations. However, in the case of punishment – particularly in the case of state punishment, from which the offender cannot just walk away as he might from a sanction imposed by a professional body – we cannot require sincerity as a condition of the successful completion of the sentence. All sorts of unrepentant offenders – the wrongfully convicted, those who have conscientiously committed a crime for good or bad reasons, the wilful or stubborn or insensitive – have to be able to earn the restoration of their civic status as a result of having done their time. This suggests that the sincerity of the apology will have to be irrelevant to the possibility of restoration. However, the objection goes, this means that the apologetic aspect of my account of punishment is really purely fanciful: in many cases no forgiveness will be earned by offenders, and on my view it is no part of the state's aim to ensure that they do earn it. We can subject the offender to proportionate condemnation by imposing deprivation of freedom, but the apology

---

[24] See my account of 'redemptive forgiveness' in Bennett, 'Personal and Redemptive Forgiveness'.
[25] This issue is further discussed in Bennett, 'Taking the Sincerity Out of Saying Sorry'. The argument of the following paragraphs summarises and develops the argument of that paper. I have tried to recast slightly the objection that arises from the need for sincerity.

aspect of the sanction – the imposition of amends – is an empty ritual. It plays no part in making the offender more able to be reaccepted. It adds nothing to the condemnatory work that would be done by the suspension of status and its return after a determinate length of time. It is simply something extra that the offender is forced to do – and if we are seeking to minimise hard treatment (where this is compatible with retaining condemnatory force) then we should do away with it.

This objection works by pointing out the limits to what the state should take itself to have a responsibility to do by way of achieving reconciliation between the offender and the moral community. However, my position accepts and has a justification for those limits. I have already argued that the state's responsibility for issuing condemnation is limited to those acts that violate the terms of the legal or political relationship. These are what, following Duff's usage, I have called 'public wrongs'.[26] The responsibility of the state is not to address or condemn all wrongs as such, but simply to address public wrongs. The state does not have a responsibility to make the offender undo his wrong in the sense in which this would require a penitent repudiation of the wrong. But it does, I have argued, have a responsibility to make the offender undo the public wrong. The question to which this objection draws our attention is 'How does the offender undo public wrong?' The answer I have proposed is that one can undo a public wrong by completing a sentence of proportionate apologetic action regardless of the spirit in which one does this. The proponent of this objection might ask how this can be enough to undo the wrong, given that in normal cases what undoes the wrong is the offender's repudiation of the offending action. But the very thing that the objection appeals to – the intrusiveness of demanding an ostensibly sincere apology from the offender – provides us with an answer. The answer is that apologetic action must be enough by itself, regardless of the spirit in which it is done, because *that is all that the state can legitimately ask the offender to do.* Therefore the state must regard the offender as being restored simply by virtue of having completed the sentence. Whether he is genuinely remorseful or not is not relevant to his relations with the state.[27]

Now again this response might not fully satisfy the proponent of the objection. The objector might continue to ask why, if we recognise the limitation such that we cannot require sincerity, the symbolism of

[26] See Duff, *Punishment, Communication and Community*, p. 61.
[27] Bennett, 'Taking the Sincerity Out of Saying Sorry', pp. 135–6.

blame and apology is really the right one. Why deploy the symbolism of reconciliation and restoration at all when it is *merely* symbolic? So let me point to one final advantage of the symbolism of apology. Using the symbolism of apology rather than merely blaming allows the state to say something about what the appropriate response to condemnation is. This is important because although in a sense the offender's response is his own business (in the sense, that is, in which the state should not punish him further for having the wrong response) this should not be taken to imply that there is no right or wrong about how he should react. He ought to react by feeling the sort of guilt or remorse that would find a satisfying expression in undertaking the penance that he has been set. The claim that this reaction is appropriate follows from the claim that the condemnation is justified. The imposition of amends therefore allows the authority to make a more symbolically specific judgement as to the seriousness of the wrong. The suspension of a person's status for six months does carry a condemnatory message. But it is a message that is far harder to interpret than the message carried by the imposition of a certain amount of amends. Setting an amount of amends is an immediate way of communicating 'this is how sorry you ought to be' – and it is hard to imagine a more intuitive way of expressing condemnation.

CONCLUSION

In this chapter I have developed the Apology Ritual theory of punishment that we initially stated in the last chapter. I have explained and defended the need for collective condemnation of crime through the symbolism of blame and apology. Such symbolism would only be appropriate if political community could legitimately be conceived of as a relationship of the sort we imagined in working out our Strawsonian defence of the retributive attitudes. But I have claimed that it can be, at least on a plausible liberal theory of the good state. I have also defended the need for collective condemnation against the objection that individuals do not have a right, let alone a duty, to condemn offenders even where they share membership of some ethical relationship. And I have defended the need for the symbolism of apology and not merely blame, for amends and not merely deprivation of freedom. I have not considered all the objections that may be made of this account. But in addressing some of the main reasons readers may have for rejecting the Apology Ritual account I hope to have cleared the way for the final chapter in which we will consider how this theory compares to some of its main rivals.

CHAPTER 8

The Apology Ritual and its rivals

In this part of the book I have proposed a theory that – like some forms of retributivism – sees punishment as aimed at expressing proportionate condemnation of wrongdoing, but is also – like the idea of restorative justice – based in the idea of restoring relationships damaged by crime. It is a theory that has common ground with a number of well-known approaches to criminal justice. In this chapter we will look at some of these rival theories and compare their merits with my own approach.

THE APOLOGY RITUAL AND RESTORATIVE JUSTICE: SOME PRACTICAL IMPLICATIONS

We will begin by returning to restorative justice. The fundamental criticism that we considered in chapter 6 is that informal restorative justice leaves out something that the political community has a responsibility to do in the wake of an offence, which is to condemn the offence. This is an important way in which the political community can do something to vindicate the victim: not doing so, treating it as though it might be just a private matter for the individuals concerned to sort out, would be a failure of solidarity with the victim. On the basis of this insight we saw that there is a role for the criminal sanction – understood as what I have called the Apology Ritual – as an expression of collective condemnation of crimes, where crimes are 'public wrongs' – morally wrong actions that affect the perpetrator's relations with their fellow citizens (where all parties are considered as participating in a certain morally structured relationship) and where it is the role of the state to express this condemnation. I argued that the most symbolically adequate form for expressing condemnation and the offender's altered relationship within the political community would be partially to suspend the offender's civil rights and liberties and to require her to do some level of penitential or apologetic action (proportionate to the offence) before she could regain her civil status. We could think of this as a restorative version of the criminal sanction, or a formalised, coercive version of restorative justice.

However, the Apology Ritual account raises the question of whether it abandons the goods of informal restorative justice in favour of the good of the collective condemnation of the offence, and if so whether this trade-off is really worth it. In this concluding chapter I want to give due weight to the important advantages of the informalist approach. In chapter 6 I claimed that informal restorative justice could bring advantages, firstly, in terms of increased *control* over the proceedings and outcomes for victims, offenders and other interested parties; secondly, the possibility of *recognition* of one's situation through the chance to tell one's story to an audience who are there to listen; and thirdly the participants' *understanding* of what is going on in terms that meet their intuitive expectations of the responsibilities the parties have to one another. I suggested that these goods are rooted in the possibility that restorative justice brings of allowing victims, offenders and other parties who are not legal professionals to participate meaningfully in the justice process. In a situation in which the use of informal restorative justice procedures was widespread – as it would be, for instance, if restorative justice were the main default approach to justice – it could have advantages including (1) catering for (at least some of) the needs of victims; (2) appealing to the moral nature of offenders rather than encouraging them to play a bureaucratic game; (3) making the structure of official justice closer to our intuitive ideas about the responsibilities of offenders towards victims and others; (4) encouraging wider community involvement; and (5) leading towards a state in which communities and citizens are – in a good sense – self-policing. However, I also suggested that these were goods of restorative justice the realisation of which our current trial-and-sanction system tends to frustrate – in part because of its centralised, cumbersome, procedure-bound nature. Yet in response to the criticisms that I made of the informalist approach I have now proposed that we do still need a centralised (and therefore presumably cumbersome and procedure-bound) criminal sanction that functions through the state to express collective condemnation of offences. In this chapter I would therefore like to look first of all at the extent to which the strong points of the laissez-faire conception can be accommodated within my conception of state punishment, and to be honest about the extent to which they must be lost. This discussion will also allow us to discuss some of the implications of my account in practice.

The Apology Ritual account sees punishment as the imposition on an offender of a certain amount of amends, the proportions of which (i.e. onerousness, duration, demandingness) symbolise condemnation of the seriousness of the crime by indicating how much the offender would have to do in order to redeem herself and normalise her relationship with the political community. One thing that seems to be necessary within this picture is that when offenders have carried out crimes of a similar degree of seriousness they are asked to make a similar level of amends. Only in this way – effectively by comparing a particular offence to others that have called for similar sanction – can the political community as a whole express condemnation of the offence in a proportionate way. We have some intuitions about *cardinal* proportionality – that is, about how onerous a sentence would 'fit' an offence of a given seriousness – on the basis of which sentencing guidelines could be drawn up. But equally important is consistency across cases of *ordinal* proportionality – involving a proportionate increase in the onerousness of sanctions as the seriousness of the offence increases. This means that the job of fixing a sentence – an amount of amends to be made by the offender – cannot be left for a restorative justice encounter to determine without entirely doing away with the idea that the job of the sentence is to express not just condemnation (since it might be argued that a mere conviction does that), but symbolically adequate condemnation of the offence as an act of a determinate degree of seriousness.

However, even though this may be the case, it does not necessarily mean that face-to-face or indirect restorative justice mediation is incompatible with the view I am putting forward. One possibility, for instance, is that restorative justice be offered as a voluntary and optional addition to the sentence for those who want it. Perhaps the state could facilitate such meetings either by setting up a service itself or else by funding and regulating voluntary sector provision. Even under this system it could become regular to ask victims and offenders whether they would be willing to engage in mediation. But such an arrangement would be an imperfect one in the sense that any involvement in restorative justice would be strictly additional to the sentence and would place an extra burden on the offender who decides to comply. A better solution might be to find a way of counting involvement in restorative justice as part of the discharge of a sentence for those who want it while not prejudicing those who do not. So we can maybe do better than the 'additional restorative justice' approach if we consider what sorts of things sentences might actually consist in on my account.

The key idea on my account is that the nature of sentencing should stay as close as possible to what a 'virtuous offender' would feel it necessary to do by way of making amends. Such an offender would, I have argued, feel the need to do what she can to alleviate the harm she has caused and to make some further penitential amends. Therefore restitution and penitential service, directed to the victim as necessary, should as far as possible be at least an element of a sentence. For instance, the offender might be asked either to make financial compensation to the victim or to make payment in kind by providing some sort of service that helps to alleviate the harm done. However, the practicality of this would depend on the offender's means and ability, as well as the victim's willingness to have further dealings with the offender. Take the question of means first of all. There is a problem with the justice of requiring financial compensation when, say, a flat-rate fine – payable to the victim – for a particular offence will affect rich and poor offenders very differently. One dimension of deciding how much amends is sufficient has to do with the wrongfulness of one's action and the seriousness of its effects. But another dimension has to do with what it will cost the offender to make these amends, where this 'cost to the offender' has to take into consideration the impact on the offender and not merely its 'flat-rate' cost. To some extent this worry could be offset if payment in kind were also acceptable (it might even be suggested that this is to be preferred on the grounds that it affects all offenders equally regardless of their ability to pay). However, even here there might be differences between offenders, as when one offender has skills that could be deployed to do something genuinely useful for the victim, while another could only bring unskilled labour, and would be unable to make a satisfactory attempt at any skilled job they were asked to do for the victim. On top of this, of course, is the willingness of the victim to have to enter into the sort of relationship with the offender that would be required if he was doing some job for her. Depending on the nature of the offence, it might not be appropriate for the offender to be asked to do something for the victim at all, let alone something that might put him in proximity with her while he carried out the work. The victim should always have a right to veto such personal restitution. In such cases what the offender should be sentenced to do is some more general form of community service, though preferably something with some symbolic link to the nature of the offence, so that it represents an activity that could meaningfully be experienced by the offender as making amends for his offence.

What these considerations show is that it will be hard to make decisions in the abstract about precisely what sort of amends will be appropriate in a given case for a given type of offender. In the abstract we might be able to say that for a given type of offence the sentence should consist in some combination of fine and community service (where this service might be carried out for the victim or not as appropriate). However, we will not be able to be more specific until we know the details of the particular offence and the details of the situation of victim and offender. This suggests that judgements about sentencing will rely heavily on the discretion of sentencers and will only be able to be lightly constrained by guidelines that are laid down in advance. The problem with this, however, is that it makes it hard to see how we could achieve consistency across cases. This is a real problem if the point of having consistency across cases is to communicate proportionate condemnation of crime.

In response to this I think that we do have to acknowledge a tension in the conception of symbolically adequate condemnation that I have put forward in this book. On the one hand, condemnation has to be meaningful if it is really to express condemnation. For this reason there is pressure to find sentences that are based as far as possible on what the virtuous offender might feel it necessary to do to make up for her offence. This might require an imaginative use of a wide range of community service or reparative activities that are hard to compare in the abstract (for instance, in a set of official sentencing guidelines). But, on the other hand, in order for the sentence to represent a symbolically adequate expression of collective condemnation, it also has to be capable of expressing consistent judgements about how serious a crime is, a task it can only fulfil if there is the possibility of making publicly defensible judgements about how the sentence in a particular case is in line with precedent elsewhere. In the face of these conflicting pressures some sort of compromise is necessary. We will have to do what we can to ensure proportionality, but on the other hand we should not forget that proportionality is a value whose importance is derived from the overall aim of symbolically adequate condemnation. Therefore we should not prioritise proportionality to the extent of allowing all the meaning to bleed out of our range of sentences. If we can strike a reasonable balance, some leeway in judgements of proportionality might be worthwhile if the overall idea of punishment as symbolically adequate condemnation is sufficiently attractive. Furthermore, the compromise might be strengthened if it allows us to accommodate some more of the benefits of restorative justice than have up to now seemed possible on the Apology Ritual account.

For these reasons we might think that a reasonable way of implementing the Apology Ritual in practice might be something like what I will call the Limited Devolution model.[1] This model essentially involves criminal justice officials collaborating with the victim and the offender to fix the sentence. As we have said, the state must retain the role of setting the level of the sentence. But it could set the level in fairly abstract terms: for instance, in terms of hours of community service. Through some sort of mediation, either indirect or face-to-face, the victim and offender could then consider how these hours should be spent, what the offender could meaningfully do to make amends for his crime. On this view something like a restorative justice meeting could then have the role of making the abstract sentence passed down by the court more determinate. It would allow the victim to decide whether the offender makes amends to her or does some more general service. Such decisions would again be subject to official review to ensure broad proportionality. And either victim or offender would have the right to veto such collaboration, in which case the authority to set the sentence would revert to state officials to set a standard community service punishment. But overall there would be an attempt to ensure that victims and offenders have at least the opportunity to determine a meaningful process of making amends within bounds overseen by the state.

The Limited Devolution model is attractive in part because it acknowledges (a) that it is victims and offenders themselves who may be best placed to tell what a meaningful sentence might be for the particular offence with which they are involved, and (b) that such sentences might be more meaningful to these parties if they have chosen them themselves. The state therefore devolves decision-making powers to victims and offenders if they want it. However such devolution can only be legitimate if the sentences that victims and offenders decide on are comparable across cases. I have suggested that they could be if state officials can make judgements about something like hours of community service, where some sort of 'tariff' for different sorts of crimes is something about which there could be guidelines that sentencers could be charged with applying consistently. However, there is a question about whether specifying a certain number of hours is by itself enough to make community service proportional. This is because, while we can obviously compare hours of community service, mere time spent is not the only way in which community service sentences differ. It also matters which activity it is that

---

[1] The Limited Devolution model might be seen as a development of the suggestion for situating a 'making amends' model within a proportionalist sentencing system in von Hirsch *et al.*, 'Restorative Justice: A "Making Amends" Model?'.

one is sentenced to do, since some are more onerous than others. But, it might be said, proportionality in this area is something that it would be very hard for guidelines to specify in advance. If the decision of victim and offender in some case is that the offender should do some relatively onerous task, then the state officials might have a responsibility to reduce the number of hours they had originally set. But while a guideline of this sort could be incorporated into official sentencing advice it might be hard to imagine how much more could be done to spell out what 'relatively onerous' means here. I think that a certain amount can be done to address this worry: for instance, the way in which we usually communicate the content of judgements such as 'relatively onerous' is by giving a range of examples. It may be that a range of detailed examples could be incorporated into sentencing guidelines in order to illustrate the sorts of things that it can be reasonable to expect offenders to do for particular sorts of offence. Furthermore we could stipulate that sentences would have to be approved by a sentencing board made up of representatives of the different criminal justice agencies and lay members. However, I acknowledge that being able to understand the policy dictated by a range of examples requires a certain amount of shared 'commonsense'. Nevertheless this will be the case in all sets of guidelines: I do not think that the problem of determinate interpretation is one that affects my suggestion in particular. Thus it may be that allowing leeway for some reasonable differences in interpretation of concepts like 'relatively onerous' is a price worth paying in light of the other benefits of the Limited Devolution model.

The concern that the Limited Devolution model aims to address is that the Apology Ritual account removes *control* over sentencing from stakeholders such as the victim and the offender. However, when I discussed the importance of the parties themselves exercising control over the proceedings (in chapter 6), I was at pains to stress that this is not the only important aspect of the restorative meeting. If the restorative meeting was just about the different parties competing to exercise the most control over the outcome then it would be more like a bargaining event than an ideal of justice. Thus I suggested that the ideal of restorative justice should be understood more on the model of a shared inquiry into what the offender was responsible for (what he can be asked to make amends for) and how he should make those amends. It is as an authorised contributor to such an inquiry, I suggested, that we can understand the importance victims and offenders ascribe to being listened to and having their view taken seriously. I talked about these as goods of *recognition*.

In the Limited Devolution model participants can still gain such recognition. Where the parties are willing, they can still stage a discussion that reviews evidence about how bad the offence was, how it came about (i.e. what was going on in the offender's life such that he came to commit it), what the mitigating factors were, and what should be done to address it. The only difference on my model is that there has already been an official verdict about what the offender is responsible for and what she can be asked to make amends for. This may seem artificially to take away much of the point of the restorative meeting which, as I have portrayed it, is an investigation into these questions. However, the fact that an official verdict has been passed on these questions – which I take it the participants would have to regard as fixed and unchanging, unless we can imagine new evidence arising in such meetings that could give rise to a right of appeal against a previous conviction or sentence – need not prevent the restorative conversation ranging over such topics. Whether or not the participants think that the verdict is something that could be overturned, it still makes sense for them to discuss these matters, particularly since the course of the discussion can affect how the sentence is actually carried out.

I have argued, then, that on the Limited Devolution model participants can continue to exercise some *control* and can continue to gain *recognition* by having the chance to tell their side of the story to a reasonably sympathetic audience. Of course, this also takes place in a context they *understand*, in the sense that it reflects their intuitive sense of what the parties to a serious wrong owe to one another in its aftermath – specifically apology and reparation. However, one of the advantages of my account is that it allows at least part of what is valuable in restorative justice to be realised even in the case in which restorative justice is not appropriate. This is because the criminal sanction itself and the nature and level of punishment are modelled on the intuitive workings of blame and apology. Therefore even victims and offenders who reject the opportunity to determine the nature of the sentence are capable of seeing in the following of the official procedures something close to what they would expect in standard non-legal cases of wrongdoing. Even where they do not get the chance to tell their side of the story and have its significance recognised by the other party, they will nevertheless be able to identify with the process.

What I have provided here is only a brief sketch of how the Apology Ritual might be implemented. This sketch no doubt betrays my background as a moral philosopher rather than a criminal lawyer. However, for the sake of completeness it seems important to include some attempt to explain the practical implications of my theory. I started the book with the complaint that our present criminal justice procedures discourage rather than build on Bryson's impulse to apologise and make amends. While my account meets this complaint to the extent that it draws the overall symbolism of punishment from the process of apology, it would be satisfying if someone like Bryson had the chance to make more than merely institutional reparation. If the criminal justice process can provide the opportunity, where appropriate, for actual contact between victim and offender and the direction of the offender's amends to the victim, my impression is that someone like Bryson would appreciate it.

THE BENEFITS-AND-BURDENS APPROACH RECONSIDERED

I have spent some time explaining how my account differs from common accounts of restorative justice, and how it might be able to accommodate at least some of what is most valuable in such accounts. I now want to have a look at how my account compares with three prominent approaches to the criminal sanction, all of them broadly retributivist, to see what can be said in favour of the approach I adopt. The three under consideration are: the benefits-and-burdens account already considered in chapter 2; von Hirsch's censure-plus-deterrent account; and Duff's theory of punishment as secular penance. We have looked at some of the problems with the benefits-and-burdens account before.[2] The main criticism of this theory is that it fails as an attempt to explicate the moral significance of retribution because it assimilates all cases of wrongdoing to those of free-riding, explaining the need to take action against the offender on the basis of the need to remove unfairly gained advantages and restore a fair balance or distribution of benefits and burdens. However, having developed the Apology Ritual account of punishment we are now in a position to see some deeper points of similarity between the two approaches.

For instance, like the cycle of blame and apology account, the benefits-and-burdens defence of retribution begins with the idea of a social group as a cooperative enterprise, where this model has a wider application than merely to the state. For instance, we can imagine Morris's model applying equally well to an informal organisation like a lottery syndicate exhibiting such cooperation (each person pays a certain amount every week in return

---

[2] For this theory, see Morris, 'Persons and Punishment'.

for a share in the winnings if there are any). The crucial thing is that membership of the enterprise brings some benefits, but they are benefits that can only be realised if in general the members are prepared to assume a certain burden. Of course this leaves a loophole occupied by the sneaky free-rider. Thus, where such an arrangement obtains, the members of the group have a certain duty of fair play: in return for the benefits they get through membership of the group they ought to be prepared to assume the burden even when that means acting against their self-interest. On the basis of this we might say that, as on my account, a group such as a lottery syndicate has a *collective interest*, in this case a collective interest in there being a fair distribution of benefits and burdens. The group considered as a collective can be concerned that no one free-rides and that everyone pays their dues. Furthermore, as on my account, we can say that the group as a collective has this interest because what wrongdoing disrupts is an intrinsically valuable relationship. It is only if the fair distribution of benefits and burdens is intrinsically valuable that we can claim that when someone takes an unfair advantage the group has a collective interest in restoring fairness. Thus we can understand the benefits-and-burdens account as an example of a view on which retribution is fundamentally a matter of bringing about the right relations between persons. Crime disrupts the right relation between persons by introducing unfairness into the system: sanction restores fairness.

This characterisation of the similarities between the two accounts allows us to see the strengths of the benefits-and-burdens argument but also where its weaknesses lie. One point where Morris's view does seem to be attractive is in its understanding of wrongdoing as a matter in which the group as a whole has a legitimate interest: wrongdoing is not just a matter that concerns private individuals but rather affects the perpetrator's relations with the group as such. This does seem to be part of our notion of retribution (tying in with the distinction between civil and criminal offence). However, Morris takes a narrow view of what sorts of actions can affect our relations with the group in this way. He assumes that such groups only have a collective moral interest in fairness and hence that it is only actions that disturb the fair balance of benefits and burdens that affect one's relationship with the group. This *might* be correct if one is only thinking of groups like the lottery syndicate, insofar as such groups are effectively just an arrangement for the pursuit of individual self-interest within fair bounds. They are not relationships in which we cooperate in furthering some intrinsically valuable activity – such as friendships, educational institutions, and so on. But Morris's view ignores the existence of richer relationships of the sort I have discussed in this book, in which members have a collective interest in one another's actions by virtue of the fact that they are cooperating together in some shared project that is a part of the good life. When we are in such relationships, I have suggested, it would be wrong to say that it is only unfair actions that disturb our relations with fellow cooperators and call for redress.

However, another way of defending the benefits-and-burdens account would be to admit these inadequacies when regarding it as a theory of the *moral* significance of retribution and to regard it instead as a specifically *political* theory about the basis of the criminal sanction in an attractively liberal state.[3] Thus the proponent of this account might acknowledge that of course there are richer relationships than that of the lottery syndicate but claim nevertheless that it is the lottery syndicate – the association for the fair pursuit of self-interest – rather than those richer relationships that is a good model for the state. After all, the argument might go, the state ought to take a limited role in the moral lives of its citizens, leaving them free as far as possible to live their lives as they see fit: being neutral as to the good, it ought not to pass moral judgement on all areas of its citizens' lives, in particular not on the morality of their actions as such.[4] Of course, this is not to say that the institution of the state and the exercise of its power are not based on any moral ideas whatsoever. Rather the guiding moral idea is that of society as a fair system of social cooperation.[5] It is this idea that gives the state – on this view – its conception of those wrongs in which there is a collective, public interest. Wrongs as such are not the business of the state; what is the business of the state are wrongs that violate the terms of fair cooperation.

Therefore on this 'political' interpretation of the benefits-and-burdens view it is not the case that *from a moral point of view* what is wrong with any criminal action is akin to free-riding. Rather it is only insofar as wrongdoing is akin to free-riding within the scheme of social cooperation *that it can properly be punished by the state* – since the role of punishment is simply to uphold the arrangement of society as a fair system of cooperation that is the central moral project of the state. However, while my account concurs with this rejection of legal moralism – agreeing that whether an act is such as to give a collective interest in condemnation

---

[3] This is the proposal put forward by Dagger that I said in chapter 2 that I would return to consider. See Dagger, 'Playing Fair With Punishment'.

[4] For some discussion of such a claim, see my 'State Denunciation of Crime'.

[5] See e.g. Rawls, *Political Liberalism*, pp. 15 ff.

depends on whether it violates the values inherent in the central moral project(s) of the political community rather than simply on whether it is wrong – it rejects the narrow view of the political community as merely a fair system of social cooperation. Cooperation for the fair distribution of benefits and burdens is not the only intrinsically valuable relationship that could be seen as informing the project of building a liberal society. For instance, I pointed (in the last chapter) to the idea of collective self-government. This self-government conception, I argued, is at the heart of an influential version of political liberalism. But of course political liberalism shares the aspiration to liberal neutrality that motivates this 'political' interpretation of the benefits-and-burdens view. If I am correct in claiming that my account of punishment is compatible with the collective self-government conception, then it is false to say that we have to resort to the benefits-and-burdens view in order to respect liberal intuitions about the need for neutrality. The collective self-government conception provides us with an example of how political community can be conceived of as precisely the sort of intrinsically valuable relationship that my account requires. If I am also correct in thinking that my account delivers a more intuitive condemnatory account of punishment than the benefits-and-burdens view then it is my account that we ought to favour.

CENSURE, SYMBOLISM AND THE JUSTIFICATION OF HARD TREATMENT

One of the attractions of the benefits-and-burdens account is its promise of demystifying the metaphor of 'righting' or 'undoing' a wrong. Having considered the benefits-and-burdens account in chapter 2, however, I suggested that a more promising way to understand the idea of 'righting wrong' is to see it as having to do with the need for censure or con-demnation. I developed this thought in chapter 5, where I discussed the way in which the idea of 'undoing a wrong' informs the practice of apologising. I have argued, therefore, that censure theories are the most promising way of developing the retributivist tradition. Hence it is to two prominent retributivist-oriented censure accounts, those of Duff and von Hirsch,[6] that I now turn in further developing and defending my own view.

---

[6] A significant part of von Hirsch's work is developed in collaboration with Andrew Ashworth. Because most though not all of the works to which I refer here are written by von Hirsch himself, it is to him that I ascribe the position being discussed.

Von Hirsch and Duff agree that the main aim of the criminal sanction is to express condemnation of an offender for an offence. However, von Hirsch's position differs from the Apology Ritual account in that he claims that this goal is not the only defining aim of punishment. First of all, he denies that the goal of expressing condemnation can in itself justify hard treatment. Thus, he asks, in a point that recalls Feinberg's conclusion to 'The Expressive Function of Punishment':

Can the institution of punishment, however, be explained *purely* in terms of censure? Punishment conveys blame, but does so in a special way – through visitation of deprivation . . . on the offender. That deprivation is the vehicle through which the blame is expressed. But why use this vehicle, rather than simply expressing blame in symbolic fashion?[7]

For von Hirsch, we cannot explain why hard treatment has to accompany censure simply by appealing to the purpose of censure itself. But, secondly, von Hirsch claims that, as well as having a duty to censure, one proper role of the state is the protection of its citizens and the prevention of crime. He rejects those penal theories that are purely deterrent, arguing that they cannot distinguish punishment from 'tiger control'.[8] Pure deterrence fails to capture the distinctively denunciatory aspect of punishment, but also fails to treat offenders as moral agents. However, he thinks that a deterrent *supplement* to censure can be justified, that will make it less likely that potential offenders will offend.[9] Therefore punishment consists of a message of condemnation addressed to the offender as a moral agent accompanied by an element of hard treatment that serves a deterrent function. And this dual nature of punishment, on von Hirsch's view, suits the nature of the human animal. Because human beings are not angels, the communication of good moral reasons for compliance is not always sufficient to make compliance likely. But because human beings are not simply beasts, it would be a failure of basic respect simply to have a deterrent sanction. Therefore the basic justification for the deployment of the criminal sanction is that an agent has performed an act that is worthy of condemnation by the state, not that it would serve the aims of crime reduction to sanction it. But mere verbal condemnation is not itself sufficient for creatures who are not perfectly moral. Therefore the criminal sanction has primarily a condemnatory function but also

---

[7] Von Hirsch, 'Punishment, Penance and the State', in M. Matravers (ed.), *Punishment and Political Theory* (Oxford: Hart, 1999), p. 69.
[8] Von Hirsch, *Censure and Sanctions*, p. 11.　[9] Von Hirsch, *Censure and Sanctions*, p. 13.

provides us with extra non-moral or prudential incentive in the shape of hard treatment.

Duff rejects von Hirsch's approach, and the Apology Ritual account lends support to two of his main criticisms. First of all, Duff regards the deterrent supplement as morally unjustified. But this does not mean that he regards hard treatment as unjustified, since – and this is the second point – he thinks that hard treatment is a necessary part of the aim of condemnation. On the first point Duff shares with von Hirsch a concern that offenders be given due respect as moral agents. As with von Hirsch it is arguably this concern that leads him to a communicative theory of punishment, since as we have seen in previous chapters engaging someone in moral inquiry – one form of which can involve subjecting their actions to moral criticism – is a prime example of treating someone as a moral agent. For Duff, however, the status of offenders (and potential offenders and other citizens) as moral agents makes any deterrent element in punishment – even one that as on von Hirsch's conception is merely supplementary – deeply problematic.[10] Duff shares the concern defended in this book that the way in which we treat offenders should be compatible with their status, where this will rule out certain sorts of manipulative treatment. In the terms of my argument we might say that the use of a deterrent supplement involves treating the offender as though it was not her own responsibility to make sure that she complies with moral standards. It is hard to see how the deterrent supplement is compatible with treating an offender as a qualified member of some joint enterprise whose responsibility it is to find out and comply with her responsibilities: the deterrent supplement aims to pre-empt or replace the agent's responsibility to do this for herself. If these arguments against von Hirsch are successful, then we should agree with Duff that the idea of a deterrent supplement will appear at best a last resort.

As I have said, however, Duff does not think that hard treatment is unjustified: he simply thinks that it is unjustified as a deterrent. His view, as with the Apology Ritual account, is that the very act of condemnation requires hard treatment. However, Duff has a different argument for this conclusion from the one presented here because it relies on his view of punishment as *communicative*. I think this emphasis on communication is likely to mislead us, making it difficult to see the true significance of hard treatment to punishment, and making it look as though our aim in punishing is more intrusive than is necessary. In this respect my account

---

[10] Duff, *Punishment, Communication and Community*, pp. 87–8.

shares with von Hirsch a rejection of Duff's penitential account in favour of something that might be better understood as an *expressive* theory of punishment. In order to see what is problematic in Duff's account, let us start with his argument that the aim of communicating with the offender requires hard treatment.

On Duff's view the only acceptable purpose of condemnation/ punishment is that of communicating with the offender, getting her to understand the nature of her offence. One central claim that Duff makes against von Hirsch's view that condemnation need not involve hard treatment is that the aim of censure is to bring the offender, not just to understand, but to accept and to repent the wrong done.[11] Thus, the point of expressing condemnation, on Duff's view, is not simply to let off steam, but to get the offender to understand why she is being condemned. This means getting her to understand not just *that* we disapprove of what she has done but *why* we disapprove, where this means understanding why there were good moral reasons not to have committed the offence in the first place.[12] In other words, in expressing disapproval we seek to justify what we are doing by explaining to the offender why the action *merits* condemnation. If the offender properly appreciates these reasons then, stubbornness or other weakness aside, she will accept them, come to understand herself as a wrongdoer, and feel guilt and remorse. Thus, Duff thinks, the proper aim in expressing condemnation is really always to induce repentance. Furthermore, Duff claims (as we have seen in chapter 5) that the 'appropriate vehicle' for the expression of guilt and remorse is penance, so someone who is appropriately penitent will be motivated to undertake penance for themselves.[13] Thus the aim of punishment is really to get the offender to see the need for penance. And we do this, according to Duff, by imposing penance. Thus our aim is to get the offender to accept the imposed penance as her own.[14] On Duff's view, therefore, the aim of inducing repentant acceptance of penance is implied by the aim of expressing condemnation.

Against this, however, von Hirsch claims that the state ought to have no such goal as inducing repentance. Duff claims that this goal is implied by the goal of expressing condemnation. But von Hirsch's position is presumably that there is a difference between the state expressing condemnation and the state aiming to induce repentance in offenders. We

---

[11] Duff, 'Punishment, Communication and Community'.
[12] Duff, *Trials and Punishments*, pp. 57–60.   [13] Duff, *Trials and Punishments*, pp. 68–9.
[14] Duff, *Trials and Punishments*, p. 251.

can identify two main reasons that von Hirsch has for rejecting the goal of inducing repentance. The first has to do with *intrusiveness*. Adopting the goal of inducing repentance involves the state making intrusive inquiries into the offender's life and personality, since it will become important to know how the blame is affecting him. Thus: 'Were the primary aim that of producing actual changes in the actor's moral attitudes . . . the condemnor would ordinarily seek information about his personality and outlook, so as better to foster the requisite attitudinal changes.'[15] But gaining such information about someone's personality and attitudes may require intrusive inquiries into areas of their life that are ordinarily thought to be private. Furthermore, even the act of inquiring into how someone has reacted to an act of condemnation can be intrusive. Von Hirsch offers this example: 'someone has acted inconsiderately toward me, and I respond in a critical manner. How far I may properly go in trying to elicit the morally appropriate response from him depends on the character of our relationship.'[16] In other words, when I want to show a stranger that I think he has done something unacceptable I may give him a sharp word or give him the cold shoulder, but it might be overbearing in addition to this to ask him whether he really understands and is sorry (though this might be acceptable, up to a point, with my partner or my father or my child). Von Hirsch is concerned to point out that, if such inquiries can be intrusive when made by one stranger to another, they must surely be even more intrusive when made by the state, which has powerful coercive machinery backing it up. A properly liberal state, von Hirsch thinks, will acknowledge limits on the extent to which it ought to concern itself with the attitudes of the offender.

The second reason von Hirsch has for rejecting the goal of repentance has to do with *proportionality*. The principle of proportionality 'calls for A and B to receive comparably severe punishments, if the gravity of their crimes is approximately the same. The aim of eliciting penitence, however, points the other way: B might have a thicker skin than A, and hence might need a tougher penance before the message is likely to penetrate.'[17] Thus offenders come with different degrees of moral sensitivity, some more penitent than others, some more open to moral considerations than others. If our fundamental aim is to induce repentance, then we might end up giving wildly variable penances in these different cases. This concern can be made most acute by considering two opposite cases, one in which

[15] Von Hirsch, *Censure and Sanctions*, p. 10.
[16] Von Hirsch, 'Punishment, Penance and the State'. [17] Von Hirsch, *Censure and Sanctions*, p. 75.

an offender is already contrite, and another in which someone has been wrongly convicted (an unfortunate but inevitable occurrence that any justification of punishment ought to take into account) and, vigorously protesting her innocence, refuses to repent. If one offender is already repentant while another is far more resistant, will not the latter have to be punished much more? Indeed, why should the contrite offender be punished at all on Duff's view?

These criticisms of Duff may strike us as plausible at least on the face of it.[18] However, if Duff is correct in arguing that the goal of expressing condemnation implies that of inducing repentance, then if the criticisms are valid von Hirsch would have to give up his claim that expressing condemnation is the proper aim of state punishment. The question at this point is whether von Hirsch can coherently hold on to his view that the state ought to issue condemnation of offenders while rejecting the goal of inducing repentance as intrusive. In articulating this point von Hirsch has claimed that we can distinguish Duff's conception of condemnation – on which there is a positive aim to change the offender's attitudes – from condemnation that deals with the offender *externally*: on von Hirsch's view '[t]he disapproval conveyed by the sanction gives the actor the opportunity to reconsider his actions and feel shame or regret. However, it is left to him to respond'.[19] However, this way of putting things is not altogether clear. It is hard to see what such 'external' condemnation can amount to if Duff is right that, when condemnation is being expressed to the offender and is not merely using him as a means to another end, it has to be an attempt to get him to accept the justice of the condemnation and change his attitudes. Therefore it is hard to see how an acceptable form of condemnation might be purely external. Furthermore it is hard to see how even on Duff's view, on which there is a positive aim to induce repentance, we could do anything other than leave the offender to make her own response. After all, we cannot force repentance.[20] Thus von Hirsch owes us an account of how the form of condemnation that he invokes differs from what Duff offers in such a way as to avoid the criticisms he makes of Duff.

Nevertheless we might think that von Hirsch is right that there is a difference between expressing condemnation and having the positive aim of inducing repentance. If one has the latter aim then there will be at least a

---

[18] For a defence of Duff's position, though, see J. Tasioulas, 'Repentance and the Liberal State', *Ohio State Journal of Criminal Law* 4 (2007), pp. 487–521, esp. pp. 497–8.

[19] Von Hirsch, *Censure and Sanctions*, p. 72.

[20] Duff, *Punishment, Communication and Community*, p. 110.

presumption that one has reason to monitor how the offender is responding to the condemnation while in the former there need not. This is something that might have quite significant implications for what one thinks are acceptable punishments. We might also think that there is something to von Hirsch's charge that the state should, in issuing condemnation, stop short of checking to see that the offender has responded to it appropriately. It seems correct to say that this is his own responsibility: in my terms this is one of the things that distinguishes a qualified participant from an apprentice. What we want to find out is therefore what can be made of the claim that what we are looking for is a form of condemnation that will in some sense deal with the offender *externally*. However, von Hirsch may draw some encouragement at this point from the fact that Duff himself seems to admit that there must be such an external form of condemnation. For instance, in response to the concern that on his account we should waive or mitigate the punishment of already repentant offenders and punish the defiant until they repent, Duff has claimed that such a lack of proportionality would undermine the aim of condemnation.[21] He claims at this point that the expression of condemnation to the offender for her offence is the main aim of punishment on his account. However, it is hard to make sense of this claim on the view that the aim of expressing censure is really to induce repentance. It raises the question of why we would think it important to continue expressing condemnation to someone who had already accepted the message. Therefore it looks as though in order to explain why censure is necessary in such a case Duff would have to accept that there *is* a role for censure that does not have to do with communication to the offender and the aim of inducing repentance but is rather, in von Hirsch's terms, external. However, if he does accept this then it leaves a question as to what his justification is for the use of hard treatment in such condemnation.[22] Duff's justification for hard treatment seems to be tied to his conception of condemnation as a communication that seeks to induce repentance.

---

[21] Duff, *Punishment, Communication and Community*, pp. 120, 122.

[22] This is also a question that could be asked of the account put forward in J. Tasioulas, 'Punishment and Repentance', *Philosophy* 81 (2006), pp. 279–322. Tasioulas thinks that the main justification for punishment is desert – punishment expresses blame – though another subsidiary consideration bearing on the question of how to – and how much to – punish is the instrumental role of punishment in inducing repentance. However, if inducing punishment is not the reason to punish, then it is not clear that Tasioulas has an explanation of what desert consists in and why it gives a compelling reason to punish. He appeals to Strawson, but is vulnerable to the criticisms that I make of Strawson in chapter 3. Nevertheless I think that his account of the basis of desert is compatible with the one I put forward in response to such criticisms.

Nevertheless this still leaves von Hirsch – and Duff – with an obligation to explain the nature and importance of this further 'external' form of condemnation. I am not sure that either writer satisfactorily provides such an account. My suggestion would be that what this external condemnation amounts to is that the offender is treated in such a way that *marks him out as an offender* in some way, but where the point of doing this is not to induce repentance. However, we still need an account of what the point of marking the offender out in this way might be if it is not to induce repentance. The trouble is that what one wants to say at this point is something that cannot be said within the terms of von Hirsch's account, though it may be compatible with some aspects of Duff's. This is that in marking the offender out in this way the state is simply reflecting *how things stand* with the offender. In order to see why this marking out is an expression of condemnation, we would have to look at the *symbolism* of such treatment, an issue on which von Hirsch is silent (indeed, as we have seen, sceptical). What I have provided in this book, however, is an account that helps us to answer this question by suggesting that we can see this marking out as condemnation insofar as it reflects the emotional structure of condemnation, that is, when it derives its symbolic force from the emotions typically evoked by wrongdoing. Particularly relevant here is the reaction of blame, which I take to be a withdrawal of goodwill or respect from the offender. Where the state marks the offender out by withdrawing such respect from him, we can see this as an expression of condemnation because it reflects our understanding of how we would be motivated to treat those who have done wrong. In other words it reflects our understanding that because of the offence it would be wrong for the state simply to treat the offender as it treats everyone else. The state has to condemn by treating the offender differently. But the point of altering the way in which the offender is treated is not primarily to get the offender to *understand* and accept the reasons for the con-demnation, etc. Rather its point is for the state to treat the offender in a way that reflects the new terms of their relationship. It is this treatment of the offender that expresses condemnation, since it symbolises the fact that the wrong has changed how things stand. This is the basis of the Apology Ritual account.

Thus what the Apology Ritual account provides is an expressive but non-communicative theory of punishment. It tells us that crimes are acts that alter the offender's relationship with the political community as a whole – and hence with the state as the agent of the political community – and that the state must treat the offender in a way that adequately symbolises the effect of what the wrongdoer has done on her standing in the political community. If it is asked why the state should do this, we can reply that the point is simply one that von Hirsch and Duff accept: the aim of expressing condemnation. What I insist, however, is that such condemnation has to be expressed in symbolically adequate terms in order to work as condemnation, and that the appropriate symbols are to be found in the narrative of alienation and reconciliation that underpins our practice of blame and apology. I think that this is a theme one can find in some aspects of Duff's account. But it involves rejecting the idea that the aim of expressing condemnation equates to the aim of inducing repentance. One can accept that one has a duty to treat the offender differently without accepting that one has a duty to induce repentance. If Duff asks whether the act of expressing condemnation must not nevertheless have as its aim that it be understood and accepted by those (including the offender) to whom it is directed, then I can agree. But I can agree with this without accepting – for the reasons von Hirsch gives – that one has a duty to concern oneself with ways in which one might most effectively induce repentance.

The problem with von Hirsch's account, on the other hand, is that he does not consider what must take place in order for condemnation actually to function as condemnation. He might question this point, and say that as long as verbal condemnation is expressed as condemnation, and this is made clear in the semantics of what is said, then an act of condemnation has taken place. However, I doubt that we can see such an act as a sincere act of condemnation. For an act to be a sincere act of condemnation we have to see it as the expression of the emotional states appropriate to cases of wrongdoing. The person who sincerely condemns is in the grip of an emotion – though she need not necessarily be 'feeling' it at the time – because what has happened is something that *matters* to her. Because it matters to her she feels disposed to behave in certain ways – those ways that express the appropriate emotion. Therefore, the person who utters a 'condemnation' but fails to behave as someone who is emotionally engaged would behave comes across as someone to whom the offence does not properly matter, and hence the condemnation appears as lacking full sincerity. Therefore, I have argued, if we want state condemnation to come across as real condemnation, if we want it to express sincere condemnation, then it has to deploy adequate symbols, symbols drawn from the ways in which the emotions are appropriately expressed. It has to involve treating the offender as blameworthy and having a duty to apologise. It is from this account of the appropriate expression of the emotions that I derive my account of why hard treatment is a necessary component of the criminal sanction. Therefore I reject von Hirsch's view that one needs to appeal to the further aim of deterrence to explain why censure has to be accompanied by hard treatment. I hope to have explained how it can be that the hard treatment *is* the censure.

Finally, von Hirsch may ask where my account leaves the thought that one important role of the state is the protection of the public from serious and avoidable harms. Does the state really have no duty to impose deterrent sanctions on offenders if this is what it would take to prevent crime? As I understand this criticism, it claims that the importance of protecting the public can, perhaps often, outweigh the importance of respecting the offender as a moral agent. In response I can claim, first of all, that, because this point will only justify overriding the claims of the offender to be respected in certain cases, it does not justify von Hirsch's *default* deterrent supplement. In response to this von Hirsch can seek to justify the blanket application of the supplement by pointing to the importance of proportionality and consistency across cases: if we start to add deterrent supplements to the sentences of some offenders but not others then we will not be being fair. However, this response will not succeed, since the addition of a deterrent supplement in any case just *is* unfair and unmerited by the individual. It does not seem justified to compound this unfairness by being consistently unfair to everyone. The importance of proportionality and consistency derives from the need for consistent and proportionate condemnation, but in this case the deterrent 'extra' has nothing to do with censure and therefore could be added as necessary in the circumstances, making it clear that no further condemnation is intended in doing so. This would of course be highly morally unsatisfactory, but it is at least honest about the moral compromises being made.

Secondly, even where giving qualified moral agents a further deterrent supplement (and hence failing to treat them as qualified moral agents) is necessary and justified, this does not cancel the wrong done to the offender. The offender is still wronged, insulted, demeaned, by virtue of having been treated as someone who is not really qualified – assuming all the time that she *can* properly be considered as a qualified agent. Even if this is necessary – as when it is necessary to break a promise to someone – it leaves a 'moral residue', a need for redress, if only for an apology. This is so because treating the offender in accordance with her status is something we owe to her, just as we owe it to the promisee that we keep a promise that we might find ourselves having to break. When we break a promise, perhaps for good reasons, all things considered, it matters in a way that it does not in a simple case in which a more important reason outweighs a less important one. What we are dealing with in this book is fundamentally what we owe to offenders, and whether there is a justification from punishment that stems simply from what we do so owe. It may be a separate question what, all things considered, is 'the thing to do' regarding criminal justice. It may be the case that von Hirsch is right that deterrence is sometimes necessary, though I doubt that he can show that it is necessary for all offenders. But if what we are interested in is getting clear about the morality of the situation, then it is important to be clear that sometimes doing what is necessary requires treating offenders in ways in which they ought not to be treated.

Another way of putting this is to say that my account here provides some moral basis for the claim that we should distinguish punishment properly so-called – a sanction that is a response to a failure of an individual to do something that it was her responsibility to do – from other actions that might be taken with the aim of preventing further crimes. Even if we see deterrence or preventive detention as necessary, why see it as part of punishment rather than as a quite different type of social agency, something more akin to health care or welfare or housing, that aims at the eradication of serious and avoidable harms? This insistence on the distinctiveness of punishment 'proper' might look like a valid but uninteresting point until we see that it is only by insisting on that distinction that we get a clear picture of the moral costs of some aspects of crime prevention – the way in which sometimes what we need to do to prevent crime involves us in wronging individuals to whom we owe better treatment.

I conclude therefore that the Apology Ritual account builds on weaknesses that we have noted in restorative justice and in relevantly similar retributive accounts such as the benefits-and-burdens account and the two censure accounts of von Hirsch and Duff. The Apology Ritual account takes it that the justification of punishment lies in the need for the expression of symbolically adequate censure. The offender is compelled to undertake proportionate apologetic action as a way of undoing public wrong. However, the state has no duty forcibly to reha-bilitate the offender, or even to aim to induce repentance in any way other than through the symbolically adequate expression of condemna-tion. Therefore the Apology Ritual account disagrees with Duff that the three 'Rs' of punishment are repentance, reform and reconciliation.[23]

---

[23] Duff, *Punishment, Communication and Community*, p. 107.

There is a type of reconciliation that the state is legitimately interested in, but it is achieved by having been subjected to proportionate condemnation no matter how one responds to it: such reconciliation is simply the return of that full civic status of which one was deprived because of one's offence. It is not part of the remit of the state to pursue the full-blown moral reconciliation that comes with repentance. The Apology Ritual is interested in the same process of repentance, reform and reconciliation that Duff is interested in – what I have called the cycle of blame and apology – but it uses it to provide the basis for adequate symbols for condemnation rather than as something actually to be achieved. Of course the world would be a better place if offenders did respond to expressions of condemnation with genuine repentance and reform. But it is not clear to me that aiming to make this happen is the business of the state, let alone the justification of the criminal sanction.

CONCLUSION

What I have offered in this book is an ideal theory of punishment. It tries to explain why punishment would be justified in the clearest, central case of responsible agency. However, as such it of course does not adequately explain how we might deal with the more messy and more challenging cases that tend to come up in the real life of a criminal justice system. For instance, where a high proportion of crime is drug-related, my blithe talk of qualified moral agents may sound somewhat simplistic. Similarly, when we live in a society in which the state is only prepared to treat some classes of people as full citizens when it wants to punish them, my account might look politically naïve, even reactionary. I would like to suggest that it is neither simplistic nor naïve, though it is necessarily at this stage incomplete. In order to proceed I have had to bracket certain issues that would otherwise make the inquiry overwhelmingly complicated. I have therefore tried to paint a picture of the conditions in which retributive punishment is justified. When the complicating conditions are reintroduced – as they are in real-life cases with our actual offenders, actual institutions, actual officials, actual inequalities of power, wealth and status – it becomes a different question whether offenders deserve to be punished and whether the state has the authority to punish them. But the normative justification that I have attempted to give here of the central cases of punishment is, I think, an essential first step in coming to an adequate view on how to deal with borderline or more problematic cases. The existence of these problem cases and the complexity of real-life situations should not blind us to the fact that there is a good retributive justification for punishment *where certain conditions are met.* If these conditions are only partially met, then it becomes an interesting and difficult question to what extent retributive punishment is still justified. But I do not see how one could answer the question whether it is justified in an actual case with such-and-such conditions unless one has a clear idea of when it is justified and what justifies it. Only then will one know what is at stake and what the relevant considerations are. A next stage in the development of this theory would therefore be to look at more nuanced cases in order to see in more detail how the theory offered here might illuminate them. But that is an inquiry for another day.

Bibliography

Adams, R. M., 'Involuntary Sins', *Philosophical Review* 94 (1985), pp. 3–31.

Allen, F., *The Decline of the Rehabilitative Ideal: Penal Policy and Social Purpose* (New Haven, Conn.: Yale University Press, 1981).

Ashworth, A., 'Rights, Responsibilities and Restorative Justice', *British Journal of Criminology* 42 (2002), pp. 578–95.

Bagaric, M., *Punishment and Sentencing: A Rational Approach* (London: Cavendish, 2001).

Baker, B., 'Penance as a Model for Punishment', *Social Theory and Practice* 18 (1992), pp. 311–31.

Barnett, R., 'Restitution: A New Paradigm for Criminal Justice', *Ethics* 87 (1977), pp. 279–301.

Baron, M., 'Kantian Ethics', in M. Baron, P. Pettit and M. Slote, *Three Methods of Ethics* (Oxford: Blackwell, 1997), pp. 3–91.

Baron, M., P. Pettit and M. Slote, *Three Methods of Ethics* (Oxford: Blackwell, 1997).

Bennett, C., 'The Varieties of Retributive Experience', *Philosophical Quarterly* 52 (2002), pp. 145–63.

'Personal and Redemptive Forgiveness', *European Journal of Philosophy* 11 (2003), pp. 127–44.

'A Problem Case for Public Reason', *Critical Review of International Social and Political Philosophy* 6 (2003), pp. 50–69.

'Recent Work on Punishment', *Philosophical Books* 45 (2004), pp. 324–34.

'State Denunciation of Crime', *Journal of Moral Philosophy* 3 (2006), pp. 288–304.

'Taking the Sincerity Out of Saying Sorry: Restorative Justice as Ritual', *Journal of Applied Philosophy* 23 (2006), pp. 127–43.

'Satisfying the Needs and Interests of Victims', in G. Johnstone and D. Van Ness (eds.), *The Handbook of Restorative Justice* (Cullompton: Willan, 2007), pp. 247–64.

Bennett, J., 'Accountability', in Z. van Straaten (ed.), *Philosophical Subjects: Essays Presented to P. F. Strawson* (Oxford: Clarendon Press, 1980), pp. 14–47.

Bentham, J., *Introduction to the Principles of Morals and Legislation*, in J. S. Mill and J. Bentham, *Utilitarianism and Other Essays*, ed. A. Ryan (Harmondsworth: Penguin, 1987).

Beyleveld, D., 'Deterrence Research and Deterrence Policies', in A. von Hirsch and A. Ashworth (eds.), *Principled Sentencing*, 2nd edn (Oxford: Hart, 1998), pp. 66–79.

Bickenbach, J. E., 'Critical Notice of R. A. Duff, Trials and Punishments', *Canadian Journal of Philosophy* 18 (1988), pp. 765–86.

Bittner, R., 'Is it Reasonable to Regret the Things One Did?' *Journal of Philosophy* 89 (1992), pp. 262–73.

Bottoms, A. E., 'Some Sociological Reflections on Restorative Justice', in A. von Hirsch, J. Roberts, A. E. Bottoms, K. Roach and M. Schiff (eds.), *Restorative Justice and Criminal Justice: Competing or Reconcilable Paradigms?* (Oxford: Hart, 2003), pp, 79–114.

Bottoms, A. E. and R. H. Preston (eds.), *The Coming Penal Crisis* (Edinburgh: Scottish Academic Press, 1980).

Braithwaite, J., *Crime, Shame and Reintegration* (Cambridge: Cambridge University Press, 1989).

'Restorative Justice', in M. Tonry (ed.), *The Handbook of Crime and Punishment* (New York: Oxford University Press, 1998), pp. 323–44.

'Restorative Justice: Assessing Optimistic and Pessimistic Accounts', *Crime and Justice: A Review of Research* 25 (1999), pp. 1–127.

'In Search of Restorative Jurisprudence', in L. Walgrave (ed.), *Restorative Justice and the Law* (Cullompton: Willan, 2002).

'Does Restorative Justice Work?' in G. Johnstone (ed.), *A Restorative Justice Reader* (Cullompton: Willan, 2003), pp. 320–52.

'Restorative Justice and a Better Future', in G. Johnstone (ed.), *A Restorative Justice Reader* (Cullompton: Willan, 2003), pp. 83–97.

Braithwaite, J. and P. Pettit, *Not Just Deserts: A Republican Theory of Criminal Justice* (Oxford: Clarendon Press, 1990).

Brink, D., 'Externalist Moral Realism', in M. Smith (ed.), *Meta-Ethics* (Aldershot: Dartmouth, 1995).

Brummer, V., 'Atonement and Reconciliation', *Religious Studies* 28 (1992), pp. 435–52.

Cavadino, M. and J. Dignan, 'Reparation, Retribution and Rights', in A. von Hirsch and A. Ashworth (eds.), *Principled Sentencing* (Oxford: Hart, 1999), pp. 348–58.

Christie, N., 'Conflicts as Property', *British Journal of Criminology* 17 (1977), pp. 1–15.

Clark, M., 'The Sanctions of the Criminal Law', *Proceedings of the Aristotelian Society* 97 (1997), pp. 25–39.

Clarke, R., 'On an Argument for the Impossibility of Moral Responsibility', *Midwest Studies in Philosophy* 24 (2005), pp. 13–24.

Coleman, J. and S. Shapiro (eds.), *The Oxford Handbook of Law and Jurisprudence* (Oxford: Oxford University Press, 2002).

Crawford, A., 'In the Hands of the Public?' in G. Johnstone (ed.), *A Restorative Justice Reader* (Cullompton: Willan, 2003), pp. 312–19.

Dagger, R., 'Playing Fair With Punishment', *Ethics* 103 (1993), pp. 473–88.

Daly, K., 'Restorative Justice: The Real Story', *Punishment and Society* 4 (2002), pp. 55–79.

Declaration of Leuven on the Advisability of Promoting the Restorative Approach to Juvenile Crime, in G. Johnstone (ed.), *A Restorative Justice Reader* (Cullompton: Willan, 2003), pp. 477–81.

Devlin, P., 'Morals and the Criminal Law', in *The Enforcement of Morals* (Oxford: Oxford University Press, 1965), pp. 1–25.

Dignan, J., 'Towards a Systemic Model of Restorative Justice: Reflections on the Concept, its Context and the Need for Clear Constraints', in A. von Hirsch, J. Roberts, A. E. Bottoms, K. Roach and M. Schiff (eds.), *Restorative Justice and Criminal Justice: Competing or Reconcilable Paradigms?* (Oxford: Hart, 2003), pp. 135–56.

Dignan, J. and M. Cavadino, *The Penal System*, 3rd edn (London: Sage, 2002).

Dilman, I., *Morality and the Inner Life* (London: Macmillan, 1979).

Duff, R. A., *Trials and Punishments* (Cambridge: Cambridge University Press, 1986).

'Penal Communications', *Crime and Justice: A Review of Research* 20 (1996), 1–97.

'Law, Language and Community: Some Preconditions of Criminal Liability', *Oxford Journal of Legal Studies* 18 (1998), pp. 189–206.

'Punishment, Communication and Community', in M. Matravers (ed.), *Punishment and Political Theory* (Oxford: Hart, 1999), pp. 48–68.

Punishment, Communication and Community (Oxford: Oxford University Press, 2001).

'Restorative Punishment and Punitive Restoration', in L. Walgrave (ed.), *Restorative Justice and the Law* (Cullompton: Willan, 2002), pp. 82–100.

Duff, R. A. and D. Garland (eds.), *A Reader on Punishment* (Oxford: Oxford University Press, 1994).

Dworkin, R., *Law's Empire* (London: Fontana, 1986).

Ezorsky, G. (ed.), *Philosophical Perspectives on Punishment* (Albany, N.Y.: SUNY Press, 1972).

Feinberg, J., 'The Expressive Function of Punishment', in *Doing and Deserving* (London: Princeton University Press, 1970), pp. 95–118.

Finnis, J., 'The Restoration of Retribution', *Analysis* 32 (1972), pp. 131–5.

Frankfurt, H., 'Freedom of the Will and the Concept of a Person', *Journal of Philosophy* 68 (1971), pp. 5–20.

Fukuyama, F., *The End of History and the Last Man* (London: Penguin, 1992).

Gardner, J., 'Rationality and the Rule of Law in Offences against the Person', in J. Gardner, *Offences and Defences* (Oxford: Oxford University Press, 2007).

Garland, D., *Punishment and Modern Society* (Oxford: Clarendon Press, 1990).

Gauthier, D., *Morals by Agreement* (Oxford: Oxford University Press, 1986).

Gibbard, A., *Thinking How to Live* (Cambridge, Mass.: Harvard University Press, 2003).

Goffman, E., *Relations in Public* (London: Penguin, 1971).

Goldie, P., *The Emotions: A Philosophical Exploration* (Oxford: Oxford University Press, 2000).

Greenspan, P., 'Guilt and Virtue', *Journal of Philosophy* 91 (1994), pp. 57–70.

Hampton, J., 'The Moral Education Theory of Punishment', *Philosophy and Public Affairs* 13 (1984), pp. 208–38.

'A New Theory of Retribution', in R. G. Frey and C. W. Morris (eds.), *Liability and Responsibility* (Cambridge: Cambridge University Press, 1991), pp. 377–414.

'Correcting Harms Versus Righting Wrongs: The Goal of Retribution', *UCLA Law Review* 39 (1992), pp. 1659–702.

Hart, H. L. A., 'Legal Responsibility and Excuses', in *Punishment and Responsibility* (Oxford: Oxford University Press, 1968), pp. 28–53.

'Prolegomenon to the Principles of Punishment', in *Punishment and Responsibility* (Oxford: Oxford University Press, 1968), pp. 1–27.

Hillyard, P. and S. Tombs, 'Beyond Criminology', in P. Hillyard, C. Pantazis, S. Tombs, D. Gordon, D. Dorling, *Criminal Obsessions: Why Harm Matters More than Crime* (London: Crime and Society Foundation, 2005), pp. 5–20.

Hillyard, P., C. Pantazis, S. Tombs, D. Gordon and D. Dorling, *Criminal Obsessions: Why Harm Matters More than Crime* (London: Crime and Society Foundation, 2005).

Hegel, G. W. F., *Elements of the Philosophy of Right*, trans. H. B. Nisbet (Cambridge: Cambridge University Press, 1996).

Honneth, A., *The Struggle for Recognition: The Moral Grammar of Social Conflicts*, trans. Joel Anderson (Cambridge: Polity, 1995).

Horton, J. and S. Mendus (eds.), *After MacIntyre* (Cambridge: Polity, 1994).

Hulsman, L., 'Critical Criminology and the Concept of Crime', *Contemporary Crises* 10 (1986), pp. 63–80.

Hume, D., *Treatise of Human Nature*, ed. L. A. Selby-Bigge and P. H. Nidditch (Oxford: Oxford University Press, 1978).

Jensen, H., 'Morality and Luck', *Philosophy* 59 (1984), pp. 323–30.

Johnstone, G. (ed.), *A Restorative Justice Reader* (Cullompton: Willan, 2001).

Johnstone, G., *Restorative Justice: Ideas, Values, Debates* (Cullompton: Willan, 2002).

Johnstone, G. and D. W. Van Ness (eds.), *The Handbook of Restorative Justice* (Cullompton: Willan, 2006).

Kant, I., *The Metaphysics of Morals*, trans. M. Gregor (Cambridge: Cambridge University Press, 1991).

Kelly, E., 'Doing Without Desert', *Pacific Philosophical Quarterly* 83 (2002), pp. 180–205.

Kleinig, J., 'Punishment and Moral Seriousness', *Israel Law Review* 25 (1991), pp. 401–21.

Kojeve, A., *Introduction to the Reading of Hegel* (New York: Basic Books, 1969).

Kolnai, A., 'Forgiveness', *Proceedings of the Aristotelian Society* 74 (1973/4), pp. 91–106.

Korsgaard, C., 'Skepticism about Practical Reason', *Journal of Philosophy* 83 (1986), pp. 5–25.

'The Right to Lie: Kant on Dealing with Evil', in *Creating the Kingdom of Ends* (Cambridge: Cambridge University Press, 1996), pp. 133–58.

Kosman, L. A., 'Being Properly Affected: Virtues and Feelings in Aristotle's Ethics', in A. O. Rorty (ed.), *Essays on Aristotle's Ethics* (Berkeley, Calif.: University of California Press, 1980), pp. 103–16.

Lacey, N., *State Punishment* (London: Routledge, 1988).

LaFollette, H. (ed.), *Ethics in Practice*, 2nd edn (Oxford: Blackwell, 2002).

Larmore, C., *Patterns of Moral Complexity* (Cambridge: Cambridge University Press, 1987).

Levy, N., 'Cultural Membership and Moral Responsibility', *Monist* 86 (2003), pp. 145–63.

Lipkin, R. J., 'Punishment, Penance and Respect for Autonomy', *Social Theory and Practice* 14 (1988), pp. 87–104.

McCold, P. and B. Wachtel, 'Community Is not a Place: A New Look at Community Justice Initiatives', in G. Johnstone (ed.), *A Restorative Justice Reader* (Cullompton: Willan, 2001), pp. 294–302.

McDowell, J., 'Aesthetic Value, Objectivity and the Fabric of the World', in J. McDowell, *Mind, Value and Reality* (London: Harvard University Press, 1998), pp. 112–30.

'Values and Secondary Qualities', in J. McDowell, *Mind, Value and Reality* (London: Harvard University Press, 1998), pp. 131–50.

MacIntyre, A., *After Virtue*, 2nd edn (London: Duckworth, 1985).

MacNaughton, D., 'Reparation and Atonement', *Religious Studies* 28 (1992), pp. 129–44.

Mackie, J. L., *Ethics: Inventing Right and Wrong* (Harmondsworth: Penguin, 1977).

'Morality and the Retributive Emotions', *Criminal Justice Ethics* 1 (1982), pp. 3–9.

Marshall, T., 'Restorative Justice: An Overview', in G. Johnstone (ed.), *A Restorative Justice Reader* (Cullompton: Willan, 2001), pp. 28–46.

Matravers, M. (ed.), *Punishment and Political Theory* (Oxford: Hart, 1999).

Justice and Punishment: The Rationale of Coercion (Oxford: Oxford University Press, 2000).

Mill, J. S., *Utilitarianism*, in J. S. Mill and J. Bentham, *Utilitarianism and Other Essays*, ed. A. Ryan (Harmondsworth: Penguin, 1987), pp. 272–338.

Miller, D., 'Virtues, Practices and Justice', in J. Horton and S. Mendus (eds.), *After MacIntyre* (Cambridge: Polity, 1994), pp. 245–64.

Moberley, W., *The Ethics of Punishment* (London: Faber, 1968).

Moore, M. S., 'The Moral Worth of Retribution', in F. Schoeman (ed.), *Character, Responsibility and the Emotions* (Cambridge: Cambridge University Press, 1987), pp. 189–219.

'Law as a Functional Kind', in R. P. George (ed.), *Natural Law Theory: Contemporary Essays* (Oxford: Oxford University Press, 1992).

Placing Blame (Oxford: Clarendon Press, 1999).

Morris, H., 'Persons and Punishment', *Monist* 52 (1968), pp. 475–501.

'A Paternalistic Theory of Punishment', *American Philosophical Quarterly* 18 (1981), pp. 263–71.

'The Decline of Guilt', *Ethics* 99 (1988), pp. 62–76.

Mulhall, S. and A. Swift, *Liberals and Communitarians* (Oxford: Blackwell, 1992).

Murphy, J. G., 'Three Mistakes about Retributivism', *Analysis* 31 (1971), pp. 166–70.

'Marxism and Retribution', *Philosophy and Public Affairs* 2 (1973), pp. 217–43.

'Forgiveness and Resentment', in J. G. Murphy and J. Hampton, *Forgiveness and Mercy* (Cambridge: Cambridge University Press, 1988), pp. 14–34.

'Hatred: A Qualified Defense', in J. G. Murphy and J. Hampton, *Forgiveness and Mercy* (Cambridge: Cambridge University Press, 1988), pp. 88–110.

'Repentance, Punishment and Mercy', in A. Etzioni and D. Carney (eds.), *Repentance: a Comparative Perspective* (Totowa, N.J.: Rowman and Littlefield, 1997), pp. 143–70.

Murphy, J. G. and J. Hampton, *Forgiveness and Mercy* (Cambridge: Cambridge University Press, 1988).

Nagel, T., 'Moral Luck', in *Mortal Questions* (Cambridge: Cambridge University Press, 1979), pp. 24–38.

'War and Massacre', in *Mortal Questions* (Cambridge: Cambridge University Press, 1979), pp. 53–74.

Nagin, D., 'Deterrence and Incapacitation', in M. Tonry (ed.), *The Handbook of Crime and Punishment* (New York: Oxford University Press, 1999), pp. 345–68.

Neblett, W., 'The Ethics of Guilt', *Journal of Philosophy* 18 (1974), pp. 652–63.

Nietzsche, F., *On the Genealogy of Morality*, trans. C. Diethe (Cambridge: Cambridge University Press, 1994).

Nozick, R., *Anarchy, State and Utopia* (Oxford: Blackwell, 1974).

Philosophical Explanations (Cambridge, Mass.: Belknap Press, 1981).

Nussbaum, M., 'Equity and Mercy', *Philosophy and Public Affairs* 22 (1993), pp. 83–125.

O'Leary-Hawthorne, J. and P. Pettit, 'Strategies for Free-Will Compatibilists', *Analysis* 56 (1996), pp. 191–201.

Pettit, P., 'Realism and Response-Dependence', *Mind* 100 (1991), pp. 587–626.

A Theory of Freedom (Cambridge: Polity, 2001).

Pettit, P. and M. Smith, 'Freedom in Belief and Desire', *Journal of Philosophy* 93 (1996), pp. 429–49.

Primoratz, I., 'Punishment as Language', *Philosophy* 64 (1989), pp. 187–205.

Rachels, J., 'Punishment and Desert', in H. LaFollette (ed.), *Ethics in Practice*, 2nd edn (Oxford: Blackwell, 2002), pp. 466–74.

Radzik, L., 'Making Amends', *American Philosophical Quarterly* 41 (2004), pp. 141–54.

Rawls, J., 'Two Concepts of Rules', *Philosophical Review* 64 (1955), pp. 3–13.

'Justice as Fairness: Political Not Metaphysical', *Philosophy and Public Affairs* 14 (1985), pp. 223–51.

'The Idea of an Overlapping Consensus', *Oxford Journal of Legal Studies* 7 (1987), pp. 1–25.

Political Liberalism (New York: University of Columbia Press, 1996).

Raye, B. E. and A. W. Roberts, 'Restorative Processes', in G. Johnstone and D. W. Van Ness (eds.), *The Handbook of Restorative Justice* (Cullompton: Willan, 2006), pp. 211–27.

Raz, J., *The Morality of Freedom* (Oxford: Clarendon Press, 1986).

Rorty, A. O. (ed.), *Essays on Aristotle's Ethics* (Berkeley, Calif.: University of California Press, 1980).

Sadurski, W., 'Theory of Punishment, Social Justice and Liberal Neutrality', *Law and Philosophy* 7 (1989), pp. 351–73.

Sayre-McCord, G. (ed.), *Essays on Moral Realism* (London: Cornell University Press, 1988).

Scanlon, T. M., *What We Owe to Each Other* (London: Belknap Press, 1998).

Scheffler, S., 'Relationships and Responsibilities', *Philosophy and Public Affairs* 26 (1997), pp. 189–209.

Schluter, M., 'What is Relational Justice?' in G. Johnstone (ed.), *A Restorative Justice Reader* (Cullompton: Willan, 2001), pp. 303–11.

Schoeman, F. (ed.), *Responsibility, Character and the Emotions* (Cambridge: Cambridge University Press, 1987).

Shapland, J., A. Atkinson, B. Chapman, E. Colledge, J. Dignan, M. Howes, J. Johnstone, G. Robinson and A. Sorsby, 'Situating Restorative Justice in Criminal Justice', *Theoretical Criminology* 11 (2006), pp. 505–32.

Sherman, L. and H. Strang, *Restorative Justice: The Evidence* (London: Smith Institute, 2007).

Skillen, A. J., 'How to Say Things with Walls', *Philosophy* 55 (1980), pp. 509–23.

Skorupski, J., 'The Definition of Morality', in *Ethical Explorations* (Oxford: Oxford University Press, 1999), pp. 137–59.

'Freedom, Morality and Recognition: Some Theses of Kant and Hegel', in *Ethical Explorations* (Oxford: Oxford University Press, 1999), pp. 160–89.

'Welfare and Self-Governance', *Ethical Theory and Moral Practice* 9 (2006), pp. 289–309.

Why Read Mill Today? (London: Routledge, 2006).

Slote, M., *From Morality to Virtue* (Oxford: Oxford University Press, 1992).

Smart, J. J. C., 'Extreme and Restricted Utilitarianism', *Philosophical Quarterly* 6 (1956), pp. 344–54.

'Freewill, Praise and Blame', *Mind* 52 (1961), pp. 291–306.

Smart, J. J. C. and B. Williams, *Utilitarianism: For and Against* (Cambridge: Cambridge University Press, 1973).

Smith, M., *The Moral Problem* (Oxford: Blackwell, 1994).

Smith, M. (ed.), *Meta-Ethics* (Aldershot: Dartmouth, 1995).

Speller, A., *Breaking Out* (London: Hodder and Stoughton, 1986).

Stephen, J. F., *Liberty, Equality, Fraternity* (London: Smith, Elder, 1873).

Stern, L., 'Freedom, Blame and Moral Community', *Journal of Philosophy* 71 (1974), pp. 72–84.

Strang, H., 'Justice for Victims of Young Offenders: The Centrality of Emotional Harm and Restoration', in G. Johnstone (ed.), *A Restorative Justice Reader* (Cullompton: Willan, 2001), pp. 286–93.

Repair or Revenge: Victims and Restorative Justice (Oxford: Clarendon Press, 2001).

Strawson, G., 'The Impossibility of Moral Responsibility', *Philosophical Studies* 75 (1994), pp. 5–24.

Strawson, P. F., 'Freedom and Resentment', in G. Watson (ed.), *Free Will* (Oxford: Oxford University Press, 1982), pp. 59–80.

Swinburne, R., *Responsibility and Atonement* (Oxford: Clarendon Press, 1985).

Tasioulas, J., 'Punishment and Repentance', *Philosophy* 81 (2006), pp. 279–322.

'Repentance and the Liberal State', *Ohio State Journal of Criminal Law* 4 (2007), pp. 487–521.

Tavuchis, N., *Mea Culpa: A Sociology of Apology and Reconciliation* (Stanford, Calif.: Stanford University Press, 1991).

Taylor, C., *Hegel* (Cambridge: Cambridge University Press, 1975).

'Responsibility for Self', in G. Watson (ed.), *Free Will* (Oxford: Oxford University Press, 1982), pp. 111–26.

'Self-interpreting Animals', in *Human Agency and Language: Philosophical Papers*, vol. I (Cambridge: Cambridge University Press, 1985), pp. 45–76.

'Social Theory as Practice', in *Philosophy and the Human Sciences: Philosophical Papers*, vol. II (Cambridge: Cambridge University Press, 1985), pp. 91–115.

Tonry, M. (ed.), *The Handbook of Crime and Punishment* (New York: Oxford University Press, 1999).

Van Ness, D., 'Creating Restorative Systems', in L. Walgrave (ed.), *Restorative Justice and the Law* (Cullompton: Willan, 2001), pp. 130–49.

'Proposed Basic Principles on the Use of Restorative Justice: Recognising the Aims and Limits of Restorative Justice', in A. von Hirsch, J. Roberts, A. E. Bottoms, K. Roach and M. Schiff (eds.), *Restorative Justice and Criminal Justice: Competing or Reconcilable Paradigms?* (Oxford: Hart, 2003), pp. 157–76.

Van Straaten, Z. (ed.), *Philosophical Subjects: Essays Presented to P. F. Strawson* (Oxford: Clarendon Press, 1980).

Von Hirsch, A., *Censure and Sanctions* (Oxford: Oxford University Press, 1993).

'Punishment, Penance and the State: A Reply to Duff', in M. Matravers (ed.), *Punishment and Political Theory* (Oxford: Hart, 1999), pp. 69–82.

Von Hirsch, A. and A. Ashworth (eds.), *Principled Sentencing*, 2nd edn (Oxford: Hart, 1998).

Proportionate Sentencing: Exploring the Principles (Oxford: Oxford University Press, 2005).

Von Hirsch, A. and L. Maher, 'Should Penal Rehabilitationism be Revived?' in A. Von Hirsch and A. Ashworth (eds.), *Principled Sentencing*, 2nd edn (Oxford: Hart, 1998), pp. 26–33.

Von Hirsch, A., A. Ashworth and C. Shearing, 'Restorative Justice: A "Making Amends" Model?' in A. Von Hirsch and A. Ashworth, *Proportionate*

Sentencing: Exploring the Principles (Oxford: Oxford University Press, 2005), pp. 110–30.

Von Hirsch, A., J. Roberts, A. E. Bottoms, K. Roach and M. Schiff (eds.), *Restorative Justice and Criminal Justice: Competing or Reconcilable Paradigms?* (Oxford: Hart, 2003).

Walgrave, L. (ed.), *Restorative Justice and the Law* (Cullompton: Willan, 2001).

'Restorative Justice for Juveniles: Just a Technique or a Fully-Fledged Alternative?' in G. Johnstone (ed.), *A Restorative Justice Reader* (Cullompton: Willan, 2003), pp. 255–69.

Walker, N., *Why Punish? Theories of Punishment Reassessed* (Oxford: Oxford University Press, 1991).

Wallace, R. J., *Responsibility and the Moral Sentiments* (London: Harvard University Press, 1994).

Wasserstrom, R., 'Why Punish the Guilty?' in G. Ezorsky (ed.), *Philosophical Perspectives on Punishment* (Albany, N. Y.: SUNY Press, 1972), pp. 328–41.

Watson, G., 'Free Agency', *Journal of Philosophy* 72 (1975), pp. 205–20.

'Responsibility and the Reactive Attitudes: Variations on a Strawsonian Theme', in F. Schoeman (ed.), *Responsibility, Character and the Emotions* (Cambridge: Cambridge University Press, 1987), pp. 256–86.

'Two Faces of Responsibility', *Philosophical Topics* 24 (1996), pp. 227–48.

Wenar, L., 'Political Liberalism: An Internal Critique', *Ethics* 106 (1995), pp. 32–62.

'The Unity of Rawls's Work', *Journal of Moral Philosophy* 1 (2004), pp. 265–75.

Wiggins, D., 'Truth, Invention and the Meaning of Life', in G. Sayre-McCord (ed.), *Essays on Moral Realism* (London: Cornell University Press, 1988), pp. 127–65.

Williams, B., 'A Critique of Utilitarianism', in J. J. C. Smart and B. Williams, *Utilitarianism: For and Against* (Cambridge: Cambridge University Press, 1973).

'Moral Luck', in *Moral Luck* (Cambridge: Cambridge University Press, 1981), pp. 20–39.

Ethics and the Limits of Philosophy (London: Fontana, 1985).

Wolf, S., 'Sanity and the Metaphysics of Responsibility', in F. Schoeman (ed.), *Responsibility, Character and the Emotions* (Cambridge: Cambridge University Press, 1987), pp. 46–62.

Freedom within Reason (Oxford: Oxford University Press, 1990).

Wright, M., *Justice for Victims and Offenders: A Restorative Response to Crime*, 2nd edn (Winchester: Waterside Press, 1996).

Zehr, H., *Changing Lenses: A New Focus for Crime and Justice* (Scottdale, Pa.: Herald Press, 1990).

Index